Gender, 'Race' and Class in Schooling

For Adam, Luke
and Siobhan

Gender, 'Race' and Class in Schooling:
A New Introduction

Chris Gaine and Rosalyn George

UK	Falmer Press, 1 Gunpowder Square, London, EC4A 3DE
USA	Falmer Press, Taylor & Francis Inc., 325 Chestnut Street, 8th Floor, Philadelphia, PA 19106

First published in 1999

A catalogue record for this book is available from the British Library

ISBN 0 7507 0758 5 cased
ISBN 0 7507 0757 7 paper

Library of Congress Cataloging-in-Publication Data are available on request

Jacket design by Caroline Archer

Typeset in 10/12 Garamond by
Graphicraft Limited, Hong Kong

Printed in Great Britain by Biddles Ltd., Guildford and King's Lynn on paper which has a specified pH value on final paper manufacture of not less than 7.5 and is therefore 'acid free'.

Contents

List of Figures and Tables   vi
Acknowledgments   vii

1   Key Ideas and Concepts   1

2   Facts and Representations   11
Women and the Economy   11
Ethnic Minorities in Britain: A Brief Descriptive Account   17
Social Class   29

3   Language   36
Language and Inequality: An Introduction   36
Gender and Language   39
'Race' and Language   47
Class and Language   54

4   Curriculum   61
Gender and the Curriculum   61
Curriculum: 'Race'   68
Curriculum: Class   75

5   The Experience of School   82
Girl's Experience of Schooling   82
Experience: 'Race'   87
Experience: Class   96

6   Achievement   102
Gender and Achievement   102
Achievement: 'Race'   106
Class and Achievement   122

7   Policy: Separatism by Default, Design or Exclusion   130
Gender and Separate Schooling   130
'Race' and Separate Schooling   137
Class and Separate Schooling   144

Bibliography   153
Index   166

List of Figures and Tables

Figure 1.1 Diagram representing physical sex differences between boys and girls 6

Figure 1.2 Diagram representing differences in height of men and women 7

Figure 1.3 Normal distribution showing height of adults 7

Figure 1.4 Speculative Normal distribution of motivation for homework 8

Figure 1.5 Speculative Normal distribution showing family support 8

Figure 1.6 Normal distribution showing achievement 9

Table 2.1 Main religious groupings amongst British ethnic minorities 28

Table 2.2 Occupations in the early 1990s 33

Table 3.1 Examples of gendered language 42

Table 3.2 Examples of 'food' words 42

Table 3.3 Examples of 'animal' words 42

Table 3.4 Words for women 43

Table 3.5 Words for men 43

Table 3.6 Examples of the relationship between 'race' and language 49

Figure 3.1 The Creole continuum 51

Table 3.7 Dialect distinctions 55

Figure 6.1 Factors relating to effectiveness of schools for ethnic minority pupils 110

Acknowledgments

In Chris's case, as the primary author of the sections on 'race' and class, this book had to be written against the competing demands of a serious illness and another project which seemed to suffer from sibling rivalry, as well as the regular demands of teaching, family life, gardening and leaking taps. The fact that it was finished at all is due to the forbearance and support of my wife, my employers and colleagues, so thanks to them.

Rosalyn, as the primary author of the sections on gender, would like to thank her family, friends and colleagues for all their help and support during this project.

Many thanks also to Falmer Press, from both of us.

1   Key Ideas and Concepts

In this book we want to explore the current situation in schools with regard to three central inequalities in education: gender, 'race' and social class. All three have been high on both teachers' and politicians' agendas in the careers of most practising teachers, and all three have been the focus of significant and recent changes.

There has been a long history in the UK of addressing educational inequalities resulting from social class — from the advent of free secondary education for all in 1944, to the intended phasing out of grammar schools beginning in 1965, and to the expansion of free higher education in 1966. All of these have had the explicit aim (among others) of increasing the lower levels of educational participation and success of the children of poorer people and those in unskilled work. By the 1970s some social and political attention was also focused on the educational performance of girls and young women in line with the advent of the Sex Discrimination Act in 1975. 'Race' came later than class to national attention and policy, though special measures were introduced via the Local Government Act of 1967 to address what were seen as particular disadvantages of immigrant pupils. It was not really until the late 1970s that the issue was firmly established on the national policy agenda and, since the 1980s, it has had a very high profile.

A good deal has happened in policy terms since 1980, some of it seemingly paradoxical. In the early years of the Thatcher governments, which began in 1979, the movement towards comprehensive secondary education continued. At the same time, the intervention of LEAs in how schools dealt with racial (and to an extent gender) inequality increased, so the early 1980s saw an expansion of explicit and official attempts to tackle inequality. We call this 'paradoxical' because in time it became increasingly clear that this was incompatible with important elements of Conservative Party philosophy. There are several strands to this: it is not that in any simplistic way Tories believe in inequality.

As regards class, they believe that people have the right to be unequal. That is to say, differences in ability and effort will naturally lead to differences in education and differences in life, so this kind of inequality is not inherently unjust. With certain exceptions they believe that on the whole there are fair chances for those who want to 'get on in life' to do so. As regards 'race' they believe that there should not be unjust or unfair barriers to success on the basis of 'race'. They also believe that the state should interfere as little as possible with individuals' actions, including discriminatory ones,[1] preferring the checks and balances of the market and having a fairly sceptical view of what they would call 'social engineering'. At the same time, they also believe that there are several things about Britain best left alone — their party title itself signals this, so there is a strong assimilationist current within the party which argues that equal treatment is conditional upon 'following British ways'. This strand *does* believe in state intervention (or at least involvement) where particular aspects of British life are involved, such as requiring 'Christian' school assemblies. As regards gender, the Conservatives believe in evolutionary rather than revolutionary change. Their strong attachment to tradition and to 'tried and tested' aspects of British society means they have some suspicion of a large scale change from women as wives and mothers to women as equal partners in the workforce.

In accordance with these different currents in Conservative thought Margaret Thatcher declared in the early 1980s that 'the pursuit of equality is dead'. The involvement of LEAs in the pursuit of educational equality was reduced in the late 1980s and 1990s, largely as a result of drastically limiting the LEAs' spending power beyond what they had to allocate to schools. At the same time, central power was taken over the curriculum as an important definer of how a society sees itself and passes on messages to its next genera- tion. Whatever specific emphasis on equality which there had been in the curriculum was given less prominence. In 1980 most secondary age pupils went to comprehensive schools maintained by LEAs with a notional shared perspective and goal of providing a common (or at least similar) curriculum in broadly similar schools. This has now changed to a situation where schools may reintroduce selection in certain circumstances and where selection is allowed to flourish in a more covert way by parental choice of school. While the relationship is more complex than it would have been two decades ago because of a more fragmented social class structure, this 'choice' is neverthe- less related to social class (these points are explored in later chapters).

At the same time, and perhaps for different reasons, patterns of inequality have changed. We have already referred to an increasingly fragmented class structure and something similar has happened with regard to 'race'. In the 1980s there was a broad pattern of relative under-achievement by the children of all post-war migrants. This is no longer true. Some groups continue to be less successful than the majority white population and others have become more successful. The situation here is again more fractured and complex, and much harder to generalize about.

If anything the situation with regard to gender has changed the most. In 1980 (and for much of the time since) all the literature about gender and school performance concentrated on the poorer performance of girls. While there were areas of greater success than boys (particularly in primary school and in language-based subjects) the overall pattern was of lower results as girls got older and a much lower take-up of A-level and higher education places. This is now entirely reversed, so that while both boys' and girls' results have steadily improved over the intervening years, girls' results have done so at a much faster rate. By 1996 they outperformed boys in every subject at both GCSE and A-level (these general statements are critically analysed in Chapter 6).

Thus the forces and processes generating inequality, and the fine detail of how they operate, may have changed from the past. It is these series of changes which have placed teachers in a new position. There are new sets of practices and official policies within which teachers have to work, and there are new sets of priorities for those seeking to engage critically with the educational world in which they work. Making sense of what has happened, and is happening, is, we believe, critical if all young people are to receive their entitlement. While the Conservative Party is not likely to see political power again until some years into the twenty-first century, their influence on the educational world we now inhabit has been profound. They have changed the landscape in which anyone concerned with educational inequality has to operate.

Our own view is the comparatively modest one that more equality is possible. In particular we believe there are aspects of language (Chapter 3), curriculum (Chapter 4) and pupils' experience (Chapter 5) which at the ideological and practical level promote inequality. We also believe that in material ways current policies will increase social class differences in education and that these will interact in intricate but reinforcing ways with gender and 'race' (Chapter 7). Our main aim for this book, therefore, is to provide an accessible summary of recent history and developments in order to promote an understanding of future trends and possibilities.

Clarifying our Terms

In view of what Ball called the 'discourse of derision' to which concern with equality has been subjected in the past two decades, there are certain key terms and ideas which need defining.

The first of these is the most obvious: ***inequality***, which we have begun to discuss already. A distinction that needs to be made is between *inequality of access* and *inequality of outcome*. If there are barriers which ought to be irrelevant but which prevent particular children getting into a school or receiving its benefits (barriers such as skin colour, sex or social background) then, on the face of it, this constitutes unequal access. If it can be justified (for there are equally good alternatives: there is different but not unequal provision; and the same desirable goals are attainable by different routes) then there is not necessarily injustice present. The inequality we are concerned with therefore is different *and unequal* treatment based on irrelevant criteria resulting in injustice. This kind of unequal access can be quite subtle, it is much more than a crude (and usually unlawful) exclusion from an entire school and can operate through the curriculum that is offered, the style of interaction in classrooms and the atmosphere in corridors — all aspects of schooling which will be discussed in the ensuing chapters.

Unequal outcomes, as such, do not necessarily present a problem for educationalists. No group of people learning netball or nuclear physics will become equally proficient in the necessary skills, and no school is likely to produce a group of pupils entirely undifferentiated in their achievements. The unequal outcomes we are concerned about are those resulting from the unequal access described above.

Equality of opportunity, therefore, means opportunities without unfair barriers or irrelevant criteria getting in the way. It does not mean every pupil's results will be the same.

Discrimination we shall take to mean more than its literal sense of simply choosing and use it in its usual sense of *unjust* choosing, that is to say treating people differently on the basis of irrelevant criteria. It is unlawful in Britain in some respects but not others. For instance, it is against the law for schools to set quotas for the number of black (or white) pupils or for them to demand a higher pass mark for girls in entrance exams in order to keep the sex ratio even. It is also unlawful to have measures or procedures which *indirectly* disadvantage some ethnic groups compared to others or one sex against the other. It is not unlawful to indirectly, covertly or even virtually explicitly advantage one social class compared to another. Legislation was passed in 1996 making most forms of discrimination against disabled people unlawful in employment, but there remain areas of unequal access. Another high profile issue is sexual orientation, where at the moment no general law requires equal treatment and some explicitly prevent it, i.e. recognition of marriage and service in the armed forces. The Race Relations Acts are less draconian than bar-room wisdom usually has it. The first law was introduced in 1965, prohibiting discrimination in restaurants, theatres and cinemas; in 1968, this was widened to key areas of employment and housing, and in rather more general terms to the provision of education and health care.[2] The more nebulous provision against 'promoting racial hatred' is almost never used, and has no connection with the mythical 'bans' on books and words which have been the subject of some media hysteria.

Positive discrimination is one of a group of ideas which are easily misunderstood and perceived negatively. There is not the space here to explore the idea fully, but in relation to pupils in schools it is indicated above where discrimination is against the law, whatever the motive, hence positive discrimination is also against the law. *Positive action*, however, can be used to ensure irrelevant barriers are not preventing someone or a particular group achieving access. Taking particular steps to undermine the 'unmacho' image of learning French, or learning to type, even though the steps require extra staff resources, is positive action and is not unlawful. When viewed in this way it is clear that, in practice, many features of school life involve positive action.

Sex and gender The usual distinction here is that sex encompasses those features which are biologically determined and gender those which are socially determined. Thus the fact that women are on average shorter and lighter than men is mostly due to sex, i.e. it is biologically determined. The fact that in western societies women often wear skirts and men almost never do is entirely social. Even the pattern on the skirt matters, since in the UK it is acceptable for some men to wear skirts if they carry a tartan pattern.

Sexism refers to actions or circumstances where one sex displays prejudiced attitudes, or more especially, actions towards the other. For sexism to
have any effect it must operate from a position of power, and, as will be
discussed in Chapter 2, in practice the opportunity to act in ways which disadvantage the other sex has historically been more open to males.

'*Race*' This term is always put in quotes in this book because it does not
mean what people think it means, but it would require many pages to explain
why not (for a slightly fuller discussion see Gaine, 1995). The key point is that
what are often thought of as 'races' — Africans, Europeans, Chinese etc. — are
only superficially different from each other. Groups which appear different
from others generally have more differences *within* the group than some of
their members do with outsiders. 'Race' is a crude and superficial classification
which began in the last century, it has no biological significance to scientists
today. Perhaps a useful working definition is 'a group of people who may
share some physical characteristic to which social importance is attached'.
Thus, the important facet of 'race' is not the skin colour, facial features or type
of hair people have but the social significance which is placed upon these.

Ethnicity and ethnic group Ethnicity is a far more preferable term
because it unambiguously refers to culture. An ethnic group is simply a group
which shares certain cultural features such as language, religion, various customs, perhaps food and clothing preferences. It usually depends on a sense of
shared peoplehood — that is to say that if a group believe themselves to be an
ethnic group based on one or more of the above features then they probably
are. Where one draws the line between different 'ethnic groups' depends on
who is drawing the line and for what purpose. It might make sense sometimes
to speak of 'Asians' as an ethnic group in Britain, but at others it will be more
appropriate to speak of specific sub-divisions.

Racism is, analogously to sexism, the belief that one 'race' (in practice
often an ethnic group) is superior to others coupled with *the power to put this
belief into practice*. This last point allows for the importance of media control,
force of numbers, institutional assumptions and power over employment and
housing. Racism in this sense is more than name-calling or simple dislike of
another ethnic group.

Left wing has traditionally been associated with the Labour Party and
with socialism. In education the left has generally had more of a concern with
equality and its promotion, and has therefore tended to be in favour of measures which reduce unfair barriers to educational success. Though for a time
broadly supported by the Conservative Party, comprehensive schools have
been more actively promoted by Labour and, for the most part, it was Labour
LEAs who initiated the 'race' and sex equality policies to which we have
already referred. Obvious potential barriers to educational success are income
and wealth, so the left has been in favour of means-tested grants to higher
education and giving extra resources to schools in poorer areas. In the past,
Labour spoke of abolishing private education, but this is no longer their policy
and they are less opposed to the surviving grammar schools.

Right wing is, correspondingly a term applied to the Conservatives, though during the 1980s and 1990s they tended to be dominated by what is generally called the *New Right*. In economics the New Right are 'liberals', seeking the de-restricting of trade, commerce and the free play of market forces. In other aspects of social life they are more restricting, favouring, for example, capital punishment, severe prison regimes, 'tradition' and only limited social recognition of gay relationships. In school terms, this means that they are likely to favour introducing what they see as efficiency- and quality-enhancing 'market forces' between schools, namely schools competing for pupils (and hence resources) and competing for good exam results. On the other hand, they have been much more authoritarian about curriculum content, favouring central control and opposing 'liberalism' in the social sense, thus favouring various aspects of tradition like academic selection and uniforms and opposing or reversing some of the changes touched upon above.

A Warning About 'Difference'

One of the difficulties in discussing and analysing group differences in performance, achievement, or any other aspect of schooling is that we can forget that in practice groups *overlap* in their characteristics, rather than possess completely different ones. However, this is not always the case, which helps to confuse matters further. Take, for instance, physical sexual differences between girls and boys. Here there is little overlap, girls possessing different sexual organs to boys with a very small number of children being born as hermaphrodites, i.e. without a clear physical sex and undeveloped organs. This could be represented diagramatically thus:

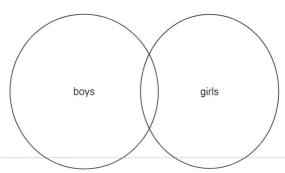

Figure 1.1:   Diagram representing physical sex differences between boys and girls

It is possible to produce a similar diagram for skin colour comparing, say, people of Pakistani descent with white people of English descent. There is still some overlap since some Kashmiri Pakistanis are very fair-skinned, some having blue eyes too, and some 'white' English people are darker-skinned than most, perhaps because of some distant Mediterranean ancestor.

Many other attributes, however, are not discontinuous. Most of the attributes we are concerned with in education are not possessed entirely by one group of people and not possessed at all by another. To take an uncontroversial example first. Men are typically taller than women, but this could not be represented in a diagram similar to the one above with almost *all* men being taller than almost *all* women. The actual picture is more like this:

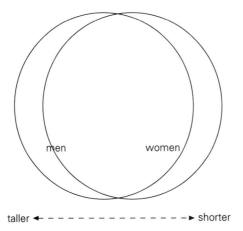

taller ◄ – – – – – – – – – – – – –► shorter

Figure 1.2: Diagram representing differences in height of men and women

Statisticians and social scientists usually represent populations not by circles as in these diagrams, but by graphs called 'normal distributions', which show more accurately the distribution of particular attributes within a population, i.e. that most people are somewhere in the centre with the numbers at either extreme falling away to zero.

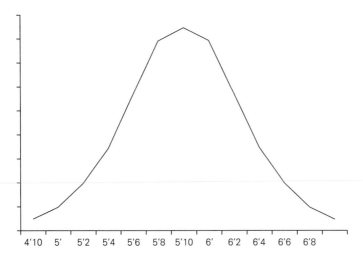

Figure 1.3: Normal distribution showing height of adults

If we split the figures by sex, we can see that most men have a height of around 5'10" and most women a height of around 5'7", but the majority of both men and women are in the range which overlaps. In any roomful of people, therefore, several of the women will be taller than several men. Sex has some relationship with height, but it alone is a weak predictor.

What would a normal distribution of motivation for homework be like? There is some evidence that girls in secondary schools are more motivated about this than boys, so we might have a pair of distributions like this:

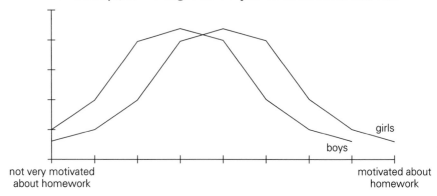

Figure 1.4: Speculative Normal distribution of motivation for homework

This shows more girls being highly motivated towards their homework than boys, *not that no boys are highly motivated or no girls have very low motivation.* You can predict from these graphs that overall the girls you teach will do more homework, but they cannot predict for you the motivation of an *individual* girl or boy. To take another case, suppose there is evidence of greater family support and encouragement for pupils of Indian background than for white ones. Such evidence would *not* support the assumption that every Indian pupil was highly supported and encouraged by her or his family, nor even that in most cases there is any difference.

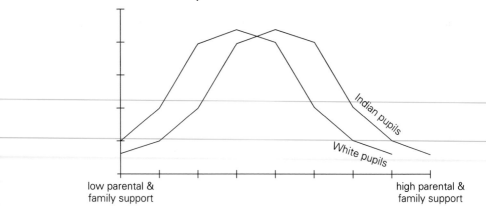

Figure 1.5: Speculative Normal distribution showing family support

The last example to illustrate this is about achievement. You will read in Chapter 6 that on average African-Caribbean boys achieve a GCSE points score some points lower than white boys. In other words, the normal distribution of scores for African-Caribbean boys has its 'peak' at a lower number. But as the distributions drawn together show, most white and African-Caribbean pupils lie in the overlapping area.

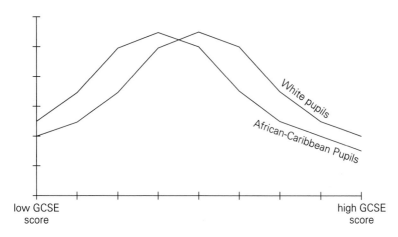

low GCSE score   high GCSE score

Figure 1.6: Normal distribution showing achievement

It is hard to over-emphasize this simple but crucial point. It is all too easy to think of differences as if they were discontinuous rather than overlapping and hence forget that ethnicity, sex and social class, while they produce significant *group* differences, are in most case weak predictors of educational outcomes for *individuals*. In any case, people are seldom, in any aspect of their lives, solely recognizable in terms of class, 'race' or gender. Most often there is a complex interweaving of all three and, more besides, like sexual orientation and age. We have nevertheless kept to these three primary categories in the organization of the book in order to structure the wealth of material and to highlight the central debates and changes in each sphere — of which a growing awareness of interlinking is only one.

Notes

1   This is an important part of Conservative philosophy and is dealt with in detail in Levitas (1986), and see also Cohen et al. (1986). In most of the last 20 years the Conservative Party annual conference has had motions submitted calling for the repeal of the Race Relations Act. Though they have never been passed, this is evidence, at least, of a view within the party that the Act is an unnecessary infringement of people's freedom.

2 The number of successful prosecutions is small. In the employment field, the Commission for Racial Equality only backs industrial tribunal claims which it thinks are absolutely solid. There were 389 of these in the whole country in 1988–89, and 22 per cent of these found the allegation of discrimination proven. For reports about education see CRE (1988a; 1992b).

2 Facts and Representations

Women and the Economy

At the beginning of the nineteenth century the family represented a working relationship which was engaged collaboratively in the production of such things as food and clothes. This work took place in the same arena as sexual relations, child bearing and child rearing. Although at that time the patriarchal role of the father was absolute, women's skills were indispensable and interdependence between the husband and wife, both being economically productive, was critical. As the nineteenth century progressed, market forces dramatically altered the structure of this working relationship. The world of the family and the world of production became separate entities. Production became part of the public sphere and the family became more and more private.

Middle-class women gradually became relatively unproductive and many working-class women, although working in the public sphere, lost many of the skills over which previously they had had control. The division of labour by gender could be characterized in the following ways: for the male, the public sphere offered waged employment, a rigid distinction between work and leisure and an income which brought with it power and independence. The middle-class woman, on the other hand, was engaged in un-waged employment, with no defined work or working hours and no defined leisure time. With no income, the woman was totally dependent on her husband and, therefore, powerless to alter or shape her destiny.

> The period from 1780–1850 was one in which the idea of separate spheres for men and women became sanctified in middle class thought and practice. Women were identified with the private domain of the home and the family as wives and mothers or unmarried dependants; men, on the other hand, were associated with the public sphere of paid work, politics and business and with economic and jural responsibility for their wives and the expected brood of children. (Purvis, 1991, p. 2)

Hence the middle-class ideology of women as domestic labourers and responsible for child care, and men in paid employment, became sedimented into British culture.

The location of women in the home was further sanctioned by Victorian scientific theory and medical practices which viewed illness as a normal state for women with their minds and bodies being controlled by their ovaries. This thinking laid emphasis on the need for middle-class women to be 'kept', if not by a husband then by an uncle, brother or other male relative. There was also an idealization of marriage in the writing of the time. John Ruskin saw the duties of wives and mothers to create a place of beauty and emotional security for her husband and her children. The home was to be a sanctuary in which the wife reigned as guardian 'angel'.

The Condition of Working-class Women

Working-class women did, however, engage in paid employment and placed politicians and policy makers in an ambivalent position in defining the parameters of their position in this respect. There was no outcry about women working as domestic servants. Women working in privately owned homes did not offend against Victorian notions of 'the angel in the house'; the role of the governess, for example, was seen as one of respectability. However, the working-class women who were engaged in 'paid work outside the home, especially in the mill or the factory, were seen as degraded beings' (Purvis, 1991) and such women needed to be 'raised' for the good of society.

> The factory system, however much it may have added to the wealth of the country, has had a deleterious effect on the domestic condition of the people . . . it has torn the wife from her husband and the children from the parents. Especially has its tendency been to lower the sacred character of woman. (cited by Purvis, 1991, p. 8)

Although the separation of women from the public and private spheres of life was more rigid for middle class than working-class women, all women were excluded from 'political' decision making, and enjoyed no rights as citizens or protection by any legal framework (Lewis, 1984).

The Twentieth Century: Women — The Reserve Army of Labour

The majority of women working during the first half of this century were young and single, most of them employed in domestic service or in the cotton industry. Men defended their skilled jobs through their trade unions and, in so doing, excluded women from other varieties of work. The First World War necessitated the recruitment of women from the cotton factories and other industries into engineering and the explosives industry to replace men entering the army. After the war, women were urged to give up their jobs for the sake of the men returning from the war effort and for the future 'welfare of the race'. However, many married women re-entered the work place and, at that time, made up 40 per cent of all working women. This resurgence of women into the labour market was seen as a threat to men's jobs, who feared that employers would break down their jobs into less skilled areas and threaten their hard won rights over entry into skilled jobs (Wickham, 1986).

During the Second World War women were re-called to the work force as they had been during the First World War. Many of these women were married and were again expected to return to the home at the end of the war to focus their efforts on child rearing and home making. The ideology that a man needed a clean, cheerful, 'looked-after' home to return to after work was one of the powerful arguments for restricting the hours and types of work women could engage in. Child development theories of the time, such as Bowlby's 'maternal deprivation thesis', which suggested that any separation of a child from their mother could lead to untold emotional damage to the child's relationships in later life, also became a forceful pressure on women to return to the home. Furthermore, the welfare state promoted a model of female dependence in marriage:

> The infamous 'co-habitation' rule has meant. . . . that a woman living with a man can have her social security payments stopped in the belief that the man should support her. If he, too, is on social security then he gets an additional allowance for her but this does not equal the value of a full single person's allowance. (Wickham, 1986, p. 20)

Nevertheless, after the war between 61–85 per cent of women did not want to go back to housework. The government had made a mistake in assuming that women would be happy providing stop-gap labour and they became concerned that the women would threaten the jobs of the returning soldiers, perhaps leading to political unrest. In the event, more than one million women were either sacked or quit their jobs.

Where Are We Now?

In 1970 the government passed the Equal Pay Act. Working women thought that the passing of such a law would mean that they would get the same rates of pay as men for the same work. Unfortunately, only a few women have benefited from this Act and more than twenty years of equality legislation has done little to shift the differences between women's and men's earning capacities. In some cases, employers have found ways of getting round the law (such as giving men different job titles from women), but more importantly men still receive higher basic hourly earnings than women because of widespread job segregation. Women work in different and lower paid occupations than men and are concentrated in the lower grades of pay structures. Full-time female manual workers earn 78 per cent of the average hourly pay of male manual workers, while female non-manual workers earn only 61 per cent of the average hourly pay of male non-manual workers. Furthermore, the earnings gap between full-time women and men is even wider for weekly take-home pay, women falling to 63 per cent of the average gross weekly pay of their male equivalents. (Weekly differentials are wider because men have longer basic hours, more access to overtime, shift premiums and other bonus payments.) Britain foots the table in Europe for pay differentials for non-manual work by women, with gross women's monthly earnings being only 54 per cent of men's, whilst in France they are 66 per cent and in Germany 70 per cent (Rubery, 1993, cited in Figes, 1994). The gap, however, between men and women on low incomes is greater, women's average earnings being just over half that of men.

Service occupations employ the vast majority of women with around 90 per cent of these being in such areas as teaching, health care, the social services, secretarial and catering. In 1993 the average weekly wage for women in the service industries fell below the 'low pay' threshold of £197. Women from minority ethnic groups tend to be in the lowest status jobs with earnings even less than white women. For example, they are more often found amongst nurses working in mental care or with the elderly (Figes, 1994). Nursing today is still one of the worst rewarded jobs. Interestingly, in the nineteenth century, nurses were paid little more than domestic servants.

Teaching originally had an unequal pay structure and women had to leave the profession when they got married. The marriage ban was lifted in 1923, but it was not until 1961 that equal pay for teachers was introduced. Nevertheless, women in schools today remain in positions of subordination and their promotion prospects look bleak. The UK figures for 1994/5 (DfEE, 1997) indicate that of teachers entering primary education 83 per cent of the intake were women. In secondary schools, women make up 51 per cent of the workforce (George and Maguire, 1997). In a recent EOC survey (Arnot et al., 1995), more than three-quarters of secondary headships were held by men. In the primary school survey, slightly over half the heads were men. This gender imbalance is reproduced throughout the education system (Maguire and Weiner, 1994).

Woolfe (1990) points out that women can and do earn more from selling their bodies than from selling their skills. In America the average secretary, of whom 99 per cent are women, earns approximately $13,000 per year. Pre-school teachers, of whom 97 per cent are female, earn $14,000 per year, and bank tellers, of whom 94 per cent are female, earn $10,500 per year. However, a Manhattan street walker can earn between $500 and $1,000 per week. It is only in modelling and prostitution where a woman can consistently earn more than men.

Women as Part-time Workers

The increase in the number of working women today is often given as one of the contributing factors to men's unemployment. However, among women of working age there has been no increase in the number of full-time working women since 1951 — it is in the area of part-time work where there has been a significant expansion. In 1993, 4.5 million women worked part-time, and 3.5 million of these workers were mothers who were unable to pursue full-time employment because of the lack of affordable childcare. In recent years the working conditions for part-timers have deteriorated with many employers taking on women for just under the number of hours necessary to make them eligible for social security benefits. They have lower incomes, lower status, little or no employment protection and very few of the benefits afforded to full-time employees, such as holiday pay. Their promotion prospects are limited and they have little access to training. Wickham (1986) reminds us that women are only half as likely to get training related to the job they actually do and are therefore more likely to be stuck in a boring low paid and repetitive job. For part-time workers, men are twice as likely to be sent on training schemes as women, even though the number of men working part-time is negligible.

Employers are aware of the fact that many women have no choice but to work part-time and, therefore, have no need to review their practices. The average salary in Britain in 1994 was £19,000, with two thirds of wage earners paid the average or below. It is estimated that a person needs to earn in excess of £20,000 per year in order to support a spouse and two children. In fact, less than 10 per cent of families are supported solely by the father. Families need the income of women, no matter how small (Figes, 1994): their earnings rarely constitute a living wage, but even the low rate of pay makes a major difference to a family with a male or single wage coming in.

Women in Old Age

Much of the recent work on gender and ageing has related to the position of women in the labour market. 'Older women face the same problem as older workers in general, but to a greater extent and earlier in their life course' (Rodhever, 1990, p. 104). Bernard and Meade (1995) examined the ways in which gendered ageism operated to disadvantage women at work, and demonstrated how the 'glass ceiling', which limited their career opportunities, frequently arose out of male managers' attitudes to women's ageing. Their research highlighted the way women sometimes internalized low expectations of their own capabilities.

Itzin (1990) confirmed the importance of employment for women in the maintenance of positive self-identity. Many women find themselves defined in relationship to their family-career roles, and some mothers may feel socially devalued when their children leave home: 'I was never me'. Itzin's research also found that many women, strengthened by the feminist movement, had found various strategies, employment being one, to 'recover some independence' and establish a positive self-image.

However, age discrimination in employment is lawful in the UK unless it can be proved that an age-bar constitutes indirect discrimination under the Sex

Discrimination Act. One survey (Metcalfe and Thompson, 1989) found that overt discrimination was common with many job advertisements specifying an upper age limit. Thus, women lack legal protection against this double discrimination of age and sex (George and Maguire, 1997). Furthermore, limited career opportunities coupled with lowered aspirations have severe consequences for women's occupational pensions. Of women over 65 in America, one in five lives in poverty. In the UK, lone women outnumber lone men by four to one and, of those, over half as many women as men need income support.

Through the Glass Ceiling

The number of women able to enter into higher paid professions is limited by the glass ceiling, a barrier essential to a highly segregated work force in which women are paid less than men whatever job they do (Figes, 1994). There are a very few women who have broken through the glass ceiling into such male preserves as accountancy, law and medicine. These few are well rewarded and have financial independence. However, as Figes (1994) points out, there are many more women who are equally able but cannot get beyond a particular point in their careers. Many careers, such as academia and medicine, demand that employees relocate in order to progress. The implications this has for women who have children is one of compromise, and often careers are put on hold until mobility becomes possible. The 'Through the Glass Ceiling Network' was initiated by a group of women in higher education in 1990 to provide peer support and career development for able women who had reached the middle management plateau in their careers. The group pooled their informal support to aid those aspiring to break through the glass ceiling, and sustained others in facing the pressures and tensions of their jobs existing in male dominated institutions.

For the women who do break through the glass ceiling there are dangers. Firstly, they may be paraded as examples of good equal opportunity practice within an organization. Secondly, with women reaching the top being so few in number, they may find themselves taking on the values and ethos of the male culture in order to survive.

> The divide has become irrelevant between the private, once female, world of the family and the more public, formerly men-only, world of work. We cannot pretend home life has nothing to do with work, when the majority of women now enter both worlds, and when men increasingly seek to spend time with their children. . . . Removing the secondary status of pay and conditions for part-time workers would encourage more men to join them and spend time with their children. Removing downward pressure on women's pay in a segregated labour market would raise the status of their skills. (Figes, 1994, pp. 231–2)

Ethnic Minorities in Britain:
A Brief Descriptive Account

Demography[1]

About one person in twenty in the UK belongs to an ethnic-minority group readily distinguishable by skin colour (a focus which is discussed in the *Introduction*). The vast majority of these have family roots outside the UK within the past 50 years. This amounts to 3 million people, or about 5 per cent of the population.

The family roots of this 3 million can be summarized as approximately:

840,000   of Indian descent (about two-thirds Panjabi Sikh, one-third Gujerati Hindu, but also some Muslims); of these 787,000 'Indian' people, perhaps 100,000 actually came from East Africa, 60 per cent being Gujerati Hindus).
500,000   African-Caribbean (predominantly Christian);
477,000   Pakistani (almost all Muslims);
157,000   Chinese;
163,000   Bangladeshi (almost all Muslims);
212,000   African (many Muslims, and from wide variety of countries);
198,000   'other Asian' (Vietnamese, Thai, etc.);
178,000   'black other' (black American; descendants of seamen in Liverpool and Cardiff, perhaps many people of mixed descent);
290,000   'other groups' (Arab, Mexican, Turkish).

About one third of the total are Muslims.

It is worth noting that less than 8 per cent of the ethnic minority population are of pensionable age (compared with 19 per cent in the total population). About a third are under 15, compared with a figure of 21 per cent in the white population. Most of those of pensionable age were born abroad, 90 per cent of those under 15 were born here.

The relative rate of growth of different groups depends upon their age structure and preferred number of children, as well as the rate of migration. The number of people of Caribbean background has declined since 1981 through people leaving. The Pakistani and Bangladeshi populations have almost doubled in the same period, partly through new arrivals; partly because new arrivals are young and young people have more children; and partly because they are more likely to have three or more children than white, Indian, African, African-Caribbean or Chinese people in Britain.

The African-Caribbean, Chinese, Arab, African and majority white populations are more likely to live in smaller households without extended families, than are Indian, Pakistani and Bangladeshi families, amongst whom more than 20 per cent of married couples live with parents.

Patterns of Settlement

The ethnic minority population is overwhelmingly urban and relatively concentrated in particular areas of English industrial cities. Indeed, they are no less concentrated than the pattern at the beginning of the 1970s (Brown, 1984; Skellington and Morris, 1992). Scotland, Wales and more rural areas of England have proportionately very few black and Asian people. London is strikingly cosmopolitan, with about 40 per cent of all ethnic minorities living there (and more than half of all British African-Caribbeans, Bangladeshis, and African Asians) though this should not be taken to mean there are whole areas of British cities which are entirely black or Asian. About one in six residents of Greater London and the West Midlands is either Asian, African-Caribbean, Chinese or mixed race, though their relative locations vary. The largest concentration of Africans is in Lambeth, Westminster has the most Chinese, and Tower Hamlets the most Bangladeshis. Brent has the highest proportion of ethnic minority groups in London, with 27 per cent.

'Ethnic minority' does not mean the same as 'immigrant' or 'dark skinned'. About 3.4 million people in Britain were born overseas, and about 2 million of these are white. It is important to see these figures in conjunction with British-born ethnic minorities, since they are often confused. In 1990, just under half of those accepted for settlement in the UK were from the Indian subcontinent: about 23,000 people.

To all intents and purposes, immigration of black and Asian people to Britain began after the Second World War. There was no immigration control for members of the Commonwealth at the time, and Britain needed — indeed, invited — new workers. Some had connections with Britain through the wartime forces; others faced new circumstances at home (for example, partition in India and restricted entry from Jamaica to the USA), and, of course, all had citizenship of the UK and colonies (later Commonwealth) which assured free entry. One of the commonest myths about 'race' in Britain is that immigration laws were originally introduced to stem an uncontrollable flood. In fact, throughout the 1950s, incoming numbers mirrored job vacancies, and families did not start joining primary breadwinners here on any scale until *after* controls were introduced in 1962. For most groups, adults came first — predominantly men in the case of Asian settlers (though there were regional variations here) but this was not so for those from the Caribbean. Immigration controls have been tightened regularly ever since. Throughout the 1980s and 1990s most Asian settlers have been the dependants of those already here; since the end of the 1970s there has been a net annual *emigration* of black people to the Caribbean.

Roots in Asia and the Caribbean

Most British Asians have original roots in four different parts of the Indian subcontinent and the countries of East Africa. Gujerat is in the west facing the

African coast (and hence the high proportion of East African Asians whose ancestors were Gujerati). The Panjab is 700 miles to the north and straddles the Indian/Pakistani border, so some British Panjabis have Pakistani roots, some Indian. Bangladesh is about 1,500 miles away to the east. People's attachment and involvement with these roots varies greatly, and we do not want to emphasize these roots at the expense of Britishness, but the numbers above will not mean very much without a clearer idea of the relevant geography. We particularly want to draw attention to the distances and differences involved, since too often there is an assumption of uniformity and similarity between all south Asian groups — the myth of the 'generic Asian' we have called it in the chapter on achievement. The four main south Asian groups contained significant differences before migration in terms of religion and language, aside from a complex patchwork of distinctions in terms of levels of education, social class, and continua such as rural/urban; traditional/modern; religious/secular; eastern/westernized (there is chart summarizing the main linguistic groupings and their relationship to religion in Chapter 3).

Thus, while we draw attention to these differences within the category 'south Asian', we are attempting not to paint a simplistic picture of the salience of these distinctions in people's lives today. Jackson and Nesbitt (1993), in discussing what they call 'multiple cultural competence' argue:

> Too easily teachers, for example, assume that a child who mixes happily at school with non-Asian peers and who competently accomplishes the tasks set is 'Westernized' and has little if anything to do with Hindu culture. All too readily non-Asians, who see evidence of children engaged in, say, temple activities, assume that they are alien, not fully British. The reality is that the nine-year-old girl who has the lead part in the Pied Piper at school, or who enjoys football, is the same child who sits in her summer shorts at home informally practising a Punjabi folk song or a Hindi film song and who, in Punjabi suit, performs in a Hindu cultural programme. (p. 175)

For some British Asians the most significant element in their identity and self image may be that they are Muslim, for others it will be that they are women; for others that they are gay; for others that they are Gujeratis; and for others that they are very poor (or very rich) and at different moments different aspects will vary in their salience (for a fuller discussion of this see Gaine, 1995; Modood, 1992; Modood and Berthoud, 1997 and for some individual accounts see Eade, 1995). 'Race' or ethnicity may routinely impact upon their lives less than other aspects of their selves, though it is likely to do so more than it does for white people, for whom whiteness is generally normal and unconscious (Albany, 1987).

A similar unpacking of the 'generic' African-Caribbean is also required. There are many different islands in the former British Caribbean (the 'West Indies') and the distances between some of them are greater than the distance from London to Rome. About half of the original African-Caribbean migrants to

Britain come from Jamaica, but roots are now considerably more complex because of intermarriage with people originating from other islands (and about 20 per cent of relationships are with whites). The islands differ markedly. Most experienced more than one colonizing and slaving power — Holland, Spain, and France as well as Britain, and these left their cultural, religious and linguistic traces. Nevertheless, there are many profoundly British things about the Caribbean. Though we briefly summarize findings about racism below it is worth stressing at this point that the original Caribbean migrants to Britain in the early 1950s felt themselves to be very British. Many had already put some of their working lives into the war effort, and they came to Britain from towns like Manchester or Kingston in counties called Cornwall, Middlesex or Surrey. They worshipped the same god in the same language; their schools had had days off from Cambridge Certificate studies on the King's or Queen's birthday; they had sung Christmas carols about snow they had never seen; and they called their sons Winston and Gladstone. As one migrant (a teacher) put it, he was so steeped in English literature that he felt he knew 'every blade of grass in Stratford upon Avon'. Their rejection by the 'mother country' was thus unexpected and painful. Feeling themselves British, at first there was no other identity in which to take shelter.

> For many black workers, still nurturing positive feelings towards the 'mother country', it was a rude awakening to discover that British society is endemically racist. (Wong, 1986, p. 112)

The Chinese are often left out of such descriptive accounts, though as can be seen from the figures above they constitute a group equivalent in size to Bangladeshis (5 per cent of the ethnic minority population of Britain). The reason for the neglect may be that with the exception of communities in London, Manchester and some other large cities, the Chinese do not have a significant presence in any one area, and even London's Chinatown is small compared with areas of minority group settlement elsewhere. The simple effect of this is that the Chinese have had a minimal effect on all but a few localized key social institutions. Few schools have had to consider their needs for language support and the maintenance of their own language; few housing authorities have had to deal with issues of harassment of Chinese tenants; and, because of their specialized niche in the restaurant trade, there has been little pressure to consider them in measures against discriminatory employment practices.

Their roots are almost entirely in Hong Kong when it was a British colony, not in China proper. Their religion may be Christian, Buddhist or Confucian (though 58 per cent described themselves in the 1997 PSI study as having no religion (Modood and Berthoud, p. 17)). High value is placed upon education, respect for elders and competence in the Chinese language. As we have already mentioned, the British Chinese are overwhelmingly involved in the restaurant trade and hence scattered over the entire country. It may make little sense to refer to them as a 'community' since active social links may be difficult, partly because a Chinese family's nearest Chinese neighbours are likely to be business competitors, and partly because of an intricate web of links and barriers through a clan system (Taylor and Hegarty, 1985).

Racism and Disadvantage

While 'race' may not be salient to individual young Asian and African-Caribbean people, racism often is, however, so that while individuals (or their friends) may not see their ethnicity as any more significant than other aspects of their lives, the evidence is that it still correlates with various important aspects of life chances — the 'ethnic penalty' as Modood and Berthoud (1997) call it.

This evidence on discrimination and 'race' is nevertheless complex, and specific details need careful analysis to avoid generalizations which are too sweeping (ignoring factors like class, age, gender, specific ethnic group and educational level, which seem to be increasingly important). Presenting black and Asian people as more-or-less helpless victims can also generate unhelpful stereotypes. However, in summary:

- Black and Asian people are more likely to suffer from racial attacks, i.e. assaults or property damage with no motive of theft or gain;
- Poverty is correlated with some ethnicities, especially Pakistanis and Bangladeshis, as are many of its key determinants: high unemployment, low pay, shift work, dependence upon social security benefits (though African Asian men now earn as much as white men, and white women — unless self-employed — on average earn less than minority women from Hindu backgrounds);
- The risk of unemployment is greater for the ethnic minority population, though there are huge variations, with 61 per cent of unqualified African-Caribbean males under 35 years old out of work in 1994, compared with 45 per cent of similar Pakistanis, 18 per cent of Indians and 19 per cent of whites;
- Racial discrimination operates in employment at the point of recruitment and selection and promotion, and has been found in recent court cases, tribunals and surveys to be present in the armed forces, at least some police forces, major national employers, government training schemes, the law and the health service. This is frequently perceived as being linked to religion;
- There is a measurably different pattern of health care provision;
- Barriers seem to exist between black and Asian people and the same welfare benefits taken up by white people;
- Black and Asian council tenants are more likely to be in poorer accommodation; ethnic minority owner occupiers are in, on average, older, smaller and less valuable properties;

- There are markedly different patterns of arrests, remands and sentences between the black and white populations. While young black males appear to be disproportionately involved in street crime in London, this is more correlated with unemployment than 'race'.

(For more details see *Skellington and Morris, 1992; Modood and Berthoud, 1997; Runnymede Trust, 1994a, b, c.*)

These general statements reveal something of the effects of racist practices, but nothing about the ideas which lie behind them. We defined racism in the introduction, including the notion that institutionalized practices and procedures can have the effect, if not the conscious intention, of racist outcomes. This should not distract us from the fact that there is a considerable degree of negativity and hostility in common attitudes and assumptions about black people and Asian people. Racism also lives inside people's heads. As Figueroa (1984) puts it there is a 'racialized frame of reference', a filter through which experiences and information is interpreted and understood in such a way that 'race' and colour are felt to be significant and important.

A further indication may be given by the responses of some of our students when asked what they have *heard* about black and Asian people, thus revealing something of their 'racial socialization' without requiring them to expose their own beliefs. We have consistently found the following, strikingly negative, recurrent themes, indicated by the frequency of key expressions (N=390):

Key expressions	*per cent*
'They should go back to where they came from'	42
'If they come over here they should accept our ways'	26
'They're just different, they don't belong here'	20
'They smell'	20
'They're violent, they cause trouble'	18
'They are thick'	16
'They take all the jobs'	14
'They're scroungers, they're lazy'	14
'They have funny food'	12
'There's too many of them'	8
'They're dirty'	6
'They have loads of kids'	4
Miscellaneous negative	26
Miscellaneous positive	2

46 per cent of the students mentioned an average of three abusive names each for black or Asian people.

In addition, as repeatedly argued elsewhere (Gaine, 1987, 1995) children and adults are not isolated from racism or without a racialized frame of reference because they are isolated from or residentially peripheral to black and Asian people. Hostile, fearful or pitying responses were found, for instance, amongst 10 year olds in the rural south-west (see also Carrington and Short, 1995).

We would argue that the evidence presents a piecemeal but consistent picture of confusion, learned misinformation and (at times) hostility in which children and young people have to grow up. It is sustained not for the most part by people's interpretations of their own first-hand contacts or by immediate fears or anxieties, but in important ways by media and political representation about violence, numbers, difference and Britishness; perceptions and interpretations in real encounters; 'folk wisdom' which may be unchallenged by schools; anecdotes from friends and relatives in a culture of unchallenged beliefs, 'jokes' and shared assumptions rooted in the past (CRE, 1992a; Norwich REC, 1994; Searle, 1989).

This is not to say, however, that there are no contradictory voices about acceptance, individual worth and justice on which young people draw, but they seem less powerful. Though it is easy for white people to feel defensive, possibly 'accused' when faced with the facts of discrimination, a survey in the *Independent on Sunday* (7 July 1991) revealed that many in the white population recognized that black and Asian people did not receive equal treatment. A significant proportion of respondents felt that non-whites were treated worse than whites, especially by employers and the police; only about a third felt that things were getting any better. This was echoed in the 1997 PSI study (Modood et al.) and in another study (IPPR, 1997) 46 per cent of white people felt that 'people in this country are quite or very prejudiced against people of other races'.

'Asian' Family Patterns

Compared to classifying people by colour it is equally easy to classify people crudely by some notion of 'culture', and equally hazardous. There is no such thing as a single 'Asian' culture and even if there were it would be constantly evolving and reinterpreting itself in Britain. This is not to say that some older settlers themselves do not try to live in a kind of 'time capsule', staying with practices and beliefs which in truth have begun to change in their original homeland in the 20 or 30 years since they migrated. But all cultures are dynamic and subject to change, despite the efforts of what could variously be described as conservatism, nostalgia or religious conviction.

It is nevertheless the case that some generalizations have to be possible about the patterned cultural differences which clearly exist between African-Caribbean, white British and Asian people, particularly as regards the place of the family and of religion in everyday life.

A great deal of negative and positive stereotyping exists in this area. On the positive side, 'Asian' families are supposed to be close knit, supportive, valuing deference and respect for elders, with strong ideals of family honour and being successful for the sake of the wider family. Though somewhat idealized, this image of 'Asian' families is not a myth, and one index of this is the large number of terms (compared to English) in South Asian languages for family members, denoting the importance and intricacy of closeness, mutual dependence and deference. Singh Ghuman (1994) suggests 'Asian' families can often be characterized as having a 'collective' orientation compared with the western 'individualist' one. As an example of this, Shaw (1988) describes very close joint families amongst Oxford's Pakistanis, with adult offspring choosing work nearby to stay within reach of the joint family and family decisions being taken about who goes to higher education, who works in the family business, and so on. Modood and Berthoud (1997) report a significantly higher level of contact with relatives amongst all Asian groups than was the case with whites (with African-Caribbeans between the two). Jackson and Nesbitt (1993) note similar patterns amongst Hindus in the Coventry area, with a strong sense that the family consisted of up to 20 immediate members, who, if not living in the same house, were not far away and merged over meals, many finances, child care and the like. There was little sense of anything like a nuclear family:

> By comparison with their non-Asian (sic) contemporaries Hindu children in Coventry spend a great deal of time socializing with kin. . . . They are brought up to regard cousins as their brothers and sisters. They grow up with a powerful sense of the family as supremely important, as the context and model of social life. (p. 44)

> By contrast [with white children in Coventry] like their non-Hindu Asian contemporaries, Hindu children spend most of their evenings and weekends with their relatives. (p. 144)

This is reinforced in all the communities by videos of family and sometimes religious events whether they took place in Pakistan or North America, further binding people into a wider sense of family and community. Jackson and Nesbitt also refer to several studies suggesting a maintenance between generations of important religious practices and beliefs and their role in reinforcing a sense of responsibility, 'obligation and reliance' for other family members as well as the deference due to some and the importance of a wider religious community. A shared culture is also reinforced by language classes and Hindi/Urdu films in all south Asian groups, though the once common sharing of a south Asian film culture is now somewhat reduced by the widespread use of videos with the family at home.

Arranged marriages need to be understood in the light of the wider sense of the family and of actions and decisions being more than simply individual ones. In such a family structure it is hard to imagine an entirely individualist orientation to any important life decision. Marriage is therefore not seen as simply the union of two individuals but of two families and therefore of legitimate concern to both. In practice, choices and options are increasing for the potential partners, with education delaying the decision for many and agencies and newspaper adverts being used to find several partners to choose from (a similar situation exists in urban India and Pakistan). Arranged marriage is not specifically required by any of the three major south Asian faiths, though it is supported by religiously framed appeals to familial and filial duty.

Such accounts are not outweighed by but need to be tempered with a recognition that there are not only differences between Hindus, Sikhs and Muslims but also great diversity within each religious group, with sects and castes emphasizing differences in doctrine and practice and social class generating other sorts of divides. Conflict and divergence from 'traditional' paths also occur. The young do not always respect the ways of their elders, some people engage with the majority population in very different ways, not all young people want an arranged marriage, not all arranged marriages last, some British Asians are gay, some choose to be single.

'Asian' Culture and Gender

It is worth making a brief comment on different expectations of boys and girls in 'Asian' culture, with yet more caveats about the risks of generalization. For the most part, Asian girls' freedom of action (and hence their reputation and family *izzat* or honour) is more circumscribed than is the case for white or black girls and there is a greater preference for keeping the sexes apart during adolescence and for modesty in dress. As with marriage this is predominantly cultural, though some religious strictures are involved too. But it cannot simply be assumed that girls will not be encouraged to pursue their education, and while this may be to make them more marriageable, more than one study has found strong parental aspirations for girls, not least among Muslim fathers — Islam placing a high value on scholarship (Siann and Khalid 1984; Singh-Raud, 1997). Haw (1995) suggests that the girls she studied wished to achieve equality within Islam not without it.

In relation to the common assertion that south Asian culture, especially Muslim culture, is sexist, it is worth citing a Muslim woman's letter to a newspaper on this subject:

> *A swift appraisal of the terrifying oppression of Western women — whose labour is cheap outside the home and free inside it, whose bodies are commodities and sales incentives in the media, who have no respect if they work and no self-respect if they do not, and who are conditioned to go to extraordinary and painful lengths to make their bodies palatable for men — a swift appraisal shows that Western women are as oppressed (if more subtly) as their sisters in Islam.*

As with other cultural features of South Asian communities there is struggle and change and negotiation in process. Eade (1995) refers to one young Bangladeshi woman who comments:

> *Fatima:* The thing is I have lived in two societies really because when I go home.... I am back to being Bangladeshi.... When I go out it is British society. I don't really like the model any western society has to give about women but then again I don't like our Bengali role of women either.... I do like the Muslim role of women because that's what I believe in and I think from what I have studied about Islam that it gives women a lot of freedom to be themselves despite the fact that people think it doesn't.... I think I would agree that in this society rather than in Bangladesh I would have more room to be myself ... In Bangladesh women are, like, dominated totally, I think. It is all, like, men telling you what to do. Even though I think this society is too ... promiscuous ... I still think it gives women room to be themselves.... (p. 33)

And another who echoes the sentiments in the letter already cited:

> *Jahanara:* I think the Islamic position I would go for ... because it has given me everything and it has got a lot to offer me.... Yes of course I think everyone has the right to stand against oppression but at the end of the day the so-called liberated woman is being used all over again.... (p. 33)

Caribbean Families

A different and more negative set of generalizations need examining in relation to African-Caribbean families, which are depicted as more often dysfunctional than white families; frequently consisting of fatherless children from casual liaisons; within a culture preoccupied with music and style; being 'laid back' and living for the moment; at best happy-go-lucky and carefree in dead-end jobs; at worst unemployed, involved in drug dealing and street crime. We touched earlier on the myths and controversies surrounding young black people's involvement (or not) with crime and with the extent of unemployment and low waged work. As to family structures and more general cultural patterns, there are aspects of Caribbean history which go back to slavery and which may be with us still.

The commonest argument here is to do with the effect of slavery on family life and parental roles. In brief, under plantation slavery black people were owned by the estate, they received no wages, bought no clothes, chose no housing — these basic necessities were provided (after a fashion) but choice was also constrained in all other aspects of life. Slaves could not necessarily marry who they liked (indeed, many were forbidden to marry at all, certainly with any benefit of clergy). A woman's children were not uncommonly sold away from her, especially if they were fathered by an overseer or owner, but also if fathered by the woman's slave partner. The consequence of this was that whereas women were in practice inevitably responsible for infant and child care, fathers had virtually no way of exercising any paternal care at all, certainly not in any material way (Clarke, 1966).

Over two centuries these kinds of conditions produced sets of cultural beliefs and assumptions, which could not suddenly disappear once conditions changed. The pattern of ultimate responsibility for children falling upon mothers was clearly still in evidence in the 1950s in Jamaica, where over 50 per cent of births were out of wedlock (Hiro, 1973) at a time when this was still extremely rare in Britain. Interestingly, it has not greatly increased in the intervening period in the Caribbean, though the rates vary on different islands (CARICOM, 1995; Stuart, 1996). Most women in time settled with a permanent partner, but he would not necessarily be the father of her children. Arguably and controversially, some of this pattern persists still, and offers some explanation of family structures which are certainly different from that of most Asians, whatever their background. Whatever the causes, a far higher proportion of Caribbean mothers compared to white mothers in Britain are not only single but have never been married.

Academic and community work is more in evidence about this in the USA than in Britain. In the 1960s Moynihan (1968) suggested there was a distinctive pattern of family structure among the poor, which many took to mean 'the blacks'. The role of fathers was a particular issue here, with concern (not just in white liberal circles) about the kind of role models young black males had in poor inner city areas, with a high incidence of unsupported mothers, high crime rates, and widespread drug abuse. In the early 1990s the Supreme Court ruled unconstitutional an attempt by a black group in Detroit to set up a school specifically for black boys, in order to counter this. In contrast, it has been argued that girls have very positive and powerful role models in generations of independent and resourceful women.

However the legacy of slavery may have found its modern expression in Caribbean lower class and urban life, it is by no means as universal as the above account would suggest. For example, in all kinds of paradoxical ways the Christian church also played a part in the development of Caribbean culture (fuelling both emancipatory and racist ideas: Fryer, 1984) and there are numerous and large congregations of black churches with clear and unambiguous doctrines of respectability, Protestant hard work, chastity and Christian marriage. One in eight of all British Caribbeans belong to such churches and this proportion is higher amongst those under 25. Rastafarianism, too, stresses ideals of marriage.

As ever, the truth is complex, and as ever we have to be aware of having too simple a view of British Caribbean 'culture', which is neither static, nor one culture, nor easily separated from forces such as class differences, divergence between generations, and the influence of American representations of blackness.

Table 2.1: Main religious groupings amongst British ethnic minorities

Religion	Main roots of British ethnic minority believers
Islam	Pakistan Bangladesh India (*Gujerat*) Middle East Africa (e.g. Morocco, Somalia, Ghana)
Hinduism	India (*Gujerat and Panjab*)
Sikhism	India (*Panjab*)
Rastafarianism	Caribbean (the faith originates in Jamaica)
Christianity	Caribbean Hong Kong

Religion

It is not possible in the space available to give more than a superficial account of the main religious groupings amongst British ethnic minorities. We have touched several times in this section on the difficulty of separating religion from culture, and it would take a very detailed account to expand on the observations already made. We propose therefore to provide no more than an *aide-memoire* about roots and to refer readers to more detailed sources.[2]

It is fair to say that the most actively religious people in Britain are its post-war migrant population, with a high level of commitment to and involvement with temples (Hindus), gurudwaras (Sikhs) and mosques (Muslims), all of them built or converted from other uses (including as Christian churches) by the voluntary contributions of the worshippers themselves. 'New' Christian groups, like Pentecostalists, Seventh Day Adventists and the New Testament Church of God have almost entirely black congregations and 'represent one of the few growth-points in Christianity in Britain today' (Modood and Berthoud 1997, p. 300). But it is too easy to over-generalize: younger people are usually less involved than the second or first generation, and this varies between the faiths with Hindus being less formally devout (Singh-Raud, 1997) — though this may be as much a feature of social class differences — and a higher proportion of Muslims stating that religion was an important part of their lives (Modood and Berthoud, 1997, p. 301).

Traditionally many Chinese were Confucian or Buddhist, though the majority of Hong Kong Chinese in Britain (if they profess any faith) are Christians.

Notes

1 The figures given in this section are derived from several sources:

 The 1991 Census;
 Skellington and Morris (1992) *'Race' in Britain Today*;
 Jones (1993) *Britain's Ethnic Minorities*;
 Modood et al. (1997) *Ethnic Minorities in Britain*;
 Runnymede Trust (1994) *Multi-Ethnic Britain: Facts and Trends*;

 These are listed in full in the bibliography.

2 The best way to appreciate the subtlety and complexity of the interplay between 'culture', religion and life in Britain is via one of the detailed studies available. For Islam we would suggest Alison Shaw's *A Pakistani Community in Britain* (1988); for Hinduism, Robert Jackson's and Eleanor Nesbitt's *Hindu Children in Britain* (1993). Sikhs have not been the subject of such a full-length study and, although old, we would nevertheless recommend Parminder Bhachu's *Parental Educational Strategies: The Case of Punjabi Sikhs in Britain* (1985). Paul Singh Ghuman's *Coping with Two Cultures* provides some comparisons not only between Sikhs, Hindus and Muslims but also between the UK and Canada.

Social Class

Class in the Past

In some obvious respects social class cannot be 'seen' in the way that 'race' and gender can — it is much less easy to recognize someone's social class on sight. In the past divisions were more starkly visible in terms of clothing, speech, housing type and location, income and type of work. Victorian Britain had such clear divisions, with clear boundaries of wealth and status and shared assumptions about immutable differences between the classes and people's 'station in life' being fairly fixed: there were those with 'breeding' and those without, 'gentlemen' and 'ladies' were different sorts of people to ordinary men and women. These divisions were expressed and sustained by a distaste for social mixing, prohibitions about marriage, and a belief that the hierarchy was God-given. As the words of a Victorian hymn put it:

> *The rich man in his castle,*
> *The poor man at his gate,*
> *God made them, high or lowly,*
> *And ordered their estate.*

There were exceptions and infringements of course. It was not unusual for upper-class men to have relationships with lower-class women, but the very fact that it would have been unthinkable for them to marry tells us the strength of the social divisions. There was also a series of grades in the middle class from respectable large shopkeepers to junior clerks, where there was perhaps more mobility.

By the immediate post-war years in Britain many of the extreme divisions and boundaries of the Victorian age had gone, but there was still a relatively small elite whose sons went to public schools and the best universities, populated the upper reaches of the civil service, the forces, the Church and the city (Glass, 1954). A clear divide existed in housing, with large council estates adding to those built before the war and greatly improving upon the facilities of cramped Victorian terraced housing (Coates and Silburn, 1970). Though renting was far more widespread, better-off people rented in different areas. There were also markedly different occupational groups — most obviously the traditional working class communities based around docks, mining, fishing, shipbuilding, steelworks and other heavy industry, and clothing.

Class Today

There are five main factors which make Britain's class structure look so different today, which make it more 'fractured' or fragmented than it was in the 1950s and less of a clear and simple hierarchy:

- the erosion and disappearance of working-class communities around traditional industries;
- the appearance and development of many new kinds of jobs, especially in non-manual and service occupations. (This alone changes the 'feel' of class divisions because there is less of a divide between the harsh manual labour of some compared to the cleaner office work of others);
- the appearance of greater social mobility, more movement between levels;
- an overall rise in living standards, not least in housing;
- the blurring of boundaries and distinctions as a result of the factors above.

Items two and three are connected: there is more mobility because there are fewer manual jobs and more non-manual ones. It is not necessarily the case that Britain has become more meritocratic — people moving above *or* below their parents in income and status because of achievements and performance. With a changing occupational structure such a process is inevitable and in fact the evidence suggests that there is little downward social mobility (because in occupational terms there is less room at the bottom). In the nineteenth century many people did different kinds of work to their parents because the economy changed rapidly from rural to urban work; the same is true today because of more recent changes. Even if every son and daughter of those already in the higher social classes took up similar jobs to their parents, some would still need to be taken by people whose own parents had never dreamed of doing such work.

Nevertheless, such structural changes force changes in attitudes too, since there is a resulting increase in social mixing as a result of it (something given additional impetus by the war). A change in the occupational structure not only forces greater mobility but also an acceptance of that mobility. This, coupled with a general rise in living standards, means that some of the old rigidities have gone.

This is not the same as saying that Britain has become a classless society. There are still marked divisions in income and wealth and, indeed, these have *increased* during the 1980s and 1990s. In the past, it was predominantly the occupational structure and its different levels of rewards which created the class structure. Everything about life chances was determined by occupation (or previous occupation — the long-term unemployed in the great depression of the 1930s were predominantly unemployed from manual work). In the 1990s some of the worst off are on low pay (hence the political attention given to a minimum wage), but the new poor are in the main those unemployed or otherwise outside the working population: pensioners, single parents, the long term sick and disabled — and, it should be remembered, their children. 'The poor' are also not all white and male: there is a preponderance of mothers amongst single parents; women's greater longevity means they form the major-ity of pensioners; and significant numbers of ethnic minorities are in low paid occupations: for instance, 30 per cent of Pakistanis in work are receiving benefits (Modood and Berthoud, 1997).

The standard of living of all these groups is decided by the state since they depend either entirely or partly upon state benefits. In 1998 an unem-ployed couple with two children under eleven would receive about £115 per week, plus help with housing costs, council tax and free prescriptions. This is about half of the average after-tax income of working families of the same size and, of course, may be the family's income indefinitely. Suggestions of various kinds have been made about how to prevent this group from growing, both to control costs and to prevent the development of a 'dependency culture'. These suggestions include better benefits to those who cannot work; financial penal-ties to single mothers who have more than one child; 'workfare' for those who can work; and a minimum wage. Whatever strategies are adopted it needs to be borne in mind that, despite myths to the contrary, benefit levels have never been generous and that large numbers of people are not living in comfortable idleness on the state.

For those in work, too, there are more marked divisions than bland statements about rising living standards would suggest. Earnings and benefits at the top end of the scale are dramatically higher than those at the bottom, and low pay and temporary, insecure work keep many on low incomes. We think an appreciation of these figures is important both to teachers' perceptions of non-working parents and to young people's perspectives and aspirations with regard to work. To sum up:

- class has not gone away though it has become more fragmented and complex;
- large economic differences persist between different groups and, in some cases, differentials have increased;
- groups unable to work (for whatever reason) form a significant proportion of those who are worst off.

Identifying Different Classes

As we have been suggesting, although they are blurred and complex, patterned differences still exist between different 'classes'. These have conventionally been charted and measured by the Registrar General's Scale (the Registrar General being the chief official of the government's statistics-gathering work), a scale first devised in 1911 to monitor class differentials in health and constantly modified since. Official publications **never** use the terms 'middle' or 'working' class (today preferring the term 'socio-economic group') though they are widely used in educational literature. Despite changes in mobility and perceptions about class in recent decades, social scientists, politicians, government officials and market researchers all work on derivations of the scale outlined below, and hence on a notion of class which is more than just in people's heads.

Conventionally, manual workers have been thought of by researchers as 'working class' and non-manual workers as 'middle class' (with the 'upper class' regarded as a small minority who are off the scale or discussed more in terms of power than income). There are persistent problems in classifying families when parents are 'in' different classes, not at all uncommon especially in the middle. The rather rough-and-ready solution in the past was to use the male's occupation as the determining one. Another difficulty lies in the focus of most class scales upon employment. As mentioned earlier, there is a section of the population some call an 'underclass', signifying they are both beneath the income levels of most of those in work and outside the work system altogether. Sociologists argue about whether these constitute a class, since historically this has always been defined in relation to occupation, and concepts like 'mobility' hardly apply to someone who is too ill to work or to a pensioner whose working life is over. Using these established criteria, however, gives the following approximate picture for the early 1990s.[1]

Table 2.2: Occupations in the early 1990s

Class	Example occupations	Female workers %	Male workers %
Professional and managerial I	Top civil servants and military officers, judges and barristers, university lecturers, doctors, directors and senior managers of large companies	14	30
Intermediate non-manual II	Teachers, nurses, managers, salespeople, engineers, small business owners, librarians	21	11
Clerical junior non-manual III	Clerical workers, secretaries, police constables, some shop staff, supervisory staff and inspectors	30	6
Skilled manual IV	Plumbers, electricians, mechanics, hair dressers, cooks, brick layers	7	31
Semi-skilled manual V	Drivers, machinists, kitchen assistants	21	16
Unskilled manual VI	Labourers, cleaners, shelf fillers	7	6

The placing of jobs in different levels is not arbitrary or idiosyncratic, though one might argue about the details. The classes correlate with various important aspects of life, so that, broadly speaking, those higher up the scale earn more and own more wealth and, hence, have more consumer goods and take more foreign holidays, while their jobs indicate that they are likely to have spent longer in education. They work in jobs with more power and, hence usually, have more social status. It should surprise no-one that those at the top of the scale are very unlikely to live in council housing. More contentiously perhaps, the evidence is that they read different newspapers and are more likely to vote Conservative, they drink and smoke less (but they drink more wine), they also divorce less, suffer from fewer and different diseases and live longer, as do their children. (All of these generalizations can be confirmed by an examination of recent editions of the government's *Social Trends* (Office for National Statistics, 1996; 1997; 1998).)

It is important to remember the point in the Introduction of this book about differences being best understood as tendencies rather than as clear discontinuities between groups. Statements comparing the two extremes can be misleading, because gaps are nothing like as clear between 'adjacent' groups. However, the differences described above *are* especially marked at the extremes: the poor of towns such as Oldham and Salford have a death rate a third higher than is found in Cambridge or the Home Counties (Dorling, 1997). Life expectancy for men in Class I is five years greater than for men in Classes V and VI, and their children have lower infant mortality rate (ONS, 1997). All the evidence shows that these are not chance correlations but real differences between groups of people. They measure real differences in lives and life chances.

Awareness of Class and Class Cultures

This brings us to another aspect of class, class consciousness, or the element of social class which is present in people's heads. There is an old dictum in social science that if people perceive a situation to be real then it will be real in its consequences, and we would suggest that this is true of class. In the Victorian and early twentieth century world described earlier, an awareness of class divisions was evident. The Labour and Conservative Parties set out to have explicit class appeal, and the trade union movement in part encapsulated the solidarity of 'the workers' as opposed to everyone else. This is less in evidence today, with almost half of the TUC's membership made up of non-manual workers and a Labour Party explicitly aiming at a broad-based appeal. The General Strike was difficult enough to organize in the 1920s, with huge efforts to promote a sense of working class solidarity. It would be impossible on the same basis today. However, there are still more than traces of a sense of social differences, of 'us' and 'them', and there are symbolic aspects which are still recognized like accent (albeit less so) and taste (higher prices aside, Waitrose seems to set out to attract a different clientele than Tesco . . .). How this is played out in terms of school choice is explored in Chapter 7.

A sense of class differences may be closely connected to notions of different class *cultures*. There is ample evidence that there was at one time a set of beliefs, orientations to life and customs which could reasonably be called 'working-class culture'. Obviously it varied in different circumstances in different parts of the country and is much more complex than aspects of it romanticized on TV in *Coronation Street* or Hovis advertisements. It is hard to know to what extent this persists or in how uniform a way since, as we have said, the structures of employment and opportunity are more fragmented than before. Traditional research (e.g. Sugarman, 1970) suggested that the conditions of working-class life produced a different orientation to life in relation to planning for the future and making long term plans, as opposed to living more for the moment and within what is predictable. In a life where one feels relatively little control or autonomy, the argument goes that it makes sense to live life a day at a time and to be fairly fatalistic. This is reflected in attitude to work: routine (as opposed to skilled) manual work brings no inherent satisfaction — it is something to be endured, literally selling one's labour in return for enough money for life's necessities and some pleasures. Work is a job, not a career, and there is little prospect of promotion and hence of higher future earnings. Buying housing is beyond one's reach, so the long-term perspective and obligation of a mortgage is not part of one's experience or aspirations. This can be seen as a rational response, not a pathological one. To constantly believe life will get better, that one will be promoted, that one will be able to buy a house next year, when all the evidence is to the contrary would signal a poor adjustment to the realities of life.

There is a clear and obvious contrast to the conditions of some traditional 'middle class' work: a secure job, a progressively rising income with the expectation of earning more in the future than at present, the security to buy a house, an almost inevitable orientation towards the future. Some sociologists would call these descriptions 'ideal types', not real views or orientations as such, but a kind of distillation of real people's approaches to life, against which subsequent real people can be compared. 'Pure' examples of these ideal types are not likely to be found, but they represent a core or cluster of real views and orientations.

And Education . . .

It does not take very much imagination to see how cultural outlook may effect orientation to education. While, of course, many working class parents will want a wider range of opportunities for their children than they have experienced themselves, many will also socialize their children into the world they know (just like middle-class parents do) and may inculcate attitudes of short-termism and relatively restricted horizons. It should also be plain that material differences effect schooling. Homes with an income (or two) rather than income support, with more space, peace and quiet, and educational resources will find it easier to prepare children for school and support them while there than poorer homes. These issues will be explored further in Chapter 6.

Note

1   Derived from *The General Household Survey*, (OPCS, 1991); *Social Trends 22* (ONS, 1992) and Modood and Berthoud (1997).

3   Language

Language and Inequality: An Introduction

We want to introduce this chapter in some detail because, in our experience, there are a good many unspoken and unexamined assumptions about language and languages which need unravelling.

Language, Social Structure and Power

First, however, we want to raise a very obvious issue about what language is for and to make the connection between language and social structure. Clearly, language is for the purpose of communication, but it also acts as a vehicle for society's culture and social structure. A simple but graphic example can be found in words for 'you'. In French (and many other languages) *tu* is used when addressing one person and *vous* when addressing several. (English lost this ability some time ago, *thou* only surviving in Yorkshire and in the *Book of Common Prayer*.) In addition, *tu* is also used when addressing people close to you and, traditionally, for 'inferiors' like servants. The use of *tu/vous*, therefore, illustrates social distance, social status, and formality. It might be considered quite offensive, for instance, if we struck up a conversation on a French train with another passenger and used *tu*, since it would suggest we were being either over-familiar or patronizing. A snob, however, might deliberately use *tu* when buying the ticket, to signify his or her superiority, and the person serving would be risking their job to use *tu* in return. Thus, with every utterance the customer can assert his or her social power and with every utterance the person serving them has to confirm it.

Another example could be found in the deep south of the USA or in South Africa, at least in the past, where adult black men were routinely addressed as 'boy' by whites. Even white children could address black adults in this way without much fear of correction from parents or (overt) negative reaction from those so addressed. A ten-year-old white girl could address her family's black gardener as 'boy' and nevertheless expect a respectful reply. In some circumstances even a black lawyer or doctor could be called 'boy' by a much poorer and less educated white person, and have to swallow it without reaction. Every time such interaction took place it had the effect of recreating, reinforcing and cementing the racialized social structure. In this sense language is *behaviour*, it is more than 'just words' it is an active element in constantly remaking social inequality. Something similar is at work in conventions about who may call whom by their first names: social power is held by those who do not need to ask permission.

We would suggest there is some parallel between this and addressing or describing adult women as 'girls' (though of course such usage is often not seen as controversial, much less offensive). However, friendly banter among genuine equals aside (for example, a group of men amongst themselves) it is fairly unlikely that a lecture theatre full of 25-year-old males would be referred to by lecturers as 'boys', whereas women of the same age would much more often be referred to as 'girls'. We do not think this is trivial and without any wider importance. It may be argued that the women concerned would consider it a compliment, even more so if they were 35 and not 25, but this is precisely the point. The older a group of *men* are the more insulted they are likely to be if referred to as children; the older *women* are the more they might regard it as a compliment. In other words, men are more valued for their age (and hence maturity, wisdom, earnings or power) and women are more valued for their youth, when they have it. In this context, it becomes more significant that there is no unproblematic word for adult women in English: 'lady' is considered polite of course, but is a bit formal and carries some connotation of superior status over other females (originally it was the pair to 'lord'). 'Woman' is considered slightly less than polite, and 'girl', we are suggesting, is also the word we use for children. The same situation does not apply for 'man' or 'men'.

There is a related, but different argument about the terms that are used for minorities in Britain who have roots elsewhere in the world, especially if they are also darker skinned. Apart from older terms, which are widely acknowledged and known to be offensive, there are many words and phrases like 'ethnic minorities', 'minority ethnic group', 'other races', 'black people', 'Asians' and 'coloured people', about which 'white' people are very uncertain. This is not surprising since, as we have said, language has to carry key messages and be actively engaged in social distinctions and hierarchies, including those we are anxious or uncertain about.

'Race' is a particularly dangerous term with misleading connotations of fundamental physical differences between different types of people. You will find we *never* use it this way and that it is *always* possible to use a more accurate and less misleading alternative: nationality (Indian, Pakistani); religious group (Muslim, Sikh); language group (Gujerati, Panjabi, Bengali); regional group (Panjabi) or ethnic group (Asian, African-Caribbean, Chinese, African).[1] To use such terms does, however, require some confidence that they will be accurate in a particular case, so there is often a need for a more general term. 'Coloured' is a term still used by many white people but by far fewer African-Caribbean or Asian people, so we do not use it, and 'ethnic' (on its own) simply obscures the point that *everyone* has ethnicity, including white English people: everyone is 'ethnic'. In practice, most comment and research about ethnicity and education in Britain refers to those with roots in the Caribbean or the Indian sub-continent, so we tend to use the admittedly sweeping term 'black and Asian'. A more general term still, which includes Africans, Chinese and groups such as Poles and Jews, is 'ethnic minority' group (or 'minority ethnic').

As for 'acceptable' terms for different social classes, our own discomfort with the available terms emerges more than once in this book. We have no solution to offer, though we suspect the uncertainty about terminology is related to the ambiguity about class divisions discussed in Chapter 2.

This issue may be demonstrated in another way with respect to gender by a well-known riddle:

> A man and his young son are out driving one day when they are involved in a serious accident. The man is killed, but the boy is rushed to hospital unconscious and very badly injured. As he is wheeled into casualty and the doctors approach, one of them says 'My God! It's my son!'

How is this possible since the boy's father has just been killed? The answer, of course, is that the doctor is his mother. Obvious when it is pointed out but infuriating and puzzling if you do not spot it at once. Some people do (a minority) but we have found that even people who have heard it before can forget and still be stumped by it. Others can be left to think about it for hours and the penny not drop, with convoluted attempts to explain what, in hindsight, is so obvious (adoption, catholic priests, mistaken identity . . .).

Why does the story work as a riddle? It is partly because of a common association of 'doctor' with 'man' (the riddle also works if you substitute 'beggar'). Here language is both reflecting the world and helping to structure it for us: we use the word 'doctor' to interpret the story and to picture the scene, to make sense of it. If this is so, then to repeat an earlier point, language can not be thought of as trivial.

These last paragraphs may cause some readers to think of the term 'politically correct', an avenue there is not time to explore in any length. The least we can do, however, is to restate that what is happening in these examples to do with class, 'race' and gender is that language is reflecting social structure, social relationships and hierarchies. It is also recreating and reaffirming them. Language is more than 'just words' and if one fails to recognize this one fails to recognize its power. Furthermore, since language both reflects and helps create social structure, relationships and hierarchies then it will also constantly change. To insist on older terms or forms of language runs the risk of ignoring significant social change, however unwelcome. Not to reflect on language change runs the risk of being imprisoned by it, an imprisonment few people would want to own up to.

Language and Notions of Superiority

Those with social power, be they defined by sex, 'race' or class, tend to reinforce their power with the status of their own language or form of language.

This is evident in Britain in assumptions about the way females use language, the alleged superiority of English over other languages, and beliefs about a hierarchy of correct and 'corrupt' forms of English. Each of these will be explored in different but related ways in the succeeding three sections.

Gender and Language

There are three key aspects we want to consider in this section, building upon the observations already made:

1 The use of 'men', 'man' etc. to include women: usually referred to as the use of *male generics*;
2 The ways in which gender differences permeate language *semantically*, that is to say the *meanings and connotations* of words;
3 *Linguistic behaviour and interaction* between males and females.

We do not intend to spell out specific implications for school and classroom life. In our experience of many years of working with teachers, the information and arguments presented here give plenty of food for thought and room for reflecting upon one's own practice and assumptions. Penelope (1990) observes 'In a man's world, language belongs to men' and the extent to which this is true is, we think, surprising to most new readers in the subject. It is paradoxical that this should be so when the balance of evidence world-wide is that girls learn to talk and read earlier than boys and do better in language-based public examinations. It is of course possible that men's control over language is slipping. . . .

1 The Issue of Male Generics (i.e. when people say 'men', 'man', 'mankind', 'his' etc. it is meant to include both sexes)

Martyna (1980) asked groups of men and women to complete sentences containing nouns which did not indicate sex (like 'officer', 'teacher' or 'motorist'). She found that women were significantly more likely to complete the sentences using alternatives to 'he' and 'his' and that 60 per cent of the men, who used masculine pronouns, reported visualizing specific males in response to the 'neutral' sentences. In another experiment respondents were asked to match pictures of stick figures to statements containing words like 'man', 'men' and 'mankind' compared to 'human being', 'individual' and 'people'. The pictures showed four people in various male/female ratios but, in general, the respondents matched pictures of two men and two women only to the *inclusive* forms, never to 'men' or 'mankind'. What this work (arguably) shows is that while at a *conscious* level many people will say 'generic' words are not gendered, this may not actually be true: numbers of men and women do not, in fact, include both sexes when they use 'generic' male pronouns.

MacKay and Fulkerson (1979) suggest further arguments about this. They gave people sentences to read like 'An old housekeeper cleaned her carpet before sunrise' and asked whether this could refer to both sexes or only to one. Only 2 per cent said it could refer to both sexes as, in other words, there was no ambiguity about the sentence. However, with 'A bicyclist can bet that he is not safe from dogs' 87 per cent said this was only applicable to males (in other words, the sentence made them visualize a male cyclist) and this percentage was not reduced even when sentences containing nouns like secretary, typist or receptionist were used while retaining the male pronoun. Swann cites Silveira (1980) as reviewing 15 such studies, all of which had similar outcomes, demonstrating that most people do not really understand 'he' as applying to women as well as men (see also Spender, 1980, pp. 155–6). Another example of this kind of ambiguity is 'To survive, man needs food, water, shelter and female companionship'. 'Man' here is clearly 'Men' masquerading as a generic.

One indication that, at root, 'man' is not a generic term is a sentence like 'Man, being a mammal, breast feeds his young'. As the sentence starts it appears to make sense but by the end it is absurd. If there are occasions when 'man' cannot be substituted for 'human' then it cannot be considered as an equivalent word.

This takes us into a related area which linguists call 'inherent masculinity', whereby particular roles are assumed to be male. The sentence 'The Ancient Egyptians allowed women considerable control over property' in effect says that the *real* ancient Egyptians were men (it is easily rewritten as 'in ancient Egypt women had considerable control over property'). Consider also 'Mr Jones owns an estate agency with his wife', where there is some implication that it is *really* Mr Jones who owns it (as opposed to Mr and Mrs Jones own an estate agency). For another example, note what is going on in this sentence:

> They said that over the previous few days, paramilitary border police had been taunting the villagers by insulting their womenfolk from the hill above the village. (*Independent*, 14 April 1989, cited in Swann (1992) p. 36)

Until half way through the sentence 'villagers' could mean either men or women, but by the end they have been defined as male (the same often happens to farmer's wives).

How has it come about that 'men' and 'man', 'his' and 'he' is seen to include women when in fact it does not? Spender (1980) argues:

> There is sexism in the language, it does enhance the position of males. Men have had control over the production of cultural forms. It therefore seems

credible to assume that males have encoded sexism into the language to consolidate their claims of male supremacy. (p. 144)

But is there any clear historical evidence for this?

Smith (1985, p. 49) argues, that 'Man' used to be only used generically, with *wif* for females and *wer* for males, but gradually *wer* dropped out of use and 'man' came to mean both males and humans. This was a gradual, *social* process, presumably reflecting social power, not something inescapably built into our language and unchangeable (though this is not to suggest that twelfth century English did not encode inequality between the sexes in other ways).

Spender and Smith both try to trace the origins of male generics and find formal evidence in the work of male grammarians. The first reference to the issue appears to be in 1560, when it was described as 'natural' to place male before female (Wilson, 1560). Kirkby in 1746 was the first to codify 'man' as inclusive, his rule 21 (of 88 grammatical rules). But to repeat, grammar is not the same thing as tablets of stone handed to Moses, the formal rules are written by 'man' i.e. in practice, men.

> (Kirkby) . . . was a member of the dominant group and had the opportunity . . . of making his subjective meanings the decreed reality. (Spender, 1980, p. 148)

The 'universality' of inclusive pronouns really became insisted upon in the nineteenth century, when the commonest usage was actually 'they' or 'their' (as in 'anyone can play if they learn' or 'everyone has their rights'). We mostly speak this way still, yet formal grammarians might say we are 'wrong'. Bodine (1975) comments:

> This usage survives in spoken language despite almost two centuries of attempts by the education and publishing establishments to analyse and regulate it out of existence. (p. 130)

and Smith (1985) adds:

> . . . the exhortations of prescriptive grammarians concerning the use of generic *he* can be seen as little more than sophisticated rationalisations for a socially motivated language change, a change once again reflecting . . . aspects of the arrangement between the sexes. (p. 51)

We are all likely to vary in our response to this in our speech or in our writing. If you examine the passage in the introduction to this chapter about *tu* and *vous* you will see 'his or her' was used on one occasion, which some people find clumsy, and we also used the singular 'their'. If we were writing about the police it is easy to say 'police officer' rather than 'policeman', and it is just as easy to say 'business people' as 'businessman'. Here are several further examples, with some possible alternatives.

Table 3.1: Examples of gendered language

Original	Alternatives
early man	early humans
man made	artificial
manpower	staff, labour
mother earth	the earth, the planet
man, being a mammal, breast feeds his young	human beings, being mammals, are breast fed
the man in the street	ordinary people
the tables were manned	the tables were staffed
she mastered the art of . . .	she completely learned the art of . . .
master copy	original

The real point, however, is that there is no neutral position here. The teacher who does not reflect upon these issues is not *avoiding* gendered language. Whatever we do about this, we are still teaching our pupils and students something. . . .

2 *The ways in which gender differences permeate language,* **the meanings and connotations** *of words*

A good deal of our assumptions about masculinity and femininity are conveyed by nuances and usages of which we are scarcely consciously familiar. Take, for instance, the number of 'food' words which are used for females and for males:

Table 3.2: Examples of 'food' words

Female	Male
honeybun, tart, crumpet, honey, peach, tasty, dish, dumpling, bit on the side	beefcake dish

There are many more routinely used for females and they are generally *sweet* foods. A more striking example is provided by animal words:

Table 3.3: Examples of animal words

Female	Male
vixen, ducky, bird, foxy, old dog, dragon, bitch, bat, kitten, pussy, sow, mare, cow, shrew, bunny, horsey, hen, cat	stallion, tiger, ram, snake, rat, worm, wolf, old goat

Apart from the greater number of words applicable to women it is also noteworthy that they are all negative (except perhaps kitten, which of course is a *baby* animal). The male ones all have sexual connotations: the first three denote sexual prowess, the last five sexual betrayal or something disreputably sexual. The contrast is even more striking when comparing words for sexually active 'promiscuous' females and males.

The following list for women is part of one collected from students in 4 minutes in 1995:

Table 3.4: Words for women

slag	tart	nympho	slapper	wanton	trampette	village bike
loose	dog	whore	prozzie	hooker	scrubber	scarlet woman
cheap	easy	slut	lilo lil	strumpet	easy lay	easy virtue
harlot	goer	trollop	jezebel	Martini	mattress back	
hussy	chips	tramp	callgirl	floozy	24 hour garage	

A comparable list for men is shorter and also contains some 'positive' words, or words which many men (perhaps secretly) would not mind being called:

Table 3.5: Words for men

Positive	**Negative**
Casanova	rat
Romeo	snake
Don Juan	tart
stallion	slag
ram	womaniser
stud	gigolo
bit of a lad	wolf
ladies man	
sowing wild oats	
philanderer	

We have noticed an increase in the use of words like 'slag' for men over the past ten years. Whether this is due to greater equality in how men's and women's sex lives are regarded, or greater caution because of HIV it is hard to say.

This is old news, of course, everyone knows about the sexual double-standard. What we want to draw attention to is the function language is performing here — in short, it is trying to keep women in their place. This array of demeaning and insulting words are *control* words. Women do not like them and girls' lives can be made a misery by such a label being applied (see Lees, 1986 for some graphic accounts) so they will plan their behaviour accordingly. (Such control is not simply exercised by males, of course. For all kinds of reasons, which illustrate the complexity of sexism, women use this vocabulary on other women.) There is also a vast array of words which in the past two centuries have been used for prostitutes (over 200). These have moved in and out of common usage (for example, 'bat' originally referred to a 'night bird') but they indicate a social preoccupation with women and sexuality. There is no corresponding vocabulary for men who use prostitutes, and no male equivalent to 'She's a right little scrubber' — 'He's a right client' does not work, somehow.

Continuing this general theme of semantic nuances, there are some interesting 'pairs' of words which are not actually pairs at all, for instance:

master	mistress
king	queen
governor	governess
lord	lady
patron	matron
sir	madam
bachelor	spinster

All of these started life as roughly equivalent but the feminine words have taken on inferior status and often some sexual connotation too. This is called *semantic degeneration*, (or derogation, or pejoration, or polarization) another example of which is the origin of 'hussy': it began life as *huswif*.

> Lexicographers have noted that once a word or term becomes associated with women, it often acquires semantic characteristics that are congruent with social stereotypes and evaluations of women as a group. (Smith, 1985, p. 48)

Inherent masculinity is another feature of sexism in language first referred to under the issue of generics, though it is highly relevant here, too. An example used already is 'to master'. Now whether you as a reader find it irritating is not the point, it is undeniably a 'male' word which signifies something esteemed, and there is no female equivalent. A study by Nilsen (1977, p. 37) showed that words with male connotations were six times more likely to convey worth or prestige than those with female connotations. With adjectives he found that feminine negative words outnumber masculine ones by 20 per cent. Perhaps we should have used the word 'penetrate' instead of 'permeate' at the beginning of this section to demonstrate that there are also some highly value-laden words with no female form, like *emasculate*, or *virile*, or *potent*. . . .

Thus, in a different way from the implications of generics, 'In a man's world, language belongs to men' (Penelope, 1990, p. 1).

3 Linguistic Behaviour and Interaction between males and females

It is widely thought that men are taciturn and more reserved, 'strong, silent types', while women are garrulous, gossiping and nagging. It is also widely thought that women use more trivial words, stop talking in mid-sentence and endlessly talk about the same things, as in the children's song with the refrain: '*The mums on the bus go chatter chatter chatter* . . .' Yet this is not borne out by the evidence. For instance, in a comprehensive review of studies in laboratories, classrooms, meetings and TV chat shows, Graddol and Swann (1989) show that men talk more.

The contrast between male and female talk is not just one of quantity however. People with less power are often obliged to be more polite. For instance, interactions between pairs with unequal power (traveller/customs official; patient/doctor's receptionist; student/teacher) are likely to be characterized by more polite linguistic behaviour on the part of the first named — not talking out of turn or interrupting, listening attentively when the other speaks, probably talking less. In analysing interaction in conversations women have been found to match this pattern, to exhibit more of what might be seen as polite behaviour:

> they give more supportive cues ('Yes, I see', 'Go on . . .');
> they interrupt less (about 2 per cent) and protest less when interrupted;
> they take fewer turns in the conversation;
> they use shorter sentences and speak for a shorter time;
> they use more 'hedge' questions ('I wonder . . .' 'Do you know what I mean? . . .' usually seen as indications of tentativeness);
> they are more likely to be addressed informally.
> (Wolfson and Manes, 1980; Fishman, 1978; others cited in Swann, 1992)

Some of these depend on context and how the speakers see their own role and the purpose of the conversation, so Edelsky (1976) for instance noted that men were big talkers in formal university committees but not necessarily in informal ones, and women students interrupted as often as males in university tutorials.

It could be argued that this is part of a learned repertoire on the part of women of successful female behaviour, that is, being linguistically subservient. It is worth noting here a study by Bornstein (1978) which examined advice given to women from the Middle Ages to the Renaissance, finding that women were advised to speak little and when they did to be 'meek, sweet, gentle and polite' (p. 133; see also Coates (1993) for a review of similar work). This is rather similar to advice given to servants and to children.

This is reciprocated of course:

> Interaction features . . . play their part in the continual recreation of gender as a social division, as well as contribute to the connotations attached to being female or male. (Swann, 1992, p. 33)

This two-fold pattern of talking less in mixed company and using more subservient or polite linguistic behaviour may not match everyone's experience, but of course it is a generalization (and some writers have suggested that this is collaborative, non-competitive behaviour at least as much as it is subservient). Clearly some groups will not follow this pattern, and women undergraduates may be one such group. On the other hand, such processes may be subliminal, as evidenced in a story of Dale Spender's about an education conference she attended. The organisers were aware that despite their best efforts they had lined up a mainly male platform of speakers, so they decided to discriminate positively towards female questioners from the floor to restore the balance somewhat. The actual ratio of questions taken from the floor was 14 male to 9 female. Then, in a later session 10 males to 4 females, but when asked afterwards 27 out of 30 respondents said there had been more female speakers. Spender (1978) comments:

> A talkative female is one who talks as much as a man, when a female talks about half as much as a man she's seen as dominating. (p. 19)

In a subsequent session during the same conference, Spender monitored the ratio of male:female speakers and their share of the 'air time'. She found that of the 32 females present those who spoke did so for a total of 26 minutes, while the five males spoke for 32 minutes . . . *and no-one noticed*, including Spender. In classrooms, this pattern of unrecognized dominance has been reported by, for instance, Sadker and Sadker (1985) and Fisher (1991) noted in her infant class that, depending on the task, the ratio of girl:boy talk could not only vary by a factor of several hundred, but that in some group tasks however much girls said they were effectively ignored.

While we need to distinguish between on-task talking in class in accordance with the agenda set by the teacher and the range of other classroom talk (from subversive to disruptive), there has been in the past unambiguous evidence that boys of all ages dominated classrooms in terms of the quantity of air time, the prevailing atmosphere and the attention 'won' from the teacher (Swann, 1992, pp. 51–2 has a comprehensive summary of this work). There has also been detailed work on how they managed this. French and French (1984) suggest it may be by giving an answer that is out of the ordinary, thus provoking a further question from the teacher. Graddol and Swann (1989) found they had to look at both the behaviour of the teacher *and* the pupils to see what was going on. It can seem as though the boys 'chip in' more, but analysis of video tapes showed that the teachers were more often *looking* at boys as they posed a question, thus inviting them to respond, albeit subliminally. 'The cues used were quite subtle, and probably operated below the level of conscious awareness' (Swann, 1992, p. 62).

At one time, argument of a particular intellectual kind was perceived by some as 'unfeminine', making it risky for adolescent girls. In classrooms teachers not uncommonly used to say 'Girls talk all the time to each other', but then in these circumstances, denied air time by the boys, they would, wouldn't they? But do they still? In the late 1990s we have seen a marked change in educational outcomes whereby it is now girls who succeed better across all subjects up to the age of 18. The admission of young women into higher education has rapidly increased and the male predominance amongst newcomers into at least some well-paid occupations (medicine, accountancy and the law) has been reversed. It may well be that this has been accompanied by an increase in girls' confidence and participation in the contested space of classroom air time. It is too early to say, but given the unconscious and un-recognized nature of much of the patterns described above, we should be wary of assuming they no longer need our attention.

Implications

As we have already suggested, it is not straightforward to simply 'read off' implications and strategies for teachers with regard to gender and language. We have five main conclusions:

- language carries many subtle messages about gender of which we are not always consciously aware;
- whether we like it or not our own use of spoken and written language teaches something to our pupils or students, so classroom materials, resources and strategies ought to take account of this;
- the dynamics of linguistic interaction have, until now, favoured males and marginalized females, though this may be changing;
- patterns of interaction are not the responsibility of one party. If boys continue to dominate classroom talk to an extent which is unfair to girls then it is likely that there is something girls, boys and teachers are all doing to allow it;
- language use is highly personal and can arouse strong feelings, so few people will change it easily or quickly.

'Race' and Language

Bilingual Children and Schooling

Language is both more and less important than is often thought in the lives and schooling of ethnic minority young people.

In the past it has too often been assumed that for some children their own language is a disability preventing them acquiring English — this implicit theory of language holds that the language capacity of the brain is like a milk bottle — only big enough to hold a certain amount, so a child's first language has to be emptied out before a new one can be put in. More technically, this model would be called 'subtractive bilingualism' — the second language grows at the expense of the first.

In our experience, the milk bottle theory has more often been applied to south Asian children than, for instance, European children. The child arriving in school speaking Russian or French is regarded as having a valued asset which the other pupils are invited to marvel at, whereas the south Asian (or African, or Turkish) child may not even be asked what language they actually speak.[2] We would not make such assumptions about other skills. If a child who was an accomplished pianist arrived at a school where violin playing was strongly encouraged, the school would not say 'Sorry, we only speak violin here' (even if they had no pianos), since it would be taken for granted that the child's understanding and knowledge of music would involve many transferable skills and could be used to help them learn the violin. In principle this has often been the implicit message to south Asian children (by far the largest bilingual group), leading the Linguistic Minorities Project (1985) to remark: 'The status of a minority language is based not on any inherent characteristics of the language but rather on the status of those who use it' (p. 106).

For the most part this is not the approach taken by parents, who regard their children's first language as crucial. An example may illustrate this:

Jasprit speaks English and Panjabi. She uses English in lessons and usually to talk with her friends (even if they are also Panjabi-speaking) though sometimes she will use Panjabi to talk about RE. When she talks to friends about football she uses English, but if they are discussing a family wedding she will use Panjabi since she has more relevant concepts in that language, but also because it is a part of herself she expresses in Panjabi. When she goes home she will switch between the two with her parents and family. Both her parents work in offices so are completely fluent in English, but they too use Panjabi for family matters, telling the children off, discussing relatives and visits, food and clothing. Jasprit also uses Panjabi when she talks with one of her uncles, who is less good at English than her parents, and whenever she goes to the Gurudwara. The Panjabi of the Sikh holy book is archaic and formal, so she does not really understand it, but the prayers are not, and there is a sense in which she cannot be a Sikh if she loses her own fluency. She is a good illustration of the usefulness of the term 'heritage language' to describe her Panjabi: it is not her first language, it is not really her mother tongue, but it symbolizes and enables her to live out her heritage in everyday life.

Though the details will vary, a similar pattern of complex language use applies to many ethnic minority children, especially where family relationships are concerned. None of this is to say that speakers of Punjabi or Urdu or Cantonese do not need to learn English. The concern of parents to ensure mother tongue maintenance is often misunderstood in this way, as evidence that 'they come over here and don't want to accept our ways'. But the assumption that 'they don't need their own language now that they're here' is a profoundly British (or English?) and monolingual one. In fact, most of the world operates in more than one language, but English is so powerful and all-pervasive that this is easy to forget. For most white British people all aspects of their identity can be expressed in their one language, but this is not the case for the examples above (which could be added to by examples from other parts of the sub-continent and from Africa), or British people with a Polish or Italian background, or the Welsh, or German speakers in Switzerland, or Greek Americans. The parents of bilingual children know very well that their children need English to succeed in Britain — after all, many of them have lived through many years of imperfect command of the language, either written or spoken, with all its consequences for employment, promotion, dealing with crucial services like health and education, and filling in forms and documents. They do not need anyone to tell them that their children will be disadvantaged without it (see Chapter 2), but at the same time they do not subscribe to the milk bottle theory. They do not want their children to be ESL but bilingual (or multilingual). To expect otherwise would be to expect people to have plastic surgery on their identity.

The most numerous and widespread are those of south Asian descent, so some key information is summarized in the following table (it may be best viewed in conjunction with the geography described in Chapter 1):

Table 3.6: Examples of the relationship between 'race' and language

Group Name	Geographical Roots	Religion	Spoken Language	Written Regional/ National Language/s	Religious Language
Bangladeshis/ Bengalis	Sylhet region of Bangladesh, itself part of Bengal	Muslim (almost always, small % Hindu)	Bengali-often called Bangla; Sylheti dialect	Bengali	Classical Arabic
Indians (Panjabis)	*Indian* state of Panjab	Majority Sikh, some Hindus	Panjabi, many understand Hindi too	Panjabi for preference, Hindi for some	Panjabi Sanskrit for Hindus
Pakistanis	*Pakistani* state of Panjab	Muslim	Panjabi and Urdu (similar to *spoken* Hindi)	Urdu (uses different script from Hindi)	Classical Arabic
Indians (Gujeratis)	Indian State of Gujerat	Mostly Hindu, some Muslims	Gujerati, many speak Hindi too	Gujerati and Hindi	Sanskrit Classical Arabic for Muslims
Chinese	Hong Kong	Christian Confucian Buddhist	Cantonese Chinese, sometimes Hakka Chinese	Chinese (shares same characters as Mandarin Chinese)	No specific language

Caribbean Language and Schooling

The situation is and has been more complex with children of Caribbean background and to understand why it is necessary briefly to explore something of Caribbean linguistic history before migration to Britain (despite the fact that in the 1990s there are virtually no migrant Caribbean children in British schools, they are all British-born).

The story really begins with West African slavery in the Caribbean (and the USA). Slaves were captured or bought from a wide area of what today includes Ghana, Nigeria and Liberia. They spoke different languages in the sense that Twi, Yoruba and Hausa have different vocabularies but came from the same language tree so they have similar structures — ways of showing the future tense, signifying plurals, emphasizing adjectives, etc. The slave owners deliberately mixed the different language groups in their purchases since it was felt that large numbers of slaves who could communicate easily with each other in one plantation would heighten the risk of rebellion. The owners, of course, spoke English (or French, Dutch or Spanish, depending on the island) and they spoke this to their slaves. It was fairly simple English. Firstly, they had no need to convey elaborate or subtle meaning, the language was merely a contact language for the simple purposes of plantation life and keeping order. They obviously knew the slaves were not fluent in English and they did not have a high opinion of the Africans' intelligence. The slaves, for their part, needed a way of communicating with each other as well as with their owners, and the only common vocabulary available was English, the only words they all heard for *water, midday, stop work, come over here, work harder* etc. were the English words (though it may be that this process began on the West African slave coast with Portuguese as the dominant language later to be superseded by others under slavery). The words of the dominant language quickly came into use amongst them, though they connected them via the linguistic rules they understood: the shared grammatical rules of their West African languages.

In a situation where several subordinate languages are brought into forced contact with one dominant language a new, relatively simple, language emerges: linguists call this language a *pidgin* and the process *pidginization*. It is not unique to the Caribbean. English and French probably began as pidgins when the Romans unified linguistically different tribes with Latin as the dominant language, and it has been studied in detail in the Far East, particularly in New Guinea. Such a language, however, has many limitations. You can trade and give orders in a pidgin but you cannot tell someone you love them, discuss things in the future conditional tense, or convey subtle shades of meaning. Pidgins are, therefore, never anyone's mother tongue because they are incapable of carrying out all the functions of a true language — 'Pidgins are by their nature auxiliary languages' (Crystal, 1987, p. 336). Where such a language is needed (as it was by the slaves in the Caribbean and in the USA), then the pidgin develops its functions and range, and becomes a full language called a *creole*.

Again this is probably the root of modern English and French. Whatever the original dominant language, the pidgins/creoles in the Caribbean are often actually called *Creole* by their speakers (or *Patois/Patwa* in some islands). Confusingly the word *creole* has also come to be popularly associated with the hybridization of French culture in the Americas generally, for instance in cooking. Linguists only use it with the specific meaning outlined above (see Dalphinis (1985) for a full discussion of this history, and Edwards (1979)).

In principle, we need to distinguish this process from anything to do with accent, or the way words are pronounced. Caribbean pronunciation differs from accents of mainland English because of the phonetic patterns and rhythms of west African languages (so 'th' becomes *t* or *d*; 'early' becomes *aarly*) and while perhaps relevant for spelling it is a relatively superficial aspect of the language and should not be confused with deeper structural processes.

The slaveholders were obviously not predisposed to regard their slaves as equals — it is not possible to permanently enslave your equals and their children — so they did not regard the language which developed amongst them as worthy of much note. In fact, they seemed to think that it was the humble attempt of primitive people who were not intellectually capable of speaking English, resulting in a kind of childlike talk 'without' tenses, plurals and the like. The owners thought they were mimicking this in speaking to the slaves in simple, baby-like phrases: 'sittee here'; 'me no like your work' and so on.

If one group really wants to dominate another, they need not only to convince themselves that their language is superior, but also to convince the group they dominate of the same thing, and so it has been with Creole. It is not 'broken English' or bad English, or slang, or an inadequate attempt by an inferior 'race' to speak a language that is beyond their powers. Well after the end of slavery, people who grew up in the Caribbean were taught to believe that it was. What is shown as a continuum below was in fact seen as a hierarchy, with full creole at the bottom.

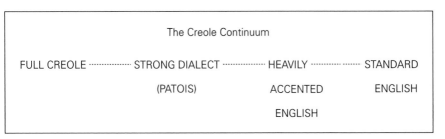

Figure 3.1: *The Creole continuum*

In a sense they were right about its inferiority in that it had less *cultural* power: it was not a language which would get children good school results and into the Caribbean middle class. It was not the language of high culture or of administration and government, but this does not make it inferior in the linguistic sense.[3] It is not necessarily less capable of conveying complex mean-ing, and it is no less governed by rules and grammatical principles. In this respect the same argument applies to dialects of English indigenous to the British mainland which are discussed in this chapter's section on class. This is not an argument about linguistics but about linguistic power, and who has power to stigmatize and prioritize. One gets a different sense of the power relations involved if one calls the language 'Broken African'.

It made good sense for Caribbean parents to stress the importance of Standard English as a tool for secure employment, but this does not necessarily imply that a version of the milk bottle theory — the *dialect inference* model need apply to Caribbean English — though, as discussed later in relation to class dialects, it is often assumed that it does. It is perfectly possible to teach children that dialects are variants from the standard and prestigious form, with different grammatical rules and different appropriateness in different situations — indeed, many would argue that it is less confusing (and undermining) to use this *repertoire* approach than to tell children that the way their parents and community speak is 'wrong' or 'bad' or 'sloppy' or ignorant (the *deficit* approach).

The relevance of this to Caribbean migrants to the UK is that they and their language met these assumptions about superiority and inferiority. Chil-dren spoke and wrote their best English according to rules they knew, but their English was not the same as Standard English. They rarely met the reper-toire approach and for some (Swann (1992), for instance, is careful to stress that this was far from universal) this inhibited their acquisition of Standard English. Historically this must have some effect on overall school performance, though it is arguable how much it does so today since few parents of school age children speak a strong Creole.

However, this leads us to a further important aspect of Caribbean English which needs exploring. For some of the reasons explored in Chapter 2, Carib-bean migrants to Britain experienced a degree of cultural alienation. Having come, as they thought, to the 'mother country', they found themselves rejected. While for British Asians the consequences have been less acute because of the distinctiveness of their religious, linguistic and cultural traditions, African-Caribbeans were much more culturally British, or so they thought. Faced with the situation of not being recognized as who they thought they were, African-Caribbeans had to construct and develop an identity for themselves. Some did this in distinctive forms of Christianity, many took part in the huge growth of Rastafarianism in Britain in the 1970s and 1980s and most swelled the grow-ing audience for Reggae. These latter phenomena gave a vehicle for the con-struction of a distinctive identity through language. This meant that young people who had never set foot in the Caribbean and who grew up speaking largely cockney or scouse (with perhaps some use of their parents' Creole) self-consciously adopted the speech forms of their parents or grandparents (sometimes much to their bemusement or annoyance) as a way of affirming an identity and as an act of cultural resistance.

The young black people of Britain who are into black consciousness and cultural awareness are keen to speak Afro-Lingua because it reinforces their awareness and gives them hope where otherwise there would be despair. (Jah Bones, 1986, p. 45)

In some respects this process has something in common with distinctive *argots* or speech forms developed by various youth cultures, but it has been far more important to young British blacks and they had a rich cultural seam on which to draw. It has been, however, a creative process rather than a mimicking one. The 'Caribbean English' spoken by many young British black people today is a new variant, called for instance 'London Jamaican' (Sutcliffe and Wong, 1986; 1992; Edwards, 1986), or by the speakers themselves as 'Jamaica talk' or 'backyard lingo' (Wong, 1986), and is used in very complex ways as an adaptation of London English. It varies not just in vocabulary and grammatical rules but also in pronunciation and rhythm. This is interwoven with aspects of black British life and with Rastafarianism for some: 'Babylon' for instance being used to signify both life in an oppressive white society and the police specifically, and 'overstand' being used to signify a non-subordinate understanding. Some words, such as *se*, which means 'that' in certain contexts, has traceable African roots. Interestingly, and reminiscent of work on white dialect speakers, Sebba (1983) reports some gender differences, with women using English more while being just as fluent as men in 'Jamaican'. It has also developed into a shared 'youth' form of language in some mixed neighbourhoods (Rampton, 1995).

In the linguistic terms discussed earlier this does not have the same educational implications, since these distinctive speech forms represent a consciously developed repertoire and hence not one with which its speakers need any help from teachers. It has some significance in terms of sub-cultural (and gendered) dynamics in many secondary schools however, (see Chapter 5) since many black students have at their disposal an identity-affirming and other-excluding form of speech which they are all the more likely to use in the face of adult exhortations to 'speak properly'.

It is not difficult to appreciate . . . why Patois or Creole soon assumed such importance, especially where it was necessary for intra-community communication that excluded others. The language became at once a source of pride as well as a barrier behind which the community survived. (Wong, 1986, p. 121)

Implications

- Class members who are not fluent in English present special challenges to the teacher as well as the pupils, but the challenge will not be met by regarding this as a deficiency or a nuisance.

- The best way of promoting children's overall linguistic skills, including their competence in English, is to acknowledge and validate the importance of other languages in their lives.
- For the foreseeable future, heritage languages will continue to be important to minority communities in Britain, just as Italian and Greek continue to be spoken in the USA.
- Government policy, which moved to a more or less exclusive emphasis on acquiring English competence in the 1990s, needs to revert to the greater support for bilingualism available in the 1980s.
- The linguistic and cultural significance of Caribbean forms of English needs to be recognized.
- Where appropriate, *repertoire* approaches need to be adopted rather than *deficit* or *dialect interference*.

Class and Language

Are Some Dialects Better than Others?

In the 'race' section we examined the status of different forms of English. There are related issues in 'mainland' English in relation to *dialects*, which can be defined for the moment as varieties of a language with differences from other varieties in pronunciation (accent), vocabulary and grammar, more often in the spoken than the written form.[4] Dialects can be either regional or social, though these are often related, the variation arising from geographical factors and/or social ones. Thus, the higher one's social status the more likely one is to speak in the high status dialect wherever one lives, and *vice versa*. Perhaps especially, but certainly not exclusively, in Britain, dialects are inextricably bound up with class as well as region.

It is important not to be distracted by accent, which is only one part of dialect. In Britain the prestigious mode of pronunciation is commonly called 'Received Pronunciation' (RP,[5] and BBC English or Oxford English, though it is not regionally specific). An RP accent does not guarantee that the speaker is using Standard English (SE) grammar and vocabulary, as Eliza Doolittle demonstrates in Shaw's *Pygmalion* when she says 'Cor blimey' in her best 'posh' voice. It sounds odd, but there is no reason why one cannot pronounce 'Ay up, Chuck, there's trouble down at t' mill' in a voice like the Queen's, and one can speak SE in any accent (take Ian Paisley for example). The essence of this issue is not about accent but about grammar, or rather grammars; what really marks out dialects is that in complex ways their grammatical rules vary.

Take the SE sentence 'Southampton is 20 mile_s_ away'. In Geordie this would be 'Southampton is 20 mile_ away', not because Geordies are ignorant about the use of 's' to pluralize nouns (they would say 'I can see six ship_s_' just like an SE speaker), but because Geordie grammar does not pluralize nouns of distance (or nouns of time as it happens, as in 'I came here 20 year_ ago'). The key point is that this is <u>rule governed</u> language, not random or ignorant variations, and the rules are applied consistently by Geordie speakers. In this example there is nothing inherently <u>linguistically</u> superior about the rule in SE or the rule in Geordie. Neither leads to confusion to speakers of that dialect or usually to listeners, since the plural is clear from the number '20'. Similarly, expressions like 'It was him what done it' represent not the stupidity of Cockney speakers, nor their laziness, nor is it 'ungrammatical' speech since it is obeying the rules of Cockney grammar. In a sense it may be 'ignorant' since it may reflect a lack of knowledge of SE grammar, a sign of formal education, but that is a literal and not derogatory sense of 'ignorant'. Linguistically, the SE and RP speaker, who does not know the rules of Geordie or Cockney grammar, is just as ignorant, but ignorance of low prestige forms does not have the same consequences.[6]

A third element of dialect is vocabulary, which we have not dwelt on here because in some ways it is more obvious. There are many regional variations in vocabulary around Britain, like *burn* (stream), *bairn* (child) in Geordie and *wee* (small) in Glaswegian, or pronunciations so specific that they are in effect different words, like the Geordie *gannin haem* (or *yem*) (going home). Usually they have their roots in the different languages which have contributed to English. For example, Scandinavian languages and Gaelic in the North East, French in the South, old Celtic forms in Cornwall, and oddities like a cup of *char* in Cockney, which was brought back by working class Londoners from service in the army in India. Sometimes, they are older words which other varieties have abandoned: *burn* (as stream) will be found in Chaucer's English; Yorkshire still has *thou*; and Geordies tend to say *cannat* (i.e. an accented 'cannot') and therefore a fuller and less abbreviated (or 'lazy'?) form than the SE 'can't'.

The following table may make some of these distinctions clearer:

Table 3.7: Dialect distinctions

Dialect	Geordie	Standard English	Cockney
Pronunciation	bath ah divn't nar	baath I don't know (RP)	baaf oy dunno
Vocabulary	bairn nowt	child nothing	kid nuffing
Grammar	three mile	three miles	three (free) miles

If some of these are combined into a sentence such as *Ah divn't nar nowt aboot that bairn's bath* there is another dialect feature not found in SE, namely the double negative, which is relatively common in non-standard forms.

There is a widespread belief that Standard English (SE), the English of the 'quality' newspapers and of this book, is somehow *proper* English and in some way superior to other forms. As Trudgill (1995) puts it

> So statusful are Standard English and the prestige accents that that they are widely considered to be 'correct', 'beautiful', 'nice', 'pure', and so on. Other non-standard, non-prestige varieties are often held to be 'wrong', 'ugly', 'corrupt', or 'lazy'. Standard English, moreover, is frequently considered to be *the* English language, which inevitably leads to the view that other varieties of English are some kind of deviation from the norm, the deviation being due to laziness, ignorance or lack of intelligence. (p. 8, original emphasis)

In fact, SE is a dialect like all the rest, only a dialect with greater social prestige and power, with historic roots in the seat of social prestige and power: London. As someone once said 'a language is only a dialect with an army and a navy', so the question 'Are some dialects better than others?' depends on whether one means linguistically or socially 'better'. SE is also the dialect most often used in print and it is what foreigners learn, so there is a third sense of 'better', meaning 'useful' for wider communication, or appropriate. In a language as widely spread and used around the world as English, there is clearly enormous value in having a standard form. At the same time it makes little sense to a child who is speaking (and possibly writing) according to a perfectly consistent and rule-governed grammar to be told that it is 'wrong' — at least the only sense that can be made of it is to deprecate the child's family and community.

Class and Code

The issue of dialect is often confused with a famous (or infamous) concept in sociolinguistics: that of social class and different linguistic *codes*. In brief, the concept was developed by Basil Bernstein from 1958 onwards and must have become one of the most taught and mistaught ideas about educational disadvantage.

Bernstein argues that middle class speech is typically more capable of abstraction and analysis than the more 'concrete' working-class speech, which he argues depends more on shared meanings and assumptions between the speakers, with all redundancy removed. Middle-class speakers are therefore more able to deal with concepts and ideas and hence at an advantage in the worlds of education and better paid work, where (in Piagetian terms) more formal operations are required. Working-class speakers are disadvantaged (the argument goes), because without shared meanings and concrete situations to refer to they are less linguistically adept, less able to organize and respond to experience linguistically in a way which is not context-bound, more 'habituated to short-run searches in their verbal planning operations' (Lawton, 1968). Their use of language is impoverished, or as Bernstein has it they use a *restricted code* in contrast to the middle class *elaborated code*.

This has nothing essentially to do with intelligence, of which Bernstein says 'The role intelligence plays is to enable the speaker to exploit more successfully the possibilities symbolized by the socially conditioned linguistic forms . . .' (1961; cited by Lawton, 1968, p. 89), and it has nothing essentially to do with dialect or vocabulary (though these are likely to be different amongst restricted code users for the reasons already discussed, and there is an undefined reference in his 1959 paper to 'poor syntactic construction'). In fact, he says that middle class people who know each other, like family members, often use restricted codes with each other, with short sentences, few adjectives or adverbs, even unfinished sentences, with gesture and tone of voice carrying meaning as well as the words. He calls this highly context-bound pattern of speech — 'particularistic'. The difference is, he argues, that middle class people are also able to use an elaborated code, with more detail in terms of description, adjectives, symbolism, logical and other relationships, and hence 'universalistic'. The example Bernstein uses to put over what he means by *code* as distinct from other features of language is the description used by two different five-year-olds of events portrayed in pictures of boys breaking a window in the course of playing football:

They're playing football . . . and he kicks it and it goes through there . . . it breaks the window and they're looking at it . . . and he comes out . . . and shouts at them . . . because they've broken it . . . so they run away . . . and then she looks out . . . and she tells them off.

Three boys are playing football and one boy kicks the ball . . . and it goes through the window . . . the ball breaks the window . . . and the boys are look-ing at it . . . and a man comes out and shouts at them . . . because they've broken the window . . . so they run away . . . and then that lady looks out of her window . . . and she tells the boys off. (Bernstein, 1970, p. 167)

The former description cannot be understood without the picture, the latter can.

Bernstein accounts for these differences in terms of the conditions of working class employment and working class domestic life, both of which he characterizes as less flexible and more contained within understood and clear boundaries, though authority may be exercised in an arbitrary way. He sug-gests speech patterns tend towards 'sympathetic circularity', that is, gaining some indication of understanding from listeners 'to enhance the solidarity of the social relationship' rather than extend curiosity or the manipulation of ideas. Arguably supporting Bernstein's case, Heath (1983) suggests some im-portant differences in the ways that written texts are used in different homes. Those who learn to use and interact with texts in a 'school-orientated' way predictably find their skills help them at school. Others learn about literacy more in group or family contexts and learn particular skills about making connections between things and situations.

There has been some debate over the years as to whether Bernstein thought of the working class speech patterns he described as inferior, as is certainly suggested by his terminology (indeed, Lawton (1968) suggests Bernstein is in effect producing a version of the Sapir-Whorf hypothesis — see note 3 on p. 60). I would suggest that at least in his earlier work there is an implication that elaborated code is better at dealing with higher order and abstract concepts and, therefore, a ready explanation for some of the pattern of lower achievement by working-class pupils.

It has to be said that Bernstein's thesis has two significant shortcomings: scant empirical evidence and a considerable lack of precision about 'middle class' and 'working class'. As regards evidence, the two extracts quoted above are not in fact quotations from *actual* boys but a distillation of the kinds of differences Bernstein encountered. Actual quotes and more detailed examples — the kind of evidence which would nowadays be commonplace in research reports — are few and far between in Bernstein's original work. To be fair, his best known work was unashamedly theorizing beyond the data, so it is not surprising that his statements are not always rigorously supported, but because of this we have to be at least cautious about its validity and reliability.

The second problem is the extent of generalization and imprecision. Is Bernstein describing 'traditional' working-class communities like mining villages or are his claims true of most families where the parents are manual workers? Indeed, are the 'middle class' he refers to homogenous? Even if the generalizations were not too sweeping in the early 1960s when Bernstein first began publishing his ideas, they must be suspect today. Given the changes in the British class structure described in Chapter 2, it would be unwise to describe it as anything other than many-layered and blurred, with few stark boundaries between different groups' experiences and educational outcomes. At the extremes, the many small gradations along the way add up to clear discontinuities and differences, but in many aspects of life, not least language codes, we think it is a mistake to think of a clear two-fold structure.

The best known rebuttal of Bernstein's work is by the American William Labov, though it is likely Labov was rebutting American versions of Bernstein's work filtered through their own assumptions about social class and 'race'. At worst, it was argued that some black children had no real language at all, that their speech was 'nothing more than a series of emotional cries' (Labov, 1972a, p. 183) and hence an extreme case of Bernstein's restricted code. A good deal of Labov's most well-known article on the subject is devoted to demonstrating that the apparent lack of speech in young black children was due more than anything to the test situation, with unfamiliar, smart, middle class, white interviewers. With these factors altered the children became much more talkative, and Labov gives a particular example of a boy who confidently discusses the abstract and subtle concept of God in what might appear to the less informed listener as 'restricted code'. Labov thereby makes two points: firstly, that working-class language, given the chance, may be more subtle and complex than middle-class prejudices allow, and secondly, that 'elaborated code' may be simply 'an elaborated, rather than a superior code or system', and at times 'turgid, redundant and empty' (p. 192).

This is not to say that there are no children growing up in circumstances where their language is impoverished, their vocabulary limited and their conceptual development thereby impeded, but it is to say that this cannot be sweepingly associated with 'the working class' and that it has no necessary connection with non-standard forms of grammar. Further, if there *were* such things as different language codes roughly correlated with working and middle class groups in the late 1950s, the fragmentation of such groups in the past 40 years makes such identification even more hazardous today.

Implications

- Varying accents and dialects need to be separated from notions of 'correctness';
- Considerable caution needs to be exercised with the notion of classes having different language codes;
- Such codes have to be clearly distinguished from non-standard grammatical forms;
- A critical questioning about language used both in and out of the classroom can have immeasurable benefits for pupils;
- Standard English is not the same as Received Pronunciation;
- While for young people to leave school unable to use SE when appropriate, condemns them to reduced job opportunities, and children whose only dialect is very close to SE are advantaged, this is not to say that others' dialects need to be extinguished. A repertoire approach can enable them to write in SE and, in speech, to switch between, say, scouse and SE (usually with a corresponding shift towards RP).

Notes

1 These are not comprehensive examples. Sikhs have been defined as an ethnic group for the purposes of the Race Relations Act and Africans, for instance, comprise many different ethnic groups.
2 Commonest spoken languages in the UK as first or second languages of bilinguals, in approximate order of number of speakers:
   Panjabi, Urdu, Bengali, Welsh, Hindi, Gujerati, Chinese (mainly Cantonese), Caribbean Creoles, Greek, Turkish, Polish, Italian, African languages (many different ones, largest groups probably being from West Africa).
3 In principle, we have no reason to believe that languages or dialects can be ranked in terms of their effectiveness, that is to say their communicative power. French is not a better or worse language than Chinese, Bengali, or Persian, though it is clearly different. Linguists' basis for saying this with confidence is their examination of the work languages have to do, the functions they have to perform, namely to fulfil the

huge range of communicative needs of a given population and to carry a good deal of its culture. An argument known to linguists as the *Sapir-Whorf hypothesis* modifies the idea that all languages are essentially equivalent to the proposition that where cultures differ significantly then languages will too, and if a particular culture does not need its language to do a particular job (like intricately to chart familial relationships like Panjabi does) then that language will be different from one which does. A 'strong' version of this hypothesis would have it that speakers of that language will have their world view shaped by it, but this is not a view held by linguists today (see Crystal, 1987). The idea that English is superior is perhaps only linguistic colonialism at work, the outcome of one language being backed by world economic power and influence (like Latin was in the past).

4   This is not a complete discussion of the word dialect, which can be defined as much socially as linguistically. See Trudgill (1995) for a concise and accessible account, and Chapter 6 of Holmes (1992).

5   As Holmes (1992, p. 143) points out it might just as well stand for 'Real Posh'.

6   We have necessarily over-simplified here. In fact, people seldom speak 'pure' Geordie or any other dialect, they generally use both standard and non-standard forms. The difference between speakers is the *frequency* with which they use different forms.

4   Curriculum

Gender and the Curriculum

In this section we want to explore how the construction of the curriculum reflects the prevailing attitudes and ideologies of its time. We will document how policy makers have supported a curriculum differentiated according to gender, for it was not until the advent of a National Curriculum that there was any requirement for boys and girls to study the same subjects up until the age of 16 years. We will also consider the development of different approaches to gender equality and consider some examples of curriculum initiatives intended to equalize provision for girls and boys.

It is often claimed that the school curriculum reflects *the values, biases, prejudices and divisions of society* (Evans, 1988, p. 94) and that the selection of knowledge for the curriculum is made by those in power, enabling them to privilege certain groups in society over others. It is, therefore, not surprising that it has only been during the last twenty years that the achievements of women living in the nineteenth and early twentieth centuries have entered into the public domain. Spender (1982) observed that many achievements of women were 'hidden from history', due to the 'domestic ideology' which confined women to the house (the chapter relating to Women in the economy explores this ideology further) and thus excluded them from the production of knowledge. Knowledge became constructed by men for men and women, who were the powerless, had to accept the content of this knowledge.

Rousseau, a philosopher whose ground-breaking treatise on education (1762) was generally viewed as progressive, enlightened and egalitarian, was, through the curriculum he advocated, calling for a return to the 'natural' order with a clearly delineated sexual division of labour. His general education theory was to benefit boys. He saw a boy's curriculum as one of freedom and self discovery without pressure to work towards any pre-determined future role. A girl's education, however, was to prepare her for her role as a future obedient wife, mother and homemaker, with a curriculum offering limited freedom. Rousseau believed that women were created for the purpose of pleasing men and that their education should equip them for this role (Darling and Glendinning, 1996).

There were, however, many women who challenged these assumptions through their writing. These early protesters about sexism and education were women like:

- Aphra Benn (1640–1689) demanded autonomy and full educational rights for women. She had written seventeen plays and thirteen novels before Daniel Defoe wrote Robinson Crusoe, 'the first novel'.
- Mary Wollstonecraft, who in 1792 wrote *A Vindication of the Rights of Woman, the Englishwoman's Journal.* Her book championed the cause of women gaining property rights within marriage and entry into male dominated professions. She saw that education was one of the major ways that men used to advance their superiority over women and argued for a national system of co-educational schooling for women where they could experience the same curriculum as boys.
- Mary Somerville (1780–1872) was one of the leading scientists of her day.
- Harriet Martineau (1800–1872) was one of the first political economists, reformer and writer.

The arguments that these women and others advanced had little influence on policy makers and, even though from 1870 onwards more women had begun to enter the teaching profession in subordinate roles, their presence had no real impact on the empowerment on girls and women. By the end of the nineteenth century basic rights to women were still denied, and it was not until 1917 that women were given the vote, not through any philanthropic concerns but through their own effects, actions and determination. Virginia Woolfe analysed the English education system in 1938 in her book *Three Guineas* and, in doing so, concluded that there was no place for women and that they would be better remaining as outsiders. While there were disadvantages in being outsiders, there were also benefits: women could remain outside the patriarchal value system which, she argued, was so destructive for men as well as women (Spender, 1982).

Policy, Practice and Legislation

Policy and practice, which supported this 'domestic ideology' for women and girls and the need for a curriculum differentiated by gender, was sustained through a series of highly influential reports. The Norwood Report (1943) identified the need for domestic subjects to be included in the curriculum for girls in order to equip them for their role in society as homemakers. Sixteen years later the Crowther Report (1959) echoed these same concerns and called for the provision of a relevant curriculum which met pupils' futures and livelihoods. The vocational resonance of this report still viewed the child's sex as an important determinant of their future careers.

> The passionate interest that many girls feel in living things can be as strong an educational incentive as the love of machines. It is not for nothing that biology is the main science taught to girls, as physics and chemistry are to boys. (Crowther Committee, 1959, p. 112)

The Newsom Report (1963) reinforced this notion of vocationalism and, whilst accepting that there may be some 'girls' whose futures lay in the scientific field, the perception of this report was that the overwhelming regard girls had for their future roles was in marriage. Darling and Glendinning (1996) observe that these reports, whilst well-intentioned, supported a gender differentiated pathway. Weiner (1994, p. 93, quoting Deem, 1981) characterizes 'the educational ideology of the post-war II period as sustaining the belief of a woman's primary place as in the home'.

The 1960s was a period when ideas of equity and freedom gained ground and some support within mainstream society. At this time much of the focus of policy makers was the relationship of scholastic ability to social class and disadvantage. While there was a failure to include a gender perspective within the analysis, this climate provided the fertile ground for the feminist critique of the state and education of the 1970s and much of the work on gender and schooling grew out of this.

The Sex Discrimination Act

The Sex Discrimination Act (SDA) of 1975 became part of British law owing to a European Economic Community (EEC) directive calling for the equal treatment of men and women (EEC directives are binding on member states). As L. Kant (1985) observed, whilst British law is rooted in individual rights it has never guaranteed basic human rights. It was because of Britain's membership of the EEC (and the United Nations, whose charter affirms fundamental human rights) that a consideration of *female* rights was forced upon the British Government resulting in the SDA.

The Act renders discrimination unlawful in employment, training and in education. The inclusion of education in the legislation required all educational establishments — for the first time — to offer equal access to all curriculum areas, plus any other benefits, to pupils of both sexes. Whilst this requirement theoretically went some way towards equalizing educational opportunity, it did little to combat the social conditioning which led to both boys and girls opting for subjects that they deemed suitable for their sex. It did, however, open up spaces for feminists to campaign for equality of opportunity in schools. The Act was interpreted by many feminists as overt governmental support towards the equalizing of society, thus giving schools a critical role to play in its implementation (Weiner, 1994). Feminist teachers began to network and gather evidence which identified the unequal treatment of girls in schools, their poorer experiences and the lowered expectations of women and girls in general.

> Teachers reported on unequal school staffing patterns, sex stereotyping in texts and reading schemes, sex specific patterns in subject choice at 13 — plus, the unacceptability of traditional vocational and career choices . . . (Weiner, 1994, p. 76)

These teachers, in successfully highlighting the importance of analysing gender issues both at school level and at the level of the Local Education Authority (LEA), called for action to follow.

It is true to say that there was some hostility and indifference to the changes called for. During the early 1980s, the Equal Opportunities Commission organized a conference on 'Girl Friendly Schooling'. At this conference nearly half the teachers present thought that boys were better at technical problems than girls; 42 per cent thought that a boy's career was more important than a girl's; and 29 per cent thought that a woman's place was in the home. Many teachers supported equal opportunities in principle, but in practice found themselves less committed, arguing that their role was to prepare pupils for society as it exists (Figes, 1994). Nevertheless, by this time, the acceptance of some equal opportunities initiatives began to take hold. Some schools had implemented posts of responsibility for equal opportunities and were developing equal opportunities policies. There were national projects set up, for example *Genderwatch*, which offered a strategic approach to both short and long term goals at school level; *Girls into Science and Technology* (GIST) a project set up to encourage girls to study science; and *Girls and Mathematics* (GAMMA). Local Educational Authorities appointed advisory teachers, part of whose remit was to raise awareness of equal opportunities issues amongst teachers, steer changes through schools by supporting the work of equal opportunities co-ordinators and setting up support networks across the education authority.

Equal Opportunities and Anti-sexist Initiatives

During this period two theoretical perspectives began to emerge. One was located in a liberal feminist model and was described as an 'equal opportunities' approach, which wished to see reform take place within existing institutional structures. The other perspective was an anti-sexist approach, which called for a radical shift in the actual structures of education. Weiner (1994) summarizes the differences in the two approaches — with equal opportunity reformists focusing on 'encouraging girls to opt for science, reviewing textbooks, analysing staffing structures of schools' (p. 79), whilst the anti-sexist lobby were concerned to reappraise the patriarchal nature of schooling and to question the dominant male value systems that shaped the curriculum and schools in general.

> What anti-sexists demanded instead was an epistemological shift in curriculum practices which allowed for herstory as well as history, promoted girl-centred science in place of conventional science curriculum and put an end to the male domination of curricula, classrooms and schools as a whole. (Weiner, 1994, p. 79)

The two approaches can be compared as follows:

Equal Opportunities (Access)
- Emphasis on improvement in teaching methods
- Equal allocation of resources
- Girls to be encouraged to move into male dominated areas of the curriculum
- Textbooks, reading books, displays and assessment papers to be scrutinized for sexist images
- Courses to be non-sexist
- Single sex mathematics groups
- Changing school organization, for example, regular uniform which is non sexist, desegregating the registers.
- Establishing posts of responsibility for equal opportunities
- Gender issues to be discussed widely in school and in local educational authority.

Anti-sexist (Girl-centred) Approach
Proponents of this approach used many of the same strategies as for the egalitarians, but based their work on the following premises:

- Feminist education means girl- or woman-centred schooling
- It has to take account of the actual (not stereotyped) experiences of women and girls
- The curriculum should draw on the past and present experiences of women and girls
- It should provide girls with the skills to take on the male system of the workplace
- It should give girls and women a sense of solidarity
- Hierarchy, competitiveness and selection should be replaced by such procedures as co-operation, democracy, egalitarianism, community
- Girl centred study for example, herstory, girls and science to replace traditional forms of study. (Arnot and Weiner, 1987, p. 356, citing Weiner, 1985)

Measor and Sikes (1992) observe that both these approaches parallel much of the work in the field of 'race' where models of multiculturalism and anti-racism have been developed and that for both 'race' and gender 'both models of intervention share some areas of concern, interest and activity, and their proponents can learn from each other, despite their fundamental differences' (p. 126).

However, in reality, most changes reflected an equal opportunities approach and took place within the existing structures of schools, classrooms and Local Education Authorities, with some changes being funded by central government. Examples of two such initiatives, which were sanctioned through official bodies, were the *Local Education Authorities Equal Opportunities Consortium* and the *Technical and Vocational Initiative*.

The Local Education Authorities Equal Opportunities Consortium (LEAEOC)

LEAEOC was initiated in 1985–6 and comprised a group of eight LEAs within London and the South East. The consortium was based at the Centre for Research and Education on Gender at the University of London, Institute of Education and had a specific brief to provide a network of support across the LEAs in the promotion of equal opportunities. The consortium, which supported several hundred schools, was represented by each LEA's advisory teacher for equal opportunities and they, together with the consortium co-ordinator, planned, delivered and hosted Inset sessions and conferences for inspectors/advisors, headteachers, school-based co-ordinators, governors and others from the education service. The whole project was managed by a steering group made up of LEA representatives who at the project's inception were at deputy director level. The project relied totally on funding from the participating LEAs and unfortunately when funding to LEAs was severely cut the consortium was unable to survive. The success of this initiative in terms of curriculum development is difficult to measure in the long term but what it did was to give equal opportunities a high profile within its sphere of influence and provide both theoretical and practical support for many teachers at all levels within the school system.

Technical and Vocational Initiative (TVEI)

TVEI was a central government initiative and one of the several vocational and science orientated programmes which can be traced back to the 1977 'Great Debate' Ruskin speech of the then Prime Minister, Jim Callaghan. In this speech, Callaghan expressed grave concern that schools were not meeting the demands of industry and were failing to equip students with the skills and attitudes needed for work, thereby rendering them unemployable. Youth unemployment at that time was increasing and was viewed as an educational problem which required a response from LEAs and schools. However, TVEI signalled a more radical departure from existing vocational courses when it was set up in 1984. It demanded the rapid and committed involvement of schools and had an expressed commitment to equal opportunities. In the first year of the project girls were recruited in similar numbers to boys. However, in the 14 projects across the country, the number of girls participating in the second year decreased dramatically. The reasons for the withdrawal of girls may have been the way the curriculum was structured by offering options which were 'girl unfriendly' and compelling girls to take non-traditional courses, though, interestingly, it was girls from single sex schools who tended to view them more favourably. There had been a concern at the project's inception that the vocational and technological nature of the initiative would inevitably lead to sex segregation unless adequate safeguards were built in. The success of the TVEI initiatives, in terms of challenging sex stereotyping, rested very much on the commitment of individual LEAs and schools to equal opportunities and an understanding that counselling and encouraging students to opt for non-traditional choices was not enough and that structural changes were necessary.

Both these projects did much to raise the issues of equal opportunities and promoted a developing awareness amongst educational institutions and teachers of the constraints of curriculum design, the distribution of resources and their impact on pupils and girls in particular.

The National Curriculum

A National Curriculum was introduced into schools as part of the Education Reform Act of 1988, an act whose significance is underlined in both the following sections. The National Curriculum for the first time *required* girls and boys to study the same subjects up until the age of 16 and claimed to provide a broad and balanced curriculum with equality of access for all pupils. It was 'aimed at widening students' range of experiences and encouraging informed choices and increasing expectations' (Measor and Sikes, 1992, p. 47).

However, the rigid and fixed nature of the curriculum has provided a uniformity rather than broad and balanced education, emphasizing particular forms of knowledge which reinforce the traditional values upheld by the white male dominated areas of knowledge. As Weiner (1994) points out, the National Curriculum is a

> British curriculum which celebrates its 'glorious' past and it is also 'woman free' ... Women's issues were accorded low priority across all the subject areas, such that very few topics were entirely devoted to women. For instance, in the early history documentation, of the named individuals white European males far outweighed any other representative group. (p. 116)

The National Curriculum is only concerned with the formal knowledge base of schooling and has done nothing to tackle the pervasive nature of the informal curriculum, so that when girls are given choices at 15 they may well opt for feminized subjects and revert to traditional sex stereotyped patterns. The National Curriculum does little to change male dominated forms of organization and management and expectations of schools and classrooms (Measor and Sikes, 1992).

Equality of access to the curriculum has made considerable progress since the days of the Norwood Report, but how far the promotion of a gender-sensitive curriculum can be sustained beyond the 1990s is questionable, especially with the considerable changes that have taken place at LEA level, the devolution of funds to individual schools and the impact of a centrally dictated curriculum. Alongside the legitimate concerns regarding the underachievement of particular groups of boys, teachers and policy makers must ensure that the significant progress made during the 1970s and the 1980s is sustained.

Curriculum: 'Race'

The Purpose of a Curriculum

Where 'race' is concerned, the curriculum has been a critical site of struggle between competing perspectives. Perhaps this is not surprising, for the school curriculum is where a society, some would say a nation, tries to embody its own sense of itself. For many, the school curriculum is the place where one would find what it is that young people need to know, what it is that they must know, in order to be appropriately raised as citizens into the society's culture.

This begs all kinds of questions about whether it makes sense to think of there being only *one* culture in British society, indeed, the use of the word 'nation' can be seen as an attempt to foreclose this debate by an implicit appeal to notions of traditional, i.e. white, 'Britishness'. In the section about social class we will explore and question the idea that there is a single set of cultural experiences and values that makes sense to and is accessible to all social classes. The same questions may be asked with regard to 'race' and ethnicity — it may make more sense to conceive of British society as comprising interlocking, overlapping but separate and changing cultures, rather than a single culture. (It would be more to the point to think of *future* British society here, since the school curriculum is in a sense a society's way of linking its past with its future, its codified way of seeing itself which it seeks to transmit to its next generations.)

An obvious example of this debate is religion. The UK is oddly alone in its approach to this, being rare amongst European countries in seeking to use the formal education system to inculcate a particular religious view. France, a country with rather higher levels of religious observance in terms of church-going, outlaws the public allegiance to a particular faith by pupils, let alone by the school authorities, much less the state. Italy, the home of the Roman Catholic Church, does not expect its schools to give pupils a Catholic view of the world. Britain, on the other hand, between 1944 and 1988 required only one subject to be taught in state schools — religious education — and had a requirement for religious assemblies. Post-1988, the other subjects of the National

Curriculum were required too, but the requirement for a daily act of worship remains, along with a (slightly later) ruling that this had to be 'in the main of a broadly Christian character'. Religious education (as distinct from worship) is also now required by law to concentrate mainly on Christianity unless a special exception is made, school by school, because of the religious backgrounds of the pupils. Of course parents can exempt their children, but we would nevertheless contend that to legally require an emphasis on one faith in schools is an example of a society (or some people in it) seeking to transmit a particular way of seeing itself into the future.

While this does not seem particularly contentious to some, to many people it clearly is, and hence the practical and symbolic importance of trying to codify it in law. Significant numbers of British citizens have no religious faith at all. Significant numbers have allegiance to other faiths. A measure which *acts as if* the vast majority of the population are practising Christians (or ought to be) when they are not has a clear ideological purpose.

1988 was a watershed year throughout the curriculum, not just in religious education, and 'race' probably had a lot to do with this. A great deal has been written about curriculum assumptions with regard to 'race', so we do not intend to rehearse the arguments at length here (see, for more detailed treatment Gaine, 1995; Klein, 1993; Sarup, 1986). The core of the debate has focused upon what an appropriate curriculum might be for a school population and a society that has become increasingly diverse linguistically, religiously and in terms of history and experience.

'Race' and the Curriculum: First Assumptions in the 1960s

Historically, the first approach has become known as 'assimilation' or 'immigrant education', in which the main goal was seen as reducing any differences between (in the 1950s and 1960s) immigrant children and the majority population. Actual or potential problems were seen as stemming from the fact that 'they' were different, so the educational task was to make them less different. The most obvious aspect of this was language, since it was indeed the case that many children who were migrants from the Indian sub-continent spoke little or no English and therefore had no access to the British curriculum whatever form it might take. We mean to imply no criticism of this as such — it would be hard to find an Asian parent who does not recognize that fluency in English is of crucial importance for their children's well-being and success in Britain. But the less obvious aspects to this approach were the assumptions of the irrelevance or downright harmfulness of key aspects of pupils' and parents' lives. The key assumption of the assimilation perspective is not only that English must be learned as quickly as possible, but that it must be learned to the exclusion of the child's first language — the 'milk bottle theory'.

The same assumption was applied to religion, history and literature in its widest sense, so that the view of the world portrayed in even early children's readers was predominantly a white one, and a middle class one at that. This is, perhaps unfairly, often parodied as giving an Enid Blyton, middle class, English, rural, Christian, nuclear family, lemonade and buns sort of view of the world to children to whom it was entirely foreign, but insofar as it happened it was entirely consistent with assimilationist assumptions. Just as students are given an 'orientation' session before undertaking a term or semester abroad, it was felt necessary to 'orientate' immigrant children at the very least. Clearly, this approach was not likely to lead to very much inclusion in the curriculum of non-Christian religious perspectives, histories of different parts of the world, Caribbean authors, Indian poets or African sculpture. In the 1950s and 1960s African-Caribbean and Asian children in British schools learned little about themselves that was positive. Their parents' countries had recently been 'granted' independence rather as a child is accorded tentative adulthood. Their histories were portrayed, in the case of the Caribbean, as a sorry tale of hapless enslavement only brought to an end by enlightened white men. Or, in the case of India, as the civilizing of chaotic teeming masses, made up either of loyal Gunga Dins or untrustworthy mutineers who put white people into black holes. Their languages, religion, culture, literature, ancient civilizations and resistance to oppression were either not appreciated or, more likely, not even known about.

There are several problems with this, which again have been explored at more length elsewhere. One is that it is founded upon something of a myth of an homogenous British culture: what is often represented as British culture carries a heavy class and male bias, as well as a regional, English one. Another mythic aspect of the notion of 'British' culture is its imagined long history, whereas in fact the royal family within living memory was German and Greek; Christmas trees were introduced from Germany only a century ago; most classical music and opera originates elsewhere in Europe; most pop music originates in the USA, until recently the most prestigious *cuisine*, as the word tells us, was French. Cricket, football and rugby were, of course, invented not just in Britain but in England, but given the significance of cricket in republican Australia and Muslim Pakistan, the allegiance to rugby in France, Wales and Afrikaner South Africa, and the now international nature of football, it is hard to claim them as uniquely English any longer.

Myth aside, another problem with an assimilationist approach is that it at least needs rethinking when the children at whom it is aimed are no longer immigrants but British-born, albeit with persisting cultural differences. At what stage, after how long, does a society stop seeing a group with cultural differences as foreign and in need of acculturation? It is not an easy question to answer, and different societies adopt different approaches. Australia and the USA, for example, both the result of large-scale immigration, have found that a mixture of aiming at common values while giving space for differences is the only strategy that works. Though this approach is less well applied to America's black population or either society's native peoples, many Americans of Italian descent continue to speak Italian to some family members, practise

Catholicism and marry other Italians a century after their great grandparents crossed the Atlantic. The curriculum issue in Britain by the early 1970s, then, was what to do about the fact that the school population had changed — and this issue was obviously posed most sharply in those schools where the change had actually happened.

'Race' and the Curriculum: Second Thoughts in the 1970s

The response which emerged at that time has become known as 'multi-culturalism' or the 'celebrating diversity' approach. As these terms imply, there was a move from the idea that Britain had essentially one culture in which everyone ought to be raised and schooled, towards the idea that there were many coexisting cultures and that the well-educated child, well prepared for adult life, would learn about them.

It is arguable whether this was educationally far-sighted or simply re-sponding to reality. Every good teacher knows that children react more posit-ively and learn more effectively when they can relate in some way to what is being taught, so it makes obvious sense to modify a curriculum so that children can see themselves in it. If a class doing a topic on food has many Caribbean-background children in it then it makes educational sense to refer to the food some of their parents make at home. It similarly makes sense to provide read-ing books with black and Asian characters and, if studying geography, to cover areas which have particular significance to members of the class.

So far so good, and up to a point the above approach became accepted wisdom in many areas by the mid-1970s. There were three ways, however, in which the multicultural approach hit difficulties which required a deeper analysis.

The first was about who the approach was for. There is no doubt that it arose in schools where there were significant numbers of ethnic minority children and, indeed, the rationale presented above is largely in terms of their needs. The question remains, however, whether or not it was appropriate for white children. Many argued that it was, that children were growing up along-side others of different backgrounds and that the future depended upon them understanding and respecting something about each other's differences. If this was true in principle, however, it was noticeable that it only seemed to apply to white children who were actually schooled alongside ethnic minorities, yet the argument ought logically apply to all white children, since they all might as adults live and work in places which are ethnically mixed. As a matter of policy, therefore, it was clear that in practice 'multicultural' education was not seen as a priority for most of the country (Gaine, 1987; Chauhan, 1988).

Another problem was a series of assumptions about 'culture'. We have touched upon the difficulties of determining a 'British' culture, taking into account the class, regional and nationalistic cultural divides that existed in the UK before post-war immigration began. Ultimately, similar problems arise in trying to define 'Asian' or 'Caribbean' culture, though these difficulties lessen the more specific one becomes in terms of language, religion, area of origin and so on. No culture is static, however, and for any teacher (whatever their own background) trying to convey the essentials as well as the changes within a particular cultural group is no easy task.

The last problem we want to identify with this early multicultural approach was the nature of the diversity it celebrated. It chose, not surprisingly, the most accessible parts: cooking, clothing, dance, music, art, and RE. Although the latter was potentially of great symbolic importance, what all these areas of the curriculum share is their relative low status. GCSEs in any of them are commonly thought (rightly or wrongly) to be worth less than 'real' subjects like maths and science. There was a risk, therefore, that multiculturalism could be practised and diversity celebrated in various ways in the primary curriculum and for low attainers at secondary level, but the subjects which really 'counted' remained untouched.

All three of these points slightly over-state the case. There were innovative schools in largely white areas of the country which pioneered multi-faith religious education without the 'incentive' of classrooms full of Muslims and Sikhs. There were science teachers who recognized that at least the hand that held the test tube illustrated in the text book did not have to be white. There were English teachers who tapped the resources of world literature in the conviction that their white pupils would benefit from them (James and Jeffcoate, 1981; Nixon, 1984). We would nevertheless argue that no significant change was under way, nor was any need for one perceived.

'Race' and the Curriculum: The Concern with Racism in the 1980s

By the late 1970s a further development was beginning. The emphasis of the previous two approaches had been on the differences between minorities and the majority population, and how to either reduce these (assimilation) or explain them (multiculturalism). The assumptions behind both were that any potential conflict, problem or hostility would arise from strangeness and unfamiliarity. The remedy, then, was to make the immigrants less strange or to make their cultures less strange to 'us'. This began to be questioned by many who felt that strangeness and unfamiliarity were scarcely the issues at all — racism, after all, has thrived in situations of long continuous contact, such as colonialism. Some teachers and people in African-Caribbean and Asian groups came to think that it was not simple ignorance on the part of whites that caused them problems, but whole patterns of beliefs and ideas. These can be summed up in the word 'racism', and include ideas about white superiority, threatened British culture, primitive religion, a civilizing colonial mission, the causes of unemployment, inherent criminality, deteriorating housing and so on. The educational answer to such racism is not a liberal celebration of diversity but anti-racism (see, for instance, ALTARF, 1984; Brandt, 1986; Twitchin and Demuth, 1985).

The ramifications of this in the curriculum were to challenge or problematize taken-for-granted assumptions. History, for instance, can examine racism (and itself) by not taking 'progress', 'superiority' and 'perspective' as read. Geography can critically examine the exploitative relationship between the rich and poor world rather than dwell on aid and pity. English can help pupils recognize and understand the relationships between dialects and power, and consider whose view of the world, whose priorities, whose values are explored in chosen fictional texts at any level (Naidoo, 1992; Oxford DEC, 1987). Mathematics, even, can note the contribution of other societies to the development of mathematical ideas, but perhaps more importantly can help young people use maths as a tool for social understanding — most obviously in statistics. In practice, these attempts at a more inclusive multicultural/anti-racist curriculum were not universal or sweeping, or accompanied by public bookburnings of 'incorrect' texts and some useful and practical guides for teachers were produced (Brown, 1990; Cohen and Haddock, 1991; Epstein and Sealey, 1990; Farrell, 1990; NUT, 1992; Thorp, 1991).

These are examples in the formal curriculum, but the anti-racist approach would also draw attention to the messages given to pupils by the hierarchies in schools, the positioning of black teachers, the way streaming and selection operated, the way incidents and various manifestations of racism are dealt with — and hence press for formalized policies, guidelines and targets. The hidden curriculum, in other words, was likely to carry as many racist messages as the formal or taught curriculum.

The Right Reacts: The Late 1980s and 1990s

This approach gained support and adherents throughout the early 1980s. It was kept on the agenda, though not supported, by the government's Swann report of 1985, which had been established in 1979 to examine black under-achievement but ended by attempting a comprehensive summary of the situation in 'race' and education. It proposed various reforms and changes in perspective, and provided a well-lit backdrop against which developing arguments and disputes could be played out. On the one hand, anti-racists felt it was riddled with official compromises and failed to grasp various nettles which bedevilled the educational scene. On the other, it began to focus a reaction from the Right against what it began to see as a serious left-wing radical onslaught on cherished British assumptions. To the Right, multiculturalism was bad enough, but to have an Establishment enquiry state that racism was endemic in much of British education was a step too far, and they began to mobilize against it (Tomlinson, 1990).

This mobilization has been described at length elsewhere (Gaine, 1993; Ball, 1995; Hill, 1989). In brief, through a series of cleverly grouped 'think tanks' and well placed negative publicity the Right effectively stopped much anti-racist development. The tragic stabbing of a Bangladeshi boy in a Manchester school was 'explained' by representing the school as having a firm anti-racist policy which 'made things worse' (Macdonald et al., 1990). A widespread myth was created about 'loony left' LEAs policing their employees' language — in truth no authority forbade expressions like blackboard and black coffee — but the myth served to trivialize and parody the concerns of anti-racists. Through increasing influence in the Conservative Party the Right secured the gradual occupation of key appointments and reversed some of the initiatives proposed by Swann (and adopted by the then Conservative Secretary of State for Education, Keith Joseph) bringing about various measures which reduced the influence of local education authorities — through their funding often the catalyst of curriculum innovation and inservice training with regard to racism (Richardson, 1992) — and, most significantly, introduced a National Curriculum.

The National Curriculum was a hugely significant event in ideological terms because, for the first time, it enshrined what 'the state' believed all its children ought to learn. As suggested earlier, 1988 was a watershed year for the British curriculum. 'Race' had a lot to do with it because, more than anything, 'race' had alerted the Right to challenges and critiques of curriculum assumptions which they felt they had to resist. There were many battles within the committees appointed to devise a national curriculum, and further battles with succeeding Secretaries of State in getting the curriculum agreed (Cox, 1991; Gaine, 1993; King and Reiss, 1993; Ball, 1994).

The National Curriculum and the Future?

The current picture is unclear. The power of the Right on key education bodies has diminished, but in a sense they need it less since their curriculum is in place. Attention has turned from the content of the curriculum to a preoccupation with standards, the implicit assumption being that the curriculum matters little in this as long as there are rigorously high expectations of everyone, regardless of ethnicity, or class, or gender. There can be no doubt that there was less radical anti-racist innovation in 1995 than there was in 1985, yet the National Curriculum *does* insist upon more in the way of competing definitions of history. There are more accounts of black resistance to slavery, forgotten histories such as that of Mary Seacole (the 'black Florence Nightingale' of the Crimean War), and different literatures than was formerly the case, and there is scope for creativity and development by individual teachers (see Runnymede Trust, 1993).

Clearly the issue has not gone away. It is still a matter which needs debating and resolving in Britain if we are to have a clearer idea of who we are and who we want to be. We are no longer simply a white, northern European, Christian, colonial power, and if the curriculum is to avoid being archaic and unconnected with lived experience then it needs to take account of this.

Curriculum: Class

Selectivity and the Curriculum: The Demands of Culture and the Economy

As became clear in the preceding two sections, any curriculum involves choices from the vast range of knowledge that is available. Choices made are contestable and it is important not to take them for granted or as in some sense 'given' — they have to be defended against competing claims on the grounds of being more worthwhile, valuable, relevant, prestigious, useful, traditional, modern or whatever. As we said in the section on 'race', the school curriculum is where a society sets down what it wants young people to know in order to be appropriately raised as citizens into the society's culture. We also asked whether it makes sense to think of there being only *one* culture in British society, and the question applies as much to social class as it does to 'race'. Allied to this is the role of the curriculum in preparing young people as future members of the workforce.

In the fixed class structure of Victorian Britain there was no question but that schools should provide one kind of education for the sons of 'gentlemen' and another for the sons of the workers (the education of daughters was not high on many agendas). The public schools' curriculum provided Latin, Greek and other subjects thought necessary to a well-rounded upbringing (including aspects of behaviour and outlook fostered on the games field), and the Board schools' curriculum contained the three Rs and enough aspects of the humanities and religion for working class children to know and understand their place. In a society with avowedly distinct class cultures and no pretence of social mobility, curriculum decisions have a certain clarity.

Decisions and choices about these issues are less clear today because it is no longer possible to decide on an appropriate curriculum simply according to a child's birth. On the whole, primary schooling assumes a common curriculum because it assumes the possibility of mobility through ability and effort. Secondary schooling may have more difficulty with a common curriculum because (in the end) they have to prepare pupils for work. Both phases, however, implicitly address the question of which skills and areas of knowledge are so highly valued that they must be offered in schools, and both (sooner or later) have to combine this with decisions about ability. While a particular form of knowledge may be valued it may also be thought too difficult for everyone, so should it be reserved for an 'able' minority? In this sense, education has both to decide what is appropriate (if anything) for all irrespective of class *origin*, and whether something different is appropriate for some depending on class *destination*. We can make these questions more concrete by contrasting the classics and bricklaying.

In a witty article called '*The sabre-toothed curriculum*' Benjamin (1971) parodies the process by which arcane and impractical knowledge comes to acquire more status than the merely useful. Latin and ancient Greek are interesting examples of this, having little practical use but carrying great prestige, being routinely taught in private schools until the late 1980s and still offered in a substantial number. There were several conventional justifications for this. As subjects they were claimed to be rigorous and disciplined and, hence, an excellent 'training for the mind'; Latin (and to a lesser extent Greek) was supposed to aid a deeper understanding of English; their study allegedly gave access to or greater understanding of many of the great works and ideas of Western civilization; and (more practically) they were needed to gain access to many degrees (especially at Oxbridge). All four combined together to confer very high status on 'classics' and reinforce their place in elite institutions.[1] In fact, and without wishing to pursue the argument at length, it can be argued that the primacy of the classics was misconceived as a preparation for the country's elite and may well have had something to do with Britain's economic decline — many of our more successful European competitors sent their future managers and leaders to study science and business.[2]

Bricklaying, on the other hand, was not taught in grammar and public schools because it has never been considered high status knowledge. It may be useful, not only for intending building workers but for anyone who may need to have an understanding of building and house maintenance, but also to develop patience, accuracy, motor skills and pride in a finished 'product'. It featured on the curriculum of some working class secondary modern schools at one time, though seldom for girls.

Both of these pursuits can, in principle, be defended as curriculum subjects. We now need to take the issue of the inherent selection involved in any curriculum and the economic and cultural demands made upon it, to account for the curriculum we have today.

Changes in the Structure of Schooling

At the end of the Victorian era the view was developing that there should be a curriculum for the manual worker, another for the worker who required knowledge of the modern world and another for those who were to be leaders. The Balfour Act of 1902 made available to the middle classes the curriculum which had previously been reserved for the 'gentleman classes', the classical curriculum being used in some new secondary 'grammar' schools with the addition of such subjects as maths, geography, English language and literature. Whilst the working classes were still to be educated in the elementary schools, the Balfour Act earmarked 25 per cent of grammar schools places for elementary school children to be paid for by the state, and this opening of the door to some social mobility was added to by the Hadow Report of 1926. This established three different types of secondary school curriculum differentiated for different 'types' of children: academic, practical or technical, a distinction given further backing by two influential reports — Spens in 1938 and Norwood in

1943. Hadow's three types of secondary schooling were maintained in the 1944 Education Act and made free to all, while also being given supposedly equal status ('parity of esteem').

Schooling established after the 1944 Act had assumed that accurate measures of ability at eleven would allow the placing of pupils in different kinds of schools according to their aptitude and ability. It was correspondingly assumed that the different schools would offer different curricula, appropriate to the likely 'destinations' of their respective pupils. Secondary 'grammar' schools focused more on 'academic' subjects, and indeed in some ways took their lead from the private sector in maintaining the position of the classics as the subjects with the highest prestige. Secondary 'modern' schools, at least for many of their pupils, pursued relevance, useable skills and ready employability (secondary 'Technical' schools were, in practice, few in number).

For many reasons the system established in 1944 did not substantially improve the position of working class children. In practice they seemed mostly to go to secondary modern schools and the route to social mobility apparently offered by grammar schools turned out to be tortuous and difficult. Some of the difficulties are discussed in the chapters on school experience and on achievement, but one issue was the curriculum. The system was clearly founded upon the notion of the appropriacy of different curricula for different eventual adult lives, but this became undermined by declining faith in IQ tests and some awareness that the tests might be loaded in favour of middle class children and hence part of the unfairness they were intended to put right. The belief grew that selection at eleven simply perpetuated social class divisions and that the common experience of primary schooling should continue for longer. As a result, comprehensive schools and the allied fading away of the eleven plus exam were the engines for curriculum change from the late 1960s onwards.

The Contest for the Curriculum

Comprehensive reform had several parents and looked a little like all of them. Harold Wilson had wanted 'grammar schools for all'; others wanted the academic/vocational divide to continue but under one roof to break down social barriers; others still wanted to create a new common curriculum which reflected neither of the main assumptions of the past. This percolated down to primary schools because there was no longer a fixed body of 'eleven plus' preparation, and some Plowdenite ideas percolated upwards too, for instance, integrating subjects and teaching more mixed ability classes. At their most innovative a fairly small number of comprehensives integrated religious education, history and geography and added sociology and economics, some mixing in English too. Separate science subjects were combined in a way which is commonplace now. Mathematics (perhaps partly integrated with science for younger pupils) was perhaps centred around lead lessons and devolving into projects and small group work. Setting by ability was replaced by mixed ability groupings, and where this continued into upper years it constituted a common curriculum, regardless of ability. Since religious education was the only subject required by law, it follows that teachers had, in principle, great autonomy over the content of the curriculum, so it was possible to depart in quite radical ways from what had hitherto been studied in history, music, art and other subjects. We want to stress again that radical departures came about in only a small number of schools, many schools simply maintaining their previous ethos and cultural identity, but this small number were significant in that they were sometimes high profile, sometimes controversial, and usually at the very least a catalyst for wider debate. In other words, by the late 1970s and probably independently of the then Prime Minister's much-cited 'great debate' speech about education, a contest over what should be in the school curriculum was in progress.

The right wing Black Papers (e.g., 1971) were part of the debate, decrying the features of the most radical schools described above both on the grounds that key aspects of national culture were being eroded, even attacked, and that the necessary preparation for an unequal adult life[3] was being replaced by a naive liberal egalitarianism or worse, a left wing radicalism.

Left wing analysts and commentators were indeed involved, beginning critically to examine the curriculum and its role in maintaining wider class divisions in society. There were several developing strands to this critique. Widely regarded as rather over-deterministic today (even by themselves) is the 'correspondence theory' of Bowles and Gintis (1976; 1981) who posited a correspondence between many aspects of schooling, including the curriculum, and the needs of the capitalist economy. It is not, however, necessary to assume that there is a simple relationship between a ruling class and what is taught in the curriculum to appreciate that there may be features of the curriculum which support the status quo. Curriculum formation is a complex process involving competing forces and processes. Teachers and schools have had (at least in the past) some autonomy. At different times and to varying extents politicians at local and national level have been involved. Pressure groups of all kinds exert pressure: family planning organizations, 'pro-life' groups, English Heritage, vested subject interests in universities, environmental lobbyists, musicians, textbook publishers, sections of the media, religious organizations, the British Association for the Advancement of Science, to say nothing of specific subject associations. Nevertheless, the arguments of those like Althusser (1971); Bourdieu (1977) and Young (1971) were that *overall* the school curriculum tended to have the effect of constructing consent and producing a notion of common sense as confirming and supporting the status quo.

In practical terms, this implied that the curriculum would tend to underplay dissent, challenge, conflict and any idea that social arrangements could be different. History examines the lives of kings, queens, 'great' men and women, Britain's advances and victories. Progress is claimed, but the role in it of working class protest and organized challenge to the state is muted, changes being portrayed as the enlightened decisions of great leaders. Part of this process is inevitably legitimating the position of elite groups, which involves legitimating their tastes and preferences in the arts and literature. The most prestigious literature is thus that of the upper classes, celebrating or at least dwelling upon the details of their lives and reflecting their concerns and interests (like who Austen's heroines are to marry). Expensive forms of music (opera, ballet, orchestral concerts) carry the most prestige. The dialects of the upper and middle classes are represented as purer, 'better' English.

This is something of a parody, but there is enough in it which is familiar to give pause for thought. Importantly, however, since what goes into the curriculum is contestable, is a site of struggle rather than being monolithically determined, it is possible to see it as potentially a means of promoting critical and questioning knowledge, hence giving young people a tool to challenge the gaps and silences in the curriculum, 'common sense' and the status quo (e.g. Giroux and McLaren, 1989). Given the exponential growth of information, knowledge and the means of accessing it, how does it come about that certain portions of it become sanctified as most suitable for schools? Why is classical music secured a place when pop music is not? Why is science represented as progress and the (at times) lethal combination of science, technology and big business underplayed? This, as Foucault (1979) would argue, is not knowledge but 'preferred discourses' which need 'denaturalizing'.

It would be wrong to suggest that these debates were the bread and butter of staff rooms throughout the land, but versions of these kinds of questions were being asked increasingly in the late 1970s and early 1980s, and in a small way were having an effect upon aspects of the school curriculum and upon examinations. (For example, the established canon of A-level English Literature was widened in 1985 by the addition of Alice Walker's *The Colour Purple*, and social science as an option at 14 alongside history and geography was growing apace.) The ideological concerns of the Right, aired in the *Black Papers*, grew and a reaction set in, fuelled by their allied concerns about 'race' explored in the previous section. This is dramatically summed up in a speech by Margaret Thatcher at the 1987 party conference:

> Too often our children don't get the education they need — the education they deserve. And in the inner cities — where youngsters must have a decent education if they are to have a better future — that opportunity is all too often snatched from them by hard-left education authorities and extremist teachers. Children who need to be able to count and multiply are learning anti-racist mathematics — whatever that may be. Children who need to be able to express themselves in clear English are being taught political slogans. Children who need to be taught to respect traditional moral values are being taught that they have an inalienable right to be gay.

As we have tried to indicate, this description is a long way from the practice of real schools, but it was part of a wide-ranging (and effective) ideological assault on the critical and questioning tendencies which were real enough. The National Curriculum was the result.

The Outcome at Present

We suggested earlier that the National Curriculum was a hugely significant event in ideological terms because for the first time it enshrined what 'the state' believed all its children ought to learn (it seemed to sacrifice, to an extent, a curriculum differentiated by ability, but in practice this is addressed by the increasing demarcation between different kinds of school, see Chapter 7). The traditionalists, the 'cultural restorationists' as they have become known, won, not only against the left but against what Ball (1994, p. 30) calls the 'modernizers' and 'vocationalists' with whom Keith Joseph had considerable sympathy.

The arguments around the content of particular subjects were resolved in favour of a particular view of class and national culture. In this 'curricular fundamentalism' 'tradition' was effectively prioritized by well-placed members of the new Right and became a key element in decisions about what was included and what was left out of 'the curriculum as museum' (Ball, 1994, pp. 35 and 39). Music prioritized the Western Classical tradition. Geography was:

> tied to an unstated politics of space. At times the proposals seem to have more to do with Margaret Thatcher's policies on Europe than good educational practice. . . . [they] isolate students in time and space, cutting them off from the realities of a single European market, global economic dependencies and inequalities, and ecological crisis. (Ball, 1994, p. 37)

As for history, Kenneth Baker announced to the 1988 Conservative Party conference that children would learn about 'the spread of Britain's influence for good around the world' and subsequent decisions made it clear that there was to be little place for the questioning stance outlined earlier. It was to be a curriculum conceived solely as knowledge as facts,

> a curriculum suspicious of the popular and the immediate, made up of echoes of past voices, the voices of a cultural and political elite; a curriculum which ignores the pasts of women and the working class and the colonized — *a curriculum of the dead.* (Ball, 1994, p. 46)

Earlier, we denied any simple correspondence between state power and the curriculum, arguing that curricula outcomes are a complex product of competing forces and human actions. Despite our account of recent curriculum 'history' we would still hold to this, and indeed the clear dominance of the cultural restorationists has waned since Lord Dearing (who belongs more in the 'modernizer' camp) reduced the statutory element of the curriculum. Nevertheless, the development of the National Curriculum represents an important shift towards central determination of what young people shall learn, and highlights the terrain over which some ideological battles are fought. These battles have not gone away, and questions about the content and purpose of the school curriculum and its relationship to inequality will continue to underpin every teacher's work.

Notes

1   Of course science and technology are expensive to teach, and the ability to use the same Latin textbooks for decades may have had something to do with its appeal.
2   Some historical perspective may also put the claims made for the classics in context. At the turn of the century British universities did not offer modern languages, modern history, even modern literature — they were not considered intellectual or demanding enough for a degree. Geography has had a long battle for intellectual recognition as a subject, and engineering suffered for many years under the label of being 'merely' practical and hence quite unsuitable for ivory towers.
3   This is not to say that Conservatives did not have genuine concerns about the fate of those who failed at school. Sir Keith Joseph, as Secretary of State, began several initiatives intended to make secondary schooling more meaningful and rewarding to those identified as 'less able'. He established the Technical and Vocational Education Initiative (TVEI) and merged the 'streamed' exams of CSE and GCSE.

5 The Experience of School

Girls' Experience of Schooling

In this section we will explore the differences in the educational experiences of girls and boys. Many studies (e.g. French and French, 1984) suggest a threefold process. First, that children learn gender identity through the primary socialization process at home, involving the media, the toys they play with, and the comics and books that they read. Second, that they consequently arrive at school with firmly embedded ideas of gender appropriate behaviour and attitudes. Third, that schools through their organizational structures both formally and informally reinforce these stereotypes.

Feminist teachers in the 1980s analysed classroom practices in order to identify the differential experiences of boys and girls. Much of their work focused upon the processes of classroom interaction, the messages conveyed through the school's staffing structure, how subject choices were influenced by gender and the representation of women in the text books used in school. Issues of sexuality were also seen as a significant contributory factor in how girls experienced school. Teachers and researchers explored how far these differential experiences disadvantaged girls in particular in terms of their participation in schooling and in the occupational choices they made. However, in recent times, due to the growing body of evidence which suggests that boys are underachieving, there has been a significant movement to include the position of boys in the debate.

Classroom Interaction

Schools and classrooms are dynamic and constantly evolving environments and teachers, in this context, are in a powerful position to guide and shape the culture of the classroom, consequently much classroom research has focused on teacher behaviour (Clarricoates, 1978; Stanworth, 1981; Delamont, 1984). Feminist researchers have suggested ways in which schools transmit messages about what counts as appropriate behaviour for girls to engage in. Clarricoates (1978) found that teachers assumed that boys would be more lively, interesting and adventurous, whilst girls were more likely to be conforming, conscientious and quiet, and many studies report on the enormous pressure placed upon girls to conform to particular codes of behaviour (Measor and Woods, 1984).

One of the most common ways adopted by researchers into the way that school students experience schooling is through studies of classroom interaction, by recording the number of and variety of ways in which teachers interact with their class and then comparing the difference between boys and girls (Darling and Glendinning, 1996; see also Chapter 3). A study by Brophy and Good (1970) found that the only form of interaction where the girls scored more highly was the frequency with which they volunteered to answer a question. Their offers of answers were, however, taken up less often by the teacher than with male volunteers. Spender's (1982) study indicated that boys were more valued than girls and that they were consistently treated more as named individuals which constantly placed girls on the margins of classroom life.

Kelly (1986) collated the various pieces of research on classroom interaction and found that studies consistently reported that boys received more teacher attention time than girls; male teachers gave less attention to girls than female teachers; girls got less criticism but less instruction; and that boys received more academic and more behavioural criticism. The girls' share of instruction was smallest amongst the oldest age groups and in mathematics, but generally subject differences were minor. Where teachers had been involved in equity training the bias was reduced. Interestingly, Acker (1994) points out that despite the apparent consistency in the finding of these studies, earlier studies of Douglas (1964) and Sexton (1969), accounted for boys' early difficulties in learning to read by teachers' preference for girls:

> The teachers tend to see the boys as less hardworking, less able to concentrate and less willing to submit to discipline than the girls. These judgements are made mostly by women, and might have been different if they had been made by men . . . (Acker, 1994, p. 92)

More recent studies of classroom interaction question the conditions under which teacher behaviour is produced. The role of prior understandings and strategies which children bring to the classroom is constantly stressed. MacIntosh (1990) found that girls were aware that teachers paid more attention to boys; the importance of this finding is that both boys and girls are encouraged to regard boys and their activities as more worthy of attention. A study by Merrett and Wheldall (1992) distinguished between primary and secondary schooling. Their study found that in primary school no significant differences in levels of praise and criticism were found between girls and boys, or between male and female teachers. In secondary school, however, boys were given both more praise and more criticism for misbehaviour than girls, while men teachers tended to give more praise to boys for their schoolwork (Darling and Glendinning, 1996).

In the context of the present debate regarding boys' underachievement, many researchers and teachers alike tend to portray boys as being disaffected while girls are not. Connell (1989) suggests that there is a powerful male subculture which condones an anti-school ethos and inhibits academic success.

Schools are held in some part responsible for the development of this sub-culture for the role they play in the construction of masculinities (Connell, 1995) and this construction is constantly reinforced through the process of interactions (see Chapter 6, as well as succeeding sections of this chapter). It could, therefore, be argued that boys should have more attention to encourage them to apply themselves and to seek academic success. However, as Riddell (1992) has observed, there is a growing body of literature which suggests that girls' passivity may also be a problem and that there is an emerging sub-group of girls who also are disaffected and rejecting of school cultures (Darling and Glendinning, 1996).

Staffing Structures

Although teaching in the UK has become a feminized profession (Acker, 1989), female access to high positions of responsibility in education has proved less possible than access to the profession overall, with very few women holding headships and other senior positions (see Chapter 3). With few visible examples of women at the top of the teaching profession, it is questionable whether schools are good sites for the promotion of equal opportunities — the people holding positions of responsibility view the world with male eyes. On the other hand, women are very visible in the classroom, especially in the early and primary years. Younger children are seen as easier to teach and nursery staff are deemed often not to need as long a training as others, their role being perceived as one of caring rather than educating. In the early 1990s the government of the day set up an initiative to train a 'mum's army' of teachers for the early years. This 'mum's army' would have been trained in a year, thus lending credence through official policy to the notion of primary school teaching (and in particular infant teaching) as work engaged in by women with less pay and lower status. It is interesting to note that male teachers in the early years, especially in nurseries, are often viewed with suspicion and their masculinity may be called into question. The relative power relations between men and women in schools, which are demonstrated through the positions of responsibility held, can be a powerful transmitter to children of future gender roles.

Subject Choices

Research on children entering into infant school at age 5 has shown them to be aware of activities and occupations being gender specific. Smithers et al. (1991) found that children clearly differentiated activities along gender lines. Activities to do with the natural sciences were viewed as male, whilst those relating to domesticity as female, even when the child had experience of seeing an adult in both roles, for example a boy whose mother was a general practitioner.

Many researchers have alerted teachers to the dangers that the 'free choice' in the early years may lead to a constrained choice in the later years, for unless the children have an opportunity to experience the full range of activities and educational experiences, they are not in a position as they get older to make choices based on experience, rather than on gender. The National Curriculum has to some extent provided a curriculum which offers a full range of subjects but the legacy of the primary socialization still has a strong bearing on option choices. When at the vulnerable age of 15 or 16 school students have to choose whether to continue with, say, science, girls and boys still seem to make sex-stereotyped choices. Girls are reluctant to make choices that will render them 'unfeminine' and boys are equally reluctant to be 'unmasculine'. The consequence may be that the sort of choices made can lead to future work in high status and highly paid professions associated with science or mathematics, or the possibility of entering the market place in a subordinate and poorly paid occupation.

There has been official concern over the lack of girls opting for science-based subjects and many of the curriculum initiatives of the 1980s focused on providing a 'girl friendly' science curriculum. Boys still outnumber girls by four to one for entry to A-level physics; and roughly 40 per cent of all women in higher education study arts subjects, languages and education, as opposed to 18 per cent of men (White et al., 1992). Today there is a further concern that the shift from an economy with a strong manufacturing base to one where service industries predominate, will leave boys without the necessary communication skills and less employable than girls.

Representations Through Curriculum Texts

Sex stereotyping through the books and displays used by schools can be very powerful and contribute to the image girls and boys have of themselves. Many of the books children use on a regular basis represent white male middle class values as the norm. There have been several studies of children's books, probably the best known being by Lobban (1974). She analysed six reading schemes used in primary schools and found that males who were represented twice as often as female, were also shown engaged in active and dominant roles. Females, on the other hand, were backgrounded and where they were visible their roles were confined to domestic tasks. Stones (1983) called for a new kind of writing for children which portrayed females as lively, complex and interesting characters and which acknowledged women's contribution to history. Today, many publishers of school texts have, through such pressure from feminist organizations, made a visible commitment to gender equality. Story books too have presented females as passive with girls doing little for themselves. However, authors such as Cole, the Alhbergs and many others have taken many traditional tales and reshaped them to reflect a dynamic and assertive female role. Measor and Sikes (1994) point out the controversial nature of rewriting tales, as some teachers find the newer versions rather artificial. It must be remembered, however, that traditional tales have always been reformulated and reshaped as they have passed from one generation to another and been retold in different cultural contexts and rewritten to reflect the issues and concerns of the time.

Sexuality

A major concern for researchers exploring power relations which characterize so much of school is the contentious area of sexual relations. Walkerdine (1981) illustrates graphically how four-year-old boys in a nursery class make use of sexist, violent and oppressive language to position themselves power-fully in relation to their nursery teacher. Lees (1986) observed that the climate of sexual relations which exists in secondary schools undermines girls' con-fidence and makes them feel a deep sense of inferiority. She adds that the sexual harassment, which is demonstrated through 'unwelcome verbal or phys-ical conduct of a sexual nature', is experienced by girls on a regular basis.

Lees describes an impossible situation in which girls were identified as being a 'slag or a drag', where you are damned if you do enter into a sexual relationship and damned if you don't. Girls are judged on 'sexual activity' whereas boys are judged on a variety of activities such as sport. Lees found that double standards operate and girls find themselves in a no-win situation. Both boys and girls call girls names and these names are derogatory and denigrate women. She further observed that any interventions made by girls in classrooms were either ridiculed or ignored. The boy's solidarity, however, was based on the collective denigration of women. This 'putting down' has become part of classroom life and by far the majority of verbal insults for men resonate with notions of femininity (sissy, wimp). This enables boys/men to maintain power and use this to control women.

Lees suggests that the sexual insults are part of the experience that pushes girls into marrying, the jobs that they take up and their perceptions of them-selves as objects of another's desire. Schools have a responsibility to support girls in schools. It is not enough to provide equal access to the curriculum, schools must not allow schools to provide the situation and backdrop for harassment to take place.

Negotiating school for gay and lesbian school students and teachers can be more hazardous. Rogers (1994) describes how in British schools compuls-ory heterosexism is as

> . . . compulsory as maths and English. Compulsory heterosexuality is implicit in the gender roles which students are expected and encouraged to adopt and within the sexist norms which prevail in our society. (p. 34)

She illustrates how the homophobic discourse is used by boys and teachers to challenge a boy's masculinity when he fails to reflect the dominant masculinist behaviour in, say, sport or in other arenas of the school life by calling him a *pansy* or *sissy*. As an Advisory Teacher for Equal Opportunities I witnessed a secondary school teacher reprimanding a boy for bad behaviour by ordering him '*to go and sit on the poofs chair*'. Lee's found that the worst insult to a girl at secondary school was being called a 'lezzie'. Again, the sexist and homophobic language is used to control and maintain and discourage any deviation from a heterosexual pathway.

What are the long term effects on children's and students' responses to schooling as reflected by these studies? Girls may do better at secondary school than boys in terms of qualifications, but their higher success rate is not reflected in their ability to attain employment or entry into higher education in equivalent numbers to boys. However, as we have indicated, the underachievement of particular groups of boys needs urgent attention. We also need to remember that young people spend more than 15,000 hours in classrooms, and it is only in the second half of this process of schooling that they even begin to look ahead to GCSE (Darling and Glendinning, p. 76). Thus, the importance placed on examination results and occupational choice by politicians and parents must be seen as only part of schooling. How children experience schooling has an impact which goes beyond examination results and into the workplace.

Experience: 'Race'

The experience of ethnic minority children at school is, of course, varied and complex, and to over-simplify or over-generalize would do nothing to aid general understanding and nothing to improve the situation for those whose experience is negative. Nevertheless, there are grounds for concern and certainly areas worth further exploration by teachers and schools.

In a diagram in Chapter 6 we suggest several aspects of life in school that might affect achievement:

- racism from teachers and other adults in school;
- the effect of peer groups and subcultures;
- racism experienced from other pupils.

We intend to focus upon these in this section.

While this focus on achievement is certainly appropriate, it needs to be said that a different school experience along 'racial' lines does not necessarily produce worse exam results. It is possible that some ethnic minority children, or groups, may even do better than others despite experiencing racism or, indeed, because of it. In my view this still constitutes a problem: few white parents would think that their children's happiness at school is irrelevant just as long as their results are good, and we do not think many people today would hold the view that children's formative experiences should be really unpleasant so as better to prepare them for life's adversity. So while results are important, we take the view that there are still issues for social justice when different groups of children's experiences at school are worse than others'.

We also need to bear in mind, when considering school experience, the wide range of other factors which affect it. For one thing, schools vary considerably in their ethnic composition. Some schools contain only a minority of white pupils, the majority sharing one different ethnic background — such as Pakistani. Others, with no greater a proportion of white pupils, contain *several* different ethnic groups, such as African-Caribbeans, Bangladeshis and Sikhs. Some schools are evenly balanced between white and black and Asian pupils, though again the Asian and black groups may not be homogenous. Yet others (most in fact) contain a minority of black and Asian pupils, though the proportion may range from more than 40 per cent to less than 4 per cent. The dynamics of interaction and the relevance of 'race' will vary in relation to these different proportions in unpredictable and complex ways (so, for instance, it is by no means clear that fewer minority children equals fewer 'problems' and less racism). We need also to remember that class and gender are critical variables which affect the salience and significance of 'race' as a factor in the experience of schooling: middle class Asian boys may encounter the formal world of schooling in very different ways from working class Asian girls. It is important that pupils of all ethnic minorities are not seen more in terms of 'race' than in terms of these other key categories.

Racism from Teachers and Other Adults in School

Most accounts of schooling which tap pupils' views reveal that there are some racist teachers, but while Wright's 1986 study cites incidents where teachers reprimand black pupils with references to the jungle, and Macdonald et al. (1990) report the deliberate wearing of pig badges around Muslim pupils, it is clearly rare for teachers to use explicit racist abuse: it is unlikely to go unreported for long and is invariably known about by all the black and Asian children within days if not hours.

On the other hand, all the key studies report explicitly racist *views* from teachers, though in varying proportions. Wright found this to be the case with a third of the teachers she interviewed. Mac an Ghaill (1988) observes 'racism was prevalent throughout the white staff, including the school management, the teachers and the administrative and domestic workers' (p. 61). Mirza (1992) produces a typology of teachers in her two schools, one of which she identifies as 'racists' (though she suggests all but one of the other groupings held 'expectations that were often characterized by overt racism on the one hand or unintentional racism on the other' (p. 83) and Mac an Ghaill, too, in his differ-ent typology identifies some explicitly racist teachers.

Readers may find this alarming and/or hard to believe. Full details can only be gleaned from the original studies themselves, but the kinds of things the authors above identify are stereotypical and fixed views about particular groups, accompanied by either a condescending or a hostile attitude. They found derogatory views about African-Caribbean and Asian cultural patterns, family lives, parenting and parental aspirations for their children, stereotypical assumptions about the intelligence of African-Caribbean pupils (low) and Asian pupils (high) and corresponding sweeping generalizations about their poten-tial threats to discipline. These assumptions were gendered (that is they were different in respect of girls and boys) but took very little account of class. They were often accompanied by assimilationist ideas about the curriculum, a pre-ference for white pupils and an unwillingness to recognize where unequal treatment may be taking place. While this reads like an indictment, we should bear in mind that none of the studies demonstrated that all aspects of the description apply to more than a minority of teachers. Readers will have to make up their own minds whether they wish to dwell on that minority or emphasize the existence of the majority.

The effect of these numbers of racist teachers is not straightforward. While Mirza notes that 75 per cent of the teachers in her study made negative re-marks about the abilities of the black girls in general (in relation to white girls, not black boys) she does not believe that a simple matter of self-fulfilling prophecies explains lower results (p. 54) because the girls do not internalize the teachers' evaluations of them, they 'challenged their teachers' expectations' (p. 83). It is clear that pupils recognize these expectations. Foster (1990) has particular teachers identified to him as treating black pupils worse, not neces-sarily in a crude way. But as one of Foster's respondents says 'They don't need to show you what they're like, you can just read them as they go along, as they do certain things, you can just read them' (p. 135) though none of his respond-ents characterize the school or its teachers as predominantly racist. Mirza's (1992) respondents also identify specific teachers who partly determine their subject choices and she cites some similar comments: 'You feel the discrimina-tion, they try to hide it but you can see through it. They try to say "We're all equal", but you can tell: they talk to you more simply' (p. 55). Mac an Ghaill (1988) found that many pupils perceive a web of factors providing obstacles to their progress, including teacher expectation of them as being low achievers:

> At junior school, teachers pretend they like black kids, as soon as you leave junior school and you get into secondary school, and you reach third, fourth and fifth that's when you learn, you realise how you are being treated and the problems in the past. As you get older you understand what you are. (p. 94)

The issue of perceptions of behaviour is a critical one (perhaps more critical than perceptions of academic ability) and there is consistent evidence that African-Caribbean boys are perceived as more aggressive, truculent, disruptive and challenging of authority than other groups. This is aptly summed up by a comment from one of Wright's (1986) teachers in the file of a well behaved and academically able pupil: 'No trouble as yet this year . . .' (p. 22). Mac an Ghaill cites a student teacher explicitly advised by the school management 'to look out for the West Indians. . . . They had a lot of trouble from them in the past' (p. 64) and that 'African-Caribbean male students tended to be seen as having "low ability" and potential discipline problems'. All in all, the evidence is that they receive more criticism from teachers who seem to treat them in more authoritarian ways than other groups of pupils, even at nursery level (Green, 1985; Smith and Tomlinson, 1989; Wright, 1986, 1992; Mac an Ghaill, 1988; Gillborn, 1990; Sewell, 1997; Connolly, 1995) and are subjected to more formal disciplinary sanctions and complete suspensions from school far more often than any other group (CRE, 1985; Gillborn and Gipps, 1996).

It may be hard not to assume that there is at least a grain of truth in these perceptions, but the perception of African-Caribbean boys takes us to the core of how complex and intricate racialized interaction in schools can be. If it was straightforwardly the case that African-Caribbean boys *are* more disruptive than others, what sense are we to make of Wright's finding in her primary school study that everyone in the school, Asian children, white children and ancillary staff, but not the teachers, saw the black boys as more picked upon? This is a finding echoed by Gillborn (1990) who instances several striking occasions when he observes African-Caribbean boys being singled out for reprimands when other white or Asian pupils were just as guilty. In fact, Gillborn calls the alleged general challenge to authority by black boys 'a myth' (in contrast to a black woman teacher in Sewell's (1995) study who asserts '. . . the disproportionate number of excluded African-Caribbean boys rests solely on the fact that African-Caribbean boys are more likely to do things that warrant exclusion' (p. 38)).

We would suggest that an understanding of these matters rests upon an appreciation of the out-of-school factors affecting black pupils such as the racism experienced by themselves and their families, the ways these experiences differ and are mediated and interpreted because of social class and gender, together with an appreciation of the way in which the sometimes conflictual character of schools, especially inner-city schools, can become racialized.

The Effect of Peer Groups and Subcultures

Partly as a result of experiences outside school as well as within them, there is a tendency for subcultures and peer groupings to be formed along 'racial' or ethnic lines, especially in secondary schools, and especially from about year 9 onwards. Mutual negative expectations are likely to become hardened, teachers expect African-Caribbean pupils, and especially boys, to be difficult so they respond to them in critical and authoritarian ways and add to a teachers' culture which legitimates this. Their pupils come to suspect most teachers of at least covert racism and locate this within other experiences and expectations, and they create a subculture which makes sense of this, which gives them value, and provides survival strategies and support. The members of the sub-culture 'resist institutional incorporation into white cultural identities' (Mac an Ghaill, 1988, p. 110) and since teachers effectively control outward symbols — clothing most obviously — more attention may be given to style and symbolic space as well as actions such as arriving late to lessons. Sewell (1995) suggests this can become interwoven with notions of macho toughness racialized ideas about masculinity, so that it becomes unmanly for black boys to be pro-school and that resulting subcultures can adopt 'the offensive language of misogyny, homophobia or hyper-heterosexuality' (p. 39).

This can be exacerbated when some behaviours are misread or read out of context. It has often been reported, for instance, that eye contact while being scolded is avoided by children of Caribbean background as a mark of humility but is read by teachers as a sign of cheek. Ways of walking, speaking or dressing can initially be a function of peer group identity relatively free of symbolic conflictual statements, but can be sucked into a pernicious cycle of misreading behaviour and cultural signals, negative responses, and correspond-ing expectations. Gillborn (1990) writes:

> The teachers were not overtly racist, yet their ethnocentrism had racist conse-quences. The teachers believed that African-Caribbean pupils were a likely source of trouble. This belief influenced their perception of African-Caribbean pupils so that any 'inappropriate' behaviour might be interpreted as a serious challenge which called for clear (negative, critical) action. (p. 42)

We would argue, then, that a hostile orientation to school in some pupils is not a myth, though one has to be aware of the danger of an account such as the one above reproducing negative expectations. All the research, if read carefully, undermines such a simplistic blanket expectation. There are fairly firmly established conflictual subcultures in some schools, but there is also a range of individual and group responses within such schools and in compari-son with others. While there are groups, like Mac an Ghaill's 'Rasta Heads' who employed a range of disruptive tactics, were seen and saw themselves as a 'gang', saw little intrinsic satisfaction to be had from school work and expli-citly drew strength from Rastafari, there were others, like those he calls the Soul Heads and the Funk Heads, who could not be seen as so systematically oper-ating outside the school's values. This range of different individual and group responses on the part of black and Asian pupils has usually been characterized by the terms 'resistance' and 'accommodation'.

There is a series of studies which suggests that some African-Caribbean girls find a way of achieving academic success, without conforming to many of the goals and values of their schools and avoiding serious conflict with author-ity by well measured deviance (Fuller, 1980; Mac an Ghaill, 1988; Gillborn,

1990, 1996; Mirza, 1992) though it should be noted that half of Mac an Ghaill's 'black sisters' were Asian and he describes them as simply a peer group who supported each other, not a coherent 'subculture'. Faced with an environment they perceive as hostile, some respond by resisting, perhaps fairly overtly and conflictually, while others evolve a more complex response involving keeping a low profile in order to win what they want from the school — academic success — without conforming to teachers' notions of ideal pupils. The 'black sisters' adopted a highly instrumental approach to their teachers — they did not identify with them but they did not reject them out of hand, they were anti-school but pro-education. He characterizes this as 'resistance within accommodation' and frequently demonstrates the role of gender as an important variable in how young people negotiate their way through adolescence, racism and schooling.

Mirza's study (1992) is the key one to explore the relationships between class, gender and ethnicity for African-Caribbean girls and their schooling. She acknowledges, of course, that girls get better results, but wants to avoid some conventional (and, she believes, simplistic and romanticized) explanations of this in terms of matriarchal families and strong female role models — pointing instead to different labour market opportunities in Britain for girls and boys of immigrant parents and their subsequent effect on aspirations and orientation to schooling.

Whether individuals choose resistance or accommodation depends on a variety of factors such as the availability, visibility and power of existing sub-cultures, gender, social class, individual personality and the demands of the moment. It is not an either/or choice but a continuum of responses and behaviour which may be utilized at different times in different circumstances in response to different teachers, phases of schooling, and locations in school. Pupils have to live in response to a myriad of different demands — it is not a matter of inflexible patterns or formulae which can be 'read off' with reference to ethnicity, class or gender. Fixed notions of 'resisting' or 'accommodating' black pupils are simply more stereotypes.

We have said little so far about Asian pupils because the evidence suggests that they are treated differently from African-Caribbean pupils, that they have different experiences of school. Mac an Ghaill (1988) suggests 'There was a tendency for Asian male students to be seen by the teachers as technically of "high ability" and socially as conformist' (p. 64) but also sly 'At least with the coloured you know where you are, with the Asians you just can't tell' (p. 69) especially, it seemed, when they were speaking their own language. Wright in her primary school study indicates that the stereotype of Asians as being more placid and conformist is clearly present. While this seems to lead to relatively high expectations for boys it can lead to girls being almost entirely marginalized: 'There was a sense in which the Asian girls seemed invisible to the teachers' (p. 17). In contrast to the black students he observed, Mac an Ghaill (1988) also describes a group of Asian pupils called the Warriors. Contrary to the common stereotype they were negative about schooling, but

When an African-Caribbean student became a disciplinary problem, it was seen by the teachers as a frequent characteristic of being 'African-Caribbean'. Any disruptions caused by Asian students were seen as individual acts of deviancy and did not challenge the teachers' idea of being 'Asian'. (p. 123)

Mac an Ghaill makes the point, borne out in the other studies, that the stereotype of Asians was of predominantly middle class Asians, but it seems a remarkably impervious stereotype, undented by what must be many experiences of pupils who do not fit it.

Racism Experienced from Other Pupils

So far we have examined interaction with teachers and its effects, though clearly relationships and behaviour of pupils is a crucial part of anyone's school experience.

It is probably harder to generalize here than it is about interactions with teachers: after all there are countless thousands of pupil–pupil interactions during anyone's school career, taking place in thousands of classrooms, corridors, playgrounds and buses home, and schools will differ in their ethnic composition as well as in their general climate. We do not think it is possible to make safe generalizations about this aspect of 'race relations' in schools. We can, however, present some evidence with an invitation to readers to observe critically for themselves.

One assumption we want to challenge is the pervasive unwillingness in many adults to recognize that young children notice 'race', a belief in the innocence of children (Menter, 1989; Epstein, 1993b; Siraj-Blatchford, 1994). This is despite evidence of negative racial attitudes in younger juniors and infants which has been available for many years: Goodman published a detailed study in 1964 — perhaps discounted as American — but there is also Milner's British work published in 1975 and updated in 1983, and Alibhai's in 1987 (see also EYTARN, 1994). These studies demonstrate that not only do children, sometimes as young as four years old, notice racial differences but that many are also aware of the different values placed upon different colours — and these evaluations are understood by children from all ethnic groups.

We realize that the belief in racially 'innocent' young children is a powerful one which cannot be dispelled in one paragraph, though we would invite readers to view critically the idea that young children do not notice colour. After all, we talk to young children a great deal in the language of colour: a green dress, a red car, a pink flower, so can it really be that they do not notice that the child next to them in their playgroup or school is brown or pink? The fact that they do not mention it may indeed be a sign that they are already aware of some adult anxiety on the subject.

Without suggesting that infant or primary schools are wracked with racial conflict, there is evidence that in some schools young black and Asian children receive racist treatment from others: Wright (1992), for instance, notes several incidents of exclusion by four year olds, comments from teachers about white children's disinclination to work with Asians and the serious bullying Asian children sometimes encountered, as do Akhtar (1986), Alibhai (1987) and the CRE (1988). Kelly and Cohn (1989) included a small number of primary children in their survey of racial name-calling, finding that about a third had had experience of it at age 10.

Name-calling is not trivial. Any teacher who has had to deal with a teased child knows that the 'sticks and stones' rhyme is wishful thinking: 'I think it's worse than being hurt physically because physical hurt heals quicker than being called names' as one of Kelly and Cohn's respondents said. The children they surveyed said it was not only the most common form of verbal abuse but also the most hurtful, and indeed its special nature was referred to by Swann (1985):

> [racial abuse] is a reference not only to the child but also by extension to their family and indeed more broadly their ethnic community as a whole. (p. 35)

We think there is more to it than this. Racist names are not just used by children; they have relevance to and reflect something about the wider adult world. Having acne or wearing glasses may affect one's employment and housing chances but not so systematically as 'race', and such attributes are unlikely to receive open abuse in the street or to give rise to political parties dedicated to your removal. For many white people it takes a great effort of imagination to remember one's own experience of being the target of name-callers and translate that experience into that of the racially abused child, who may well know that his or her grandmother has to experience something similar in the street. The evidence about racism, presented in Chapter 2, is in some sense known about by even quite young black and Asian children, so when they hear 'Paki' in the playground they may hear it as an echo from the world outside.

While this indicates something about the experience of 'race' in classrooms and playgrounds, it does not mean, as Troyna and Hatcher (1992) point out, that crude attitudes can be 'read off' from abusive names. They examine the salience of 'race' in young children's lives through a model which considers and links the key processes, influences and forces which define experiences as 'racially' salient to children (p. 40).

They argue not that children are 'racist' or 'not racist' but that shifting and at times contradictory sense-making takes place. They dwell mostly on actual interactions and incidents, distinguishing between 'hot' and 'cold' racial name calling: the former often taking place between friends in a temper, meant to hurt but having no commitment to their content; the latter being used to deliberately taunt other children 'for fun'. Both draw on (and arguably reinforce) pervasive negative ideas, but in neither case is the relationship between beliefs and behaviour simple and straightforward. Children may have an individualist language for someone they know or might imagine in their class, but no information or concepts which might enable them to construct different views about black and Asian people as a whole, other than those which circulate, by default, in the 'common-sense' they grow up into. This can often be reflected in their positive and accepting behaviour towards a black or Asian pupil, coupled with a strong antipathy towards 'blacks' or 'Pakis' as a whole.

> ... 'race' and racism are significant features of the cultures of children [...] ... [but] racism has conditional status in people's lives; conditional, that is, on the extent to which it can be used to make sense of their world. ... The intricate web of social relations in which children live their lives and the particular set of material and cultural circumstances in which this is embedded have the potential to heighten the salience of racism as an appealing and plausible explanation for 'the way things are'. (1992, p. 196)

What is especially significant about Troyna and Hatcher's work is that it was undertaken not in stereotypical multiracial schools but in 'predominantly white primary schools'. Gaine has produced two studies which focus on pre-dominantly white secondary schools where race was 'not a problem', as indeed have Roberts (1988) and Massey (1987, 1991) and the Swann Report in the mid-1980s:

> [A] ... major conclusion which we feel must regrettably be drawn from the findings of this project, is in relation to the widespread existence of racism, whether unintentional and 'latent', or overt and aggressive, in the schools visited. ... The project revealed widespread evidence of racism in all the areas covered, ranging from unintentional racism and patronising and stereotyped ideas about ethnic minority groups combined with an appalling ignorance of their cultural backgrounds and life styles and of the facts of race and immigration, to extremes of overt racial hatred and 'National Front' style attitudes. ... (DES, 1985, p. 234)

It cannot be that this widespread evidence of hostile myths and stereotypes about ethnic minorities fails to communicate itself to the small numbers of ethnic minority pupils in the schools concerned.

All young people have to pick their way through these competing voices and different levels of action and understanding. Behaviours, responses and interactions vary in the rich complexity of school life. The least we can do as teachers is recognize that 'race' is real in their lives. We also need to recognize that the problem is beyond solving by individual teachers although some may make some progress in these very stormy waters.

Experience: Class

In the previous chapter aspects of the formal or taught curriculum were examined. Here we want to examine the 'hidden curriculum', the ways in which pupils' class backgrounds[1] may affect their experience of schooling; how the daily and accumulated experiences may produce different meanings and consequences for different children and young people, whether or not they are sitting alongside each other in apparently the same circumstances. The things which pupils learn at school are not necessarily on the timetable.

In the sections on 'race' and gender we made the point that different (and worse) experience does not necessarily produce lower achievement — indeed, in the case of certain ethnic minority groups and middle class girls, it may be that they achieve better school results *in spite of* certain negative aspects of their time at school. We do not think the same can often be said of lower working class children. They are more likely not only to have an experience of schooling which is qualitatively worse in many ways, but also one which leaves them less qualified and in possession of fewer of the benefits which schools are supposed to confer.

Some factors already discussed will have an affect on a pupil's experience of school. For instance, if a pupil is used to a different language code or if she is linguistically impoverished, then the highly language-dependent world of the school will present challenges which the upper middle class pupil will not have to face. The curriculum, too, can produce a sense of alienation, of lesson content not being relevant or related in any way to particular children's lives. The new aspects of experience at school which we want to consider are teacher expectations, the effect of peer groups and cultural 'messages' conveyed by the school.

Teacher Expectation

The core of this issue is that pupils have a tendency to perform according to people's expectations of them (as do we all). This is not to say, of course, that a pupil automatically works well or less well in accordance with messages about their ability or general worth — some will consciously defy such messages — but it is to say that teacher expectation is a powerful force which is hard to ignore. The best known study of this phenomenon was carried out by Rosenthal and Jacobson in 1968, and although there have been many criticisms of it and failures fully to replicate its dramatic results, it is fair to say that it provides, at the very least, a powerful warning to teachers. (The researchers picked out some children at random and without their knowledge, telling the teacher that in a year's time they would have made striking academic progress, and they did.)

It is probably inevitable that teachers work at least to some extent with a notion of an idealized pupil, likely to be drawn from their own experience and lifestyle (Hargreaves et al., 1975). In the pressures of teaching there emerge teacher coping strategies of identifying bright, conforming and trouble-making students, and these are inevitably permeated by assumptions about class (and indeed about 'race' and gender, as we have already explored). This is not to present a simplistic and negative picture of teachers. Any teacher or ex-teacher recognizes the near-impossibility of having no expectations of groups of pupils as well as the ease with which a cycle of mutually confirming expectations can develop. Ideally, this kind of argument and evidence should be taken as an indication of how hard a teacher's job is rather than an easy way to condemn them. Nevertheless, teachers do bear some responsibility if unquestioning stereotypes are employed and resulting expectations become fulfilled. The willingness always to be surprised by pupils' work and potential is an important attribute in teachers, needing careful balancing with a knowledge of generalizations derived from research (including their own).

Social class is fertile ground for expectations. There are signals of clothing, speech and 'style' as well as teachers' knowledge of research that working class pupils on average do less well. There are abundant stereotypes on which to draw about cultural deprivation and inadequate parenting, even when they take a benign form and parents are not 'blamed' for their apparent lack of knowledge about how to help their offspring achieve at school.

Peer Groups, Sub-cultures and Ability Grouping

This was discussed in the section about 'race', partly with reference to earlier work on social class groupings in schools. There are several classic and well-known studies of what can happen when assumptions about social class combine with labels about ability and become built into school structures — i.e. in rigid streaming systems — and thence into distinctive sub-cultures which become a fundamental part of school life. The best known studies are about boys in secondary schools (Hargreaves, 1967; Lacey, 1970; Willis, 1977; Corrigan, 1979) but many primary school teachers may recognize the same processes at work, albeit not within a structure where separate streamed classes have such an impact upon school dynamics, and some studies look at the operation of looser banding from the same perspective (Ball, 1981). A study of girls' peer groups was undertaken by McRobbie (Centre for Contemporary Cultural Studies, 1978).

As with 'race', a key process involves a clash between teacher's idealized view of what a pupil 'ought' to be and the reality. Notions of what constitutes ability, good behaviour, conformity, respect and belief in certain goals are used by teachers (inevitably) in making judgments about pupils, and these are inextricably embedded in assumptions about social class (via speech, catchment area, clothing, subtle behavioural cues, parents' work, and so on). Ball's (1981) study, among others, showed that streaming or banding was often done partly on the basis of judgments about behaviour, so that pupils perceived as more 'suitable' were allocated to upper bands while behaviour was also used as a reason to move people down — bright lower class pupils often 'percolating downwards'. In cases where evaluations are already publicly declared, as it were, in streams, it can happen that pupils who feel they cannot succeed in the way most valued by the school — academic success — find some other source of self-esteem. When this becomes a collective endeavour a subculture can develop which appears to value different things from the school. In the male examples given earlier this meant valuing certain displays of toughness and apparently aggressive masculinity, rewarding (by peer group approval) the skilful disruption of lessons, challenges to authority in the form of clothing, arriving late, not having equipment, and not doing homework. For girls it may, for instance, result in a subculture which values fashion and appearance, or childbearing, as alternative sources of self-esteem.

This can all too easily become locked into a cycle of mutually reinforcing stances, and as Willis's (1977) study suggested, while apparently being a resistant subculture actually prepares 'the lads' for exactly the role the school may have pigeonholed them for: routine, unskilled factory work, where the monotony is broken with the skills partly learned at school: having a laugh and disrupting work without getting the blame.

Cultural Messages Conveyed by the School

Allied to some of the experiences young people may have through school subcultures, are the lessons schools may teach about power. Bowles and Gintis (1976) argue as part of their 'correspondence theory' that young people are intended to learn obedience, anonymity, the acceptance of hierarchy and inequality through their schooling. The hidden curriculum implicitly teaches them that acquiescence to authority, rules, and to those in authority over them (including prefects), is the route to success in school and in work. They argue that this is particularly significant for lower working class pupils, offering the illusion of equal opportunities while teaching subservience.

One of the most influential scholars in the study of social class and its relationship to the culture of the school is Pierre Bourdieu. He maintains that children arrive at school with an accumulation of 'cultural capital' and that pupils from the middle and upper classes benefit from this 'cultural capital' far more than children from lower working class backgrounds. The reason, he suggests, is that children whose values and attitudes from home are already in tune with those of the school are more likely to succeed than children whose cultural dispositions do not reflect the dominant class. Bourdieu is not suggesting that one culture is superior to another, but that the power of the dominant class enables it to impose its culture on others. In school terms the dominant culture is the 'legitimate one' and defines what constitutes 'knowledge and intelligence' (see Chapter 4). There is a real contrast, he suggests, between those pupils and their parents who *understand* the subtle processes of schools success from the inside and to whom it readily makes sense in the context of their own employment. This was discussed in Chapter 2, the point being made that parental orientation to life and work will inevitable rub off on their children. It is not that lower working class children without prior familial involvement in higher education and 'careers' do not have aspirations for goals which have in the past been out of reach, but it may be that the messages are more subtle, the reorientation of the self which is required is somehow less explicit and hence more easily missed. In some ways this issue arises again in Chapter 7, when parents' involvement in school 'choice' is considered.

Though now very old, a study by Jackson and Marsden in 1962 gives some useful insights with its exploration of the conflict between working class and middle class ways of life. They studied 88 working class children at grammar school, finding that despite their parents' encouragement and commitment to children's success, parents as well as children felt themselves patronized and out of their depth on occasions such as grammar school parents' evenings, unsure of what to say and what to ask about careers and higher education. The material differences of their homes in terms of somewhere to study and noise levels, together with conflicts to do with their neighbourhood friends attending the secondary modern school, all contributed to obstructing their achievement. Jackson and Marsden observed that the working class child who did make it to grammar school had either to assimilate the values of the school (and hence move away from the values of their home) or find themselves in conflict with them. Those children who left before the sixth form were the most likely to remain firmly entrenched in their working class culture, whilst those who stayed on, when they became adults, identified themselves as classless. In employment terms the working class children from the grammar school did get better jobs than their counterparts from the secondary modern school, but they were not as good as the jobs obtained by their middle class school friends. The study suggests that the entry of the working class children into a grammar school at the age of eleven did almost nothing to reduce class divisions.

There is a sense, then, in which schools are a different cultural world to that experienced by some children and young people. We have already touched upon the curriculum and the ways in which it may be alienating when it makes no connection with people's lives and experiences (an issue developed by Keddie, 1973). We have also covered the issue of language, and the subtle or overt value which may be put upon different forms of speech. While the Jackson and Marsden study is more than 30 years old, the widespread coverage of comprehensives came about barely 20 years ago: we are therefore only just reaching the stage when most parents of secondary school pupils had comprehensive schooling themselves.

Cultural Deprivation Theory

A different interpretation of the cultural gap between some homes and schools is that contrary to Bourdieu's argument some families *are* deficient. The term 'cultural deprivation' became popular in the 1960s among educationalists, especially psychologists, as a way of referring to the complex of factors which they believed were responsible for holding back certain pupils in school. 'Culturally deprived' became a euphemism for the working classes and minority ethnic groups whose cultures were viewed as inferior to the mainstream culture of society, thus rendering their children less educable. The adoption of government programmes (derived from others in the USA, especially Head Start) institutionalized this concept of deficiency and arguably contributed to some of the stereotyping already discussed. The most far reaching policy put in place by the government was the introduction of Educational Priority Areas (EPAs), their intention being:

> to raise the educational performance of children, to improve the morale of teachers, to increase the involvement of parents in their children's education, to increase the 'sense of responsibility' for their communities of the people living in them. (Halsey, 1972, p. 38)

The areas contained high proportions of families in poverty, poor housing, and thus, arguably, high proportions of 'culturally deprived' families. While some involved in EPAs, such as Midwinter (1972), argued that while they were unable to resolve underlying problems of material deprivation the community involvement with schools brought great benefits, others were unconvinced. Keddie (1973) fiercely criticized the whole concept of cultural deprivation, arguing that a family or community cannot possibly be deprived of its *own* culture, though it may be a culture rather less valued than the dominant one. She goes on to argue that locating the educational failure of the child with the home, rather than with the school, is tantamount to blaming the poverty on the child and family, thus drawing attention away from the structural cause of educational inequality and hence any necessity for action. Interestingly, all of the aims of the EPA's resonate powerfully with the current government plans for 'Educational Action Zones'.

Conclusions

It is clear that pupils from different kinds of backgrounds experience school in very different ways, to the advantage of some and disadvantage of others. Wider differences between social classes suggest that in ways which cannot be discounted as individual differences, pupils approach school with different skills and orientations and are in turn responded to in ways which are related to social class. The resulting interactions produce a new set of dynamics that affect group processes, how the formal curriculum is received, and a series of 'lessons' about adult life. It is unlikely that the effect of these processes will diminish very much by trying to 'compensate' for or repair supposedly inadequate parental cultures, but it seems equally unlikely that schools in the climate described in Chapter 4 will be able to make creative and flexible curricular innovations.

Note

1   As before, it needs to be recognized that the terms 'working class' and 'middle class', while widely used in the literature, can produce confusion (and be much too sweeping) if they are taken to signify patterned differences between everyone in manual work and everyone else. We intend, therefore, to describe and explore differences between what we have called 'lower working class' and 'upper middle class' families and pupils.

6   Achievement

Gender and Achievement

During the years since the introduction of the GCSE there has been an increasing concern amongst politicians, policy makers and parents which has focused upon the differences in achievement between boys and girls. During the 1970s and 1980s the concerns about achievement were directed towards girls. These concerns regarding the education and achievement of girls arose out of the growing body of feminist research and literature which critiqued the state and highlighted the disadvantageous position of women both in employment and in education.

Policy makers, both at national and local level, responded by setting in place a number of initiatives as a means of opening up access to girls. These initiatives targeted the curriculum and resources offered to girls. LEAs employed advisory teachers to support schools in developing whole school policies on equal opportunities and in developing a girl-friendly curriculum and environment. There were attempts by feminists to shift the conceptual horizons of policy makers and to revolutionize the existing structures, for example Weiner (1985) developed an anti-sexist curriculum which critiqued the patriarchal nature of schooling, and attempted to empower girls. (This was looked at in more detail in Chapter 4.) However, the majority of the work remained compensatory in nature and took place within established institutional structures and organizations. These initiatives could be seen to have enjoyed a degree of success in so far as there was greater participation by girls in their education indicated by a larger number of girls staying on after the end of compulsory schooling, and, furthermore, the end of the 1980s saw girls doing well in school and 'beating' the boys in academic achievement as measured by examination results at GCSE.

How far the compensatory programmes adopted by schools and LEAs at this time were to account for this shift in outcome is difficult to measure, but the attitudinal changes of the girls demonstrated by active choices being made with regard to their education, coupled with the expectations parents had of their daughters' educational opportunities needs acknowledgement. It is important to note that for many years girls had lagged behind boys with very little attention being given to the problem. In the 1950s and 1960s it was acknowledged that girls literacy and numeracy were superior to those of boys and, as a consequence, to achieve a grammar school place girls had to score far higher than boys in the 11+ examination.

Are girls really outperforming the boys? The EOC (1995) found that at ages 7, 11, and 14 in National Curriculum assessments in English, girls did, in fact, do better than boys. However, in science and mathematics the assessments remain broadly similar. At GCSE, girls are more successful in most major subjects, they are even achieving success in those subjects traditionally seen as 'boys' subjects, (mathematics, computer studies, chemistry, combined science and design and technology). However, their performance is usually less good in these curriculum areas. Boaler (1997) alerts us to the fact that whilst girls as a percentage are gaining the same number of mathematics passes at GCSE, the number of boys obtaining an A or A* continues to far outnumbers girls and they continue to do significantly less well than boys in GCSE physics.

At A and A/S level this seeming pattern of difference in performance is not repeated. Boys tend to score more top and bottom grades than girls. Furthermore, whilst girls are achieving better exam results than boys at age 16, there is little evidence to indicate that this is leading to improved post-sixteen opportunities in the form of training, employment, career development and economic independence. The majority of young women still go on in later life to have poorer incomes and lower employment success than men. These statistics raise many important questions with regard to the culture of schooling. Are schools focusing on the academic achievement of girls and neglecting the important and complementary skills of individual development and decision-making which enable young people to maximize their opportunities later on? Are schools challenging traditional expectations and roles in order to improve pupils' aspirations and strengthen their life choices and chances? Research by Carolyn Dixon, reported in the Times Educational Supplement (TES) (28 June 1996), highlights how at school 'being a lad is vital to their self image, and detention or being sent out of class is viewed as a badge of courage'. In 60 hours of videotaping Dixon found only one incident of indiscipline or challenge to the discipline and behaviour structures of the school being perpetrated by a girl. The male agenda was about having a joke with your mates, playing around and not being seen as a 'girl'. However, this laddish behaviour does not apply to *all* boys, the research also suggests how it was the white working class boys who were losing out, not only to girls but also to Asian boys.

Gender and Class

It is dangerous and inaccurate to imply that all boys under perform and all girls do well. The gender gap is widest in comprehensive schools and least pronounced in independent and grammar schools. Research by Gillian Plummer (TES, 23 January 1998) points out that we do not have a hierarchy in the UK where girls are the top 50 per cent and boys the bottom 50 per cent. Her research maintains that it is social class which continues to have the single most important influence on educational attainment, with those from the more affluent backgrounds getting a string of As and A*s and the most disadvantaged getting none at all. The strong correlation between social class and achievement can be seen as early as the infant school, and the gap widens as the children grow up. GCSE results illustrate an even stronger correlation. The need for detailed research on the educational failure of working class girls has been hidden by the focus upon the statistics which highlight the success rate of girls in examinations and these statistics are supposed to represent all girls.

Furthermore, the majority of boys and girls from socially advantaged families do better in all subjects at GCSE than the majority of girls from disadvantaged families, girls' schools holding the top places in GCSE having proportionally fewer socially disadvantaged girls.

Sally Power's research 'Able boys succumb to complex pressures' (TES 23 January 1998) found that boys attending independent schools did worse than girls educated in the same sector in terms of examination results. The girls tended to have better A-levels and better degree classifications than the boys. However, boys with poorer qualifications were far more successful in gaining entry to the highest status universities. Sally Power suggests that the middle class pre-occupation with male underachievement reflects their concerns that the family influence and the old boy networks are no longer as powerful to 'open doors' because of the increasing competition from women for the same jobs.

Connell (1995) describes all the attention given to this phenomenon as a 'minor moral panic' and maintains that the outcry 'against' the success of girls is a result of several interweaving strands. Firstly, there is the backlash politics, that is, girls have been enjoying positive discrimination at the expense of the boys for 'too long' and now its the boys' turn. Secondly, there is the issue of how boys become alienated from the process of schooling, for instance learning to read later than girls. Thirdly, there are concerns articulated by class teachers of boys being a discipline problem, or having a lack of interest in school.

The under-performance by boys highlighted by BBC's Panorama programme *Men aren't working* (October 1995) lends weight to these arguments. Of the children of 15+ interviewed, it was agreed amongst them that girls have a confident and positive attitude towards education whilst boys need to be pressurized into doing any work since 'girls would get the jobs anyway'. None of the boys interviewed thought that acting the fool in class was macho but nevertheless they continued to do so. The Panorama programme linked this disenchantment to the boys perceived inevitability of unemployment as conventional work opportunities have been lost through de-industrialization and the subsequent loss of apprenticeships.

The collapse of the manufacturing industry and the introduction of new technologies in the workplace have conspired to make working class boys feel useless and unwanted. The disaffection has spread to the classroom. (Martin Bright, *The Observer*, 4 January 1998)

The current research looking at boys at risk in terms of part-time or full-time employment has found that there are slight differences but it is in fact the *girls* who are still worse off. The earning potential of women is still far worse than it is for men, with women still earning 80 per cent of a man's wage (see Chapter 3). Whilst the position of women in the economy and the labour market has shifted with the loss of many traditional male areas of work, the different and constrained pathways in terms of stereotypical occupations are still in evidence. Women still occupy the low ranks in most areas of work especially in the business sector. Among working class women, higher education also remains a less than common experience with only 0.8 per cent going to university. The Commission for Social Justice (1993) found that

Only 1 per cent of women whose fathers are from social class V hold an undergraduate degree or equivalent, compared with 41 per cent of men from social class 1. (TES 23 January 1998)

The Way Forward

Do we need a strategy for boys' education? Are the equal opportunities initiatives that were set in place for girls appropriate for boys' education? How far are schools responsible for underachievement by boys? The studies which have looked at boys' responses to schooling since the early 1970s (e.g. Willis, 1977) suggest the regimented and regulated systems of the school have alienated boys from the process of schooling, and the strict discipline systems have contributed to constructions of masculinity. In fact, boys' performance has in terms of examination results also improved year on year but not as quickly as girls.

The positive action programmes put in place for girls during the 1980s (see Chapter 4) may not be appropriate for boys. The relationship many boys have with school and the contribution that schools make to the construction of masculinity and its implication with discipline, violence and disruption all need addressing. Historically, it has been boys who have dramatically outnumbered girls in special needs classes and in schools for children with learning difficulties and emotional and behavioural problems. Boys have been more likely to get expelled or truant from school and are five times more likely than girls to be excluded. Boys make up 83 per cent of permanent exclusions from school and 28,500 leave school at 16 every year without qualifications. These issues cannot be considered in a gender neutral way. The failure of boys, particularly working class boys, is said to be one of the most disturbing factors in the education system in 1998. Failure is explained by the decline of unskilled male manual work and also the anti-swot culture among teenage boys. Teenage girls are seen as more diligent at school and are encouraged to succeed. However, a closer look at the situation of the working class girls in terms of examination performance, further education and working practices would draw attention to the problems that underlie their failure which are equally harmful as those affecting boys, for instance, withdrawal, anorexia, and early pregnancy.

During the past two decades concerns about gender reform have focused on inequalities in the curriculum and the process of schooling, dwelling upon how this process contributed to the different futures for girls and boys through what they learnt and how they developed, not just by examination score (Yates, 1997). Schools need to analyse the culture of their institutions and the impact this culture may have on children of different gender, 'race' and class background. Schools alone cannot restore the loss of jobs for unskilled school leavers but they can restore rights.

> The issue of boys achievement must . . . be seen within the context of the overall issue of the provision of equality of opportunity for girls and boys. Girls currently achieve relatively well at age 16, but we have serious concerns about some aspects of their education too; not least the serious fall off after 16 in their participation in subjects which could lead to careers in science, engineering and technology. Any national debate about education and gender must take continual account of both sexes in an attempt to ensure not that they achieve equally, but that each has equal opportunity to reach their full potential. Girls and boys need an education which prepares them equally for the challenges and opportunities presented by the changing world of work. (EOC, 1996)

Achievement: 'Race'

The commonest generalization about 'race' and achievement is that Asians do well and African-Caribbeans do badly, in relation both to each other and to white pupils. It is a generalization rooted in research which goes back to the mid-1970s (Coard, 1971; Redbridge CRC, 1978) and which was given extra credibility by the Swann Report of 1985. This was set up by the then Secretary of State for Education early in 1979 with a specific brief to 'give early and particular attention to the educational needs of and attainments of pupils of West Indian origin . . .' (1985, vii) and although the final report identified other groups doing badly in schools (including Bangladeshis) it reinforced the existing generalization.

Six Problems with Accepted Wisdom

We want to argue that this generalization, now firmly part of accepted educational wisdom, is misleading to the point of being unhelpful, even damaging. There are six reasons for this:

1   It is now so widely 'known', even by beginner teachers before they start their training, that there is at least some risk that the generalization has become a self-fulfilling prophecy. Expectations of both 'Asian' and African-Caribbean pupils may have become part of the complex web of factors which actually *cause* patterned differences in attainment. As Foster (1990) argues (in a book which generally exonerates teachers from most charges of racism):

> It seems that informal gossip within the teaching profession can sometimes lead to the transference of racist myths from one institution to another. This perhaps, combined with impressions gathered from the media, can influence teachers' attitudes. . . . (p. 131)

2   The evidence on which the generalizations are made span many years in which almost everything has changed, so we need to be sensitive to the date of any research. Primary-age children, who arrived in the later 1950s direct from the Caribbean or the Indian subcontinent, having been separated from parents in some cases for years and facing a huge mismatch in styles of schooling, had very different experiences from those who were British born in the 1980s. It is, therefore, misleading to lump together research on outcomes from those two periods simply because the people being studied *look* the same. Immigrants obviously have some things in common with British-born children with the same roots and background, but there are likely to be significant differences too. Even if the outcomes were similar — i.e. systematic school failure during both periods — the underlying reasons may differ.

Swann certainly bears some responsibility for this conflating of groups of children with different experiences, a failing the Report compounded by considering whether 'West Indians' as an (apparently self-evidently) homogenous group might be biologically less intelligent than whites.

Another aspect of the problem of time and change, is that *all* results have risen. It is not necessarily that particular groups are not performing any better than they were 20 years ago but that the *rate of increase in achievement* of different groups varies over time or even within and between different secondary schools. Some of the gaps identified some time ago are not being closed, but, as we shall see, some groups seem to have overtaken others.

3   Rather caricatured figures of the generic 'Asian' and the generic African-Caribbean stalk most of the research literature, with insufficient distinction being made between sub-groups within these broad categories. Most obviously, perhaps, there is considerable variation amongst British 'Asians'. Distinctions are often made on the basis of religion, but boundaries could be re-drawn by

using language instead, or whether original roots were rural or urban, or by date of migration and settlement, let alone by occupation and education. Similar distinctions could be drawn within the category 'African-Caribbean', only half of whom, for instance, have roots in Jamaica and who are often lumped together in research with Africans (who are lumped together in turn). The dangers of not making relevant distinctions may be illustrated by the Chinese — often invisible in this area of research or assumed to be grouped together with 'Asians' — but who are *twice as successful* as whites at getting into the older established universities. All of these potential or actual groupings may or may not be relevant to school achievement, but to assume their irrelevance is simplistic research.

This weakness in the literature has two causes. The first simply results from one of the practicalities of research: to take account of some of the internal distinctions already mentioned requires large samples. If 1,000 pupils do not include more than a handful of, say, Barbadans or Muslim Gujeratis then the researcher either has to use a bigger sample with its resultant greater cost and time demands, or merge these groups with others, or leave them out entirely. A second reason is to do with the source of the data and its reliability. In practice the ethnic monitoring of school results which are often used by researchers is carried out by schools, or more accurately, by teachers, to a set of categories originally determined by the former Department of Education and Science. For the most part the pre-set categories do not sub-divide as we have suggested they ought to because teachers were not confident about getting them right.[1]

4   A key distinction which we nearly always make when looking at white children's attainment in Britain is social class: we know that for various reasons parents' occupation, the primary determinant of what we call 'class' in short-hand, has a powerful relationship with eventual school success or failure. Why then should this not be true of ethnic minorities? Part of the answer lies above, sample sizes would have had to have been unaffordably large to subdivide not only by specific roots but also by class, so it was not generally done. This factor is again affected by the period when the research was carried out, since there is a sense in which the early settlers in the 1950s and 1960s were reasonably homogenous in occupational terms: most were factory or low-paid workers and most lived in relatively poorer urban areas. However, since then all kinds of gaps and differences have opened up, and class needs to be treated as a crucial variable within ethnicity today. In addition, it needs to be said that even when class *is* taken into account, African-Caribbean and Asian men are more likely to be unemployed than whites of the same social class (Runnymede Trust, 1994a). There may be a compounding 'race' factor giving an extra twist to class disadvantage, an 'ethnic penalty' (Modood et al., 1997).

5   It may be obvious by now that there is another key distinction which has too seldom been made, that of gender. Again, we know that white British

girls and boys have different educational outcomes so we have to expect gender to be relevant to the school results of Asian and African-Caribbean children, not least because not all groups have the same patterns of gender roles and expectations.

6   A final note needs to be made of the age of the children or young people studied, since differences apparent at Key Stage 1 or at age 11 may have narrowed or changed by the time the pupils involved reach the age of 18. Despite continuing evidence of under-performing African-Caribbeans at 16+ in Birmingham, recent monitoring by the LEA suggests that African-Caribbean *infant* pupils are significantly outperforming whites at ages 5 and 7 (Gillborn and Gipps, 1996). It is also known, for instance, that in some LEAs Bangladeshi and Pakistani pupils of primary age achieve less well than other groups, but Sammons' nine year study in London shows that 'Asians' overtook everyone else during their teenage years, and it has been the case for some time that 'Asians' tend to stay in education longer than whites after the compulsory leaving age. In fact, by the age of 18 'Asians' are the most highly qualified of all groups and most minority groups (except Bangladeshis, though see below) are *more* successful at getting into the former polytechnics than whites, sometimes quite significantly so (though frequently less successful at getting into the established universities: Modood and Shiner, 1994).

Current Knowledge

These weaknesses in research design and inevitable gaps in the data persist today and continue to make generalizations hazardous. Amongst the most thorough and reliable recent results available are cited by Gillborn and Gipps in their study for *Ofsted*. They examine Brent's results between 1991 and 1993, which appear to show the stereotyped pattern: 'Asians' doing better and African-Caribbeans doing worse, a widening gap between them, with whites remaining roughly in the middle — but there are no distinctions within 'Asian' and there is no class analysis.

  With these caveats, we would tentatively suggest that there may be a group of African-Caribbean boys who are systematically underachieving, even in relation to working class whites, and are leaving schools with lower average results. Recent research from some (but not all) LEAs even suggests that the rate of improvement in average results nation-wide may not be matched by this group, indeed they may even be falling below previous levels (Gillborn and Gipps, 1996, p. 22). There is also uneven evidence of underachievement by Bangladeshis, a much lower proportion up to now going to university compared with their working class white neighbours (Eade, 1995) though there is simultaneously evidence of younger Bangladeshis dramatically raising achievement levels (Tower Hamlets LEA, 1994). But there are also successful groups: Indians, for instance, whether girls or boys, seem to be doing better than anyone else, including white pupils, though this difference probably disappears if class is controlled.

The Web of Interacting Processes

We now propose to elaborate on these patterns and the complexities of generalizing by means of Figure 6.1. It needs to be viewed with caution, since it aims to

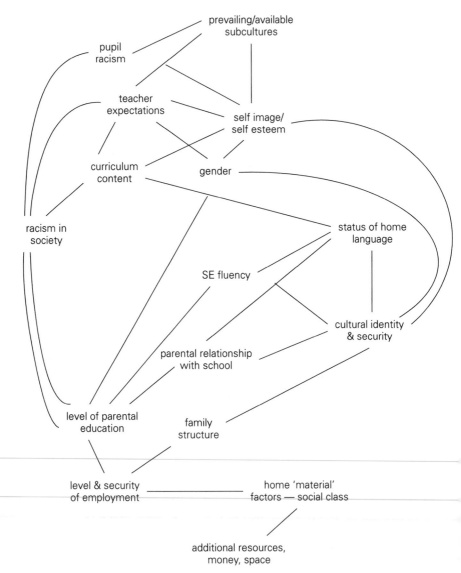

Figure 6.1: Factors relating to effectiveness of schools for ethnic minority pupils

chart or describe the entire network of factors which contribute to ethnic minorities' school performance, rather than argue that the worst case systematically happens to every ethnic minority child. It is not, therefore, intended as an exercise in deterministic victimology. It is deliberately not linear, since it should be self-evident that these processes do not operate in so simple a fashion.

Home Material Factors

Many studies in the past three decades have shown that significant proportions of some ethnic minority groups are both poor and live in poor areas, with relative lack of play space, unsafe roads and little access to leisure facilities of various kinds (Rose et al., 1969; Shaw, 1988; Runnymede, 1983; 1994b). They may also experience higher than average levels of unemployment, part-time and shift work, insecure unemployment, low pay, frequently exacerbated or even caused in the first place by racism in employment practices or in housing allocation (Maughan and Dunn, 1988; Runnymede Trust, 1994a and b; Modood et al., 1997). These material circumstances, though in part caused by racism, are likely to have the same sorts of effects as they would for white children: potentially less parental attention and energy resulting from long working hours in manual shift work, especially if combined with single parenthood; and fewer resources in terms of books, CD ROMs and educational trips. This says nothing about parents' wish for and interest in a good education for their children, only that there are more obstacles in their way than there are for others (including well-off ethnic minority families) who live in spacious surroundings with higher levels of income and leisure.

Nationally, a higher proportion of African-Caribbeans are in low paid work or unemployed than 'Asians' as a whole, though their rates are not very different from urban Bangladeshis. There is no particular reason why these factors should bear down any more or less on African-Caribbeans than on specific Asian sub-groups, though it may be that where a wider family is present — common but by no means universal amongst British Asian groups — then the effects on education of parental poverty and isolation may be offset.

Poor housing as an index of class position does not affect all ethnic minority groups equally. East African Asians, both Panjabi and Gujerati, were a middle class group in East Africa (Hiro, 1973). This meant that upon arrival in Britain, even though as refugees and with few if any material resources, they came with cultural capital in the form of business skills and experience, secondary and often higher technical qualifications. Whatever other effects this has had, it has affected their quality of housing and the areas in which they live and hence the affects of material deprivation on their children. The same may be true for Hindu Panjabis from India (Taylor, 1976; Jackson and Nesbitt, 1993; Modood, 1992; Gillborn and Gipps, 1996).

It is not necessarily the case, however, that class factors always mask 'race' ones. Recent analyses of SATs results for reading and maths at KS1 in

Wandsworth show that even when economic disadvantage was taken into account African-Caribbeans were still performing relatively less well, and indeed there appeared to be a widening gap at year 6.

Overall, we cannot be sure of the extent to which 'race' results are skewed by social class factors, since few large scale studies have had the resources to gather and analyse data at this level of sophistication. Maughan and Dunn's study (1988) found that there was a much less straightforward relationship between simple measures like parental occupation and free school meals (common surrogates for 'class' in much research) than there was for white youngsters, arguably because migrant groups are often in jobs which do not correspond with their education and skills. The Brent figures cited earlier may well be skewed by the social class composition of white Londoners, who tend to be more working class than the population as a whole.

Mismatch Between Expectations of and Experience of Schooling

There were several common features in the education of Pakistani, Indian, Bangladeshi and African-Caribbean parents in their countries of origin: it was formal, employed physical punishment and usually took place in large classes. While it was recognizably traditionally British, it was nevertheless not the same as the schooling they encountered through their children in the UK, increasingly influenced as it was by notions of child-centredness, negotiated learning and mixed ability teaching with different assumptions about discipline and control. To some extent there is also a gap between the experience of older white parents and their children's education — many finding a 'progressive' approach hard to understand or to trust, but this gap was wider and harder to bridge in the case of ethnic minorities because it was further widened by language, by experiences of racism from various aspects of officialdom, and by the network of subtle cultural pitfalls which lay in wait to confuse or humiliate the uninitiated. In short, if parents are mistrustful, uncertain or confused by their children's schools it may diminish their ability to give help and support.

Language

This is explored in more detail in Chapter 3, but needs summarizing here in relation to the flow chart. In short, language makes less difference and holds more surprises than superficial observations would suggest, and certainly it is fluency in English which is the issue, not bilingualism.

Language skills in English are obviously important: the ILEA's *Junior School Project* in 1985 (Mortimore et al., 1988) found that by the age of eleven children less fluent in English both made slower progress in reading and had lower attainment in reading (children's abilities in writing, on the other hand, showed no significant differences). This is old research, but it is worth citing because of its very large sample of pupils (2,000) and schools (50) and because there is no reason to suppose that the effect of low fluency will have decreased. A more recent study (ENCA, 1992) concluded that fluency in English and particularly whether English was spoken at home played a significant part in Key Stage 1 results, but it could not explain poorer results by Pakistanis in relation to Indians, (where perhaps class data would have helped). Recent analyses of KS1 results in Wandsworth show a similar pattern of lower results for Chinese, Indians and Pakistanis in reading probably related to English fluency, with the same children getting higher results in maths. Evidence from Tower Hamlets in 1994 shows a marked relationship between fluency and GCSE passes, with only 5 per cent of beginners gaining 5 or more A-G passes compared to 85 per cent of those who were fully fluent in English.

Cultural Differences in Domestic or Family Life and Their Effect upon Education

We attempt a brief descriptive account of 'Asian' family patterns in Chapter 2, so our intention here is to relate this to education. Despite our comments about the dangers of generalizing we think it is worth citing Bikhu Parekh, one of the original members of the Swann Committee and a long time commentator on ethnicity and education, who says very explicitly '. . . several family values play an extremely important part . . . an emphasis on learning, and seeing the individual as a representative individual, that he is the bearer of the family's hopes' (BBC, 1996), echoing the reference to 'generic Asians' adopted by Taylor in her comprehensive synthesis of all research completed in 1985. Clearly, any group which migrates half way across the world does so for a better life, and it would be absurd not to recognize that (for the most part) great hopes are invested in children — almost certainly to a greater extent than in the white population, who have not made such enormous upheavals and sacrifices — the 'migrant effect' as Mirza (1992) calls it.

What many accounts understandably highlight is the communal, entrepreneurial and aspiring future-orientation of some of south Asian British cultural life, and the importance of wider family relationships and networks. If there is a specific culture-based factor in 'Asian' school performance then it surely lies here.

This is likely to be true even where parents do not have the knowledge to give specific help. Eade (1995) cites a Bangladeshi young woman who explains:

> My parents wanted me to go to college and do my A-levels but they didn't know the system enough to tell me what to do. All the information they got was from me and my elder sister so they weren't really clear. (p. 14)

On the other hand, many teachers bemoan aspects of precisely this closely integrated family life, particularly extended visits to the subcontinent or prolonged wedding or religious celebrations during school time and late into the evening, arguing that these are to the detriment of school performance. At the same time teachers (but not necessarily the same teachers) speak of 'unrealistic aspirations' amongst Asian teenagers and their parents.

Sweeping positive accounts also underplay the extent to which individuals (or families, or one parent) may be sometimes also fatalistic, not aspiring and not necessarily supportive of or understanding about their children's educational ambitions, or may at times prioritize the education of boys. Asian youth, too, can be as dismissive as white youth of the value of education, the necessity of qualifications to secure a good job, and the worldly wisdom of their elders (especially in a new society). There is at least the potential for conflict between the individualistic western view of the autonomous individual and a more corporate sense of identity and family honour.

Social class, both here and in parents' original homelands, also plays its part in modifying this picture: people with commercial, professional or aspiring outlooks on life in India or Pakistan bring these with them; those with little education or experience beyond their village and family may well retreat into what they know when faced with the pace of change in Britain and uncertainties or ignorance about the education system. Another significant variable is gender, whose effect is neither straightforward nor simple (this is dealt with separately below).

That there should be a difference in attitudes and orientation between minorities with a recent history of migration and the white majority is not surprising. What is more puzzling to explain, given some evidence of different school results, is the apparently divergent attitudes between Asians and African-Caribbeans — and here lies more negative stereotyping, initially discussed in Chapter 2.

The notion that some kind of cultural inadequacy in Caribbean child-rearing is solely responsible for the pattern of poorer results is inadequate in itself. For instance, the numerous supplementary or Saturday schools set up and run by black parents and communities around the country hardly fit the stereotype. These concentrate upon 'the basic' three Rs and often some elements of black and Caribbean history too, and claim effectiveness in raising aspirations and achievement (Chevannes and Reeves, 1987; Berkshire LEA, 1989; Stone, 1981). Clearly they represent enormous concern and action and to some extent must replicate the continuity and sense of community which many Asian children get from language classes and their time at the mosque, gurudwara or temple. There have also been reports in recent years of African-Caribbean parents sending their British-born children back to stay with relatives in the Caribbean so that they can attend school there. The underlying parental beliefs behind both of these phenomena is that their sacrifices and extra work are needed not to overcome a flawed African-Caribbean culture but a British school system which is failing their children, especially their sons. How much this is related to social class, both here and originally in the Caribbean, has not, to our knowledge, been researched.

It is as well to remember that assumptions about cultural differences may have driven earlier research. In the largest digest of such work into African Caribbean pupils' achievement — Monica Taylor's *Caught Between* (1979) — almost all of the work she reviewed dwelt on family and culture. This was not her responsibility — she could only review what was available — but it is significant that very little had then been done on interactions *within* school and their role in achievement, to which we will now turn.

School Processes

It may be useful to untangle the different elements of this for the sake of clarity.

Curriculum

While this was discussed in Chapter 4, we want to emphasize here the argument that negative portrayals or absences in the school curriculum had a material effect in the results of African-Caribbean and Asian children. Briefly the argument goes that a negative or partial portrayal in the curriculum has an effect on the learner's self esteem and motivation, in much the same way as tales of male derring-do in wartime hold little that girls can actively identify with. This, as far as it goes, is the nub of the 'racist curriculum' argument. It should be noted, however, that we are not claiming that the portrayal of African-Caribbean and Asian people in the curriculum has been the same — though there may be little to choose between them as regards which is worse. Stereotypes have always been different, as have been the effects of the stereotypes on their subjects.

Teacher Attitudes

We cannot, however, take the curriculum in isolation, since it is encountered and negotiated by children and teachers in a context of wider racism in the press and in the media generally. In our view none of us can help but be influenced by this context. We would argue that news coverage on balance has portrayed a negative image, especially with respect to African-Caribbeans, and fictional representations follow a similar pattern (Twitchin, 1988; Dixon, 1977; van Dijk, 1993). Racist and partial representations do not *cause* teachers to view ethnic minority children in a particular light, they can however help set the agenda and define the constructs through which black and Asian people are perceived, the implicit assumptions by which their comments, actions and appearance are interpreted.

In the case of African-Caribbean pupils, this has a long history. Coard (1971) produced a hugely influential pamphlet called *Why the West Indian*

Child is made Educationally Sub-normal in the British School System high-lighting the disproportionate numbers of referrals of African-Caribbean pupils, especially boys, to ESN schools. One of the factors he cites is not just low but negative expectations of them. This was given some formal recognition by Swann (1985):

> . . . research findings and our own evidence have indicated that the stereo-types teachers tend to have of West Indian children are often related to a particular and generally negative, expectation of academic performance. (p. 25)

Swann had, of course, been set up in response to the 1970s evidence about black underachievement but also to what Foster (1990) refers to as a perception of their 'increasing threat to order' (p. 36). There was undoubtedly a high level of black disenchantment with schools, and as early as 1974 Dhondy wrote of *The Black Explosion in Schools*. Foster (1990) cites one of his inform-ants, a deputy head, recalling his arrival at the school in 1975:

> [There was] a very considerable tension in the school between the black pupils and quite a number of the staff . . . we remember feeling there's quite a lot of simmering tension here, antagonism and dislike . . . It seemed to me to be almost constantly the black kids who were up in front of the deputies and the head and the other senior teachers as well . . . (p. 36)

By the time of his research, Foster (1990) argues that in this school teachers were much more even-handed and less racist than many researchers found elsewhere. The school in question had a relatively long history of multi-cultural and anti-racist work and the African-Caribbean students were not over-represented in disciplinary matters in the way reported by the deputy head in the past. All but two of the teachers 'were unwilling to categorize or gen-eralize about students in terms of their race or ethnicity' (p. 128) while those two recited the common litany of complaints about African-Caribbean pupils, especially boys, being boisterous and excitable. He is, however, almost alone in this finding amongst academic researchers. While Gillborn (1990) and Mac an Ghaill (1988) are at pains to point out the positively expressed attitudes and a genuine wish to promote equal opportunities on the part of many teachers, nevertheless these seemed to coexist with stereotyped beliefs. Related findings by Wright (1986 & 1992), Connolly (1995) and Mirza (1992) are covered in Chapter 5.

A vicious twist to all this is currently being added by the predominance (by a factor of six) of African-Caribbean boys in school suspension figures. It may seem barely credible that this is entirely due to the sort of processes already discussed and that objectively there is no difference in the behaviour of these boys, they are simply treated differently. Nevertheless, this was pre-cisely the conclusion reached in a Commission for Racial Equality report on Birmingham LEA in 1985, investigating the disproportionate numbers of black boys being suspended. In reality, of course, there is no such thing as 'objective' behaviour in school: it is always a matter of interpretation and the outcome of a myriad of previous interactions and responses. In their review of the evidence, Gillborn and Gipps (1996) argue:

> Teachers (in their daily interactions with pupils) and schools (through the adoption of various selection and setting procedures) may play an active, though unintended, role in the creation of conflict with African-Caribbean pupils, thereby reducing black young people's opportunity to achieve. (p. 56)

When it comes to stereotypes, Asian pupils are subject to some consistent with those about their families: they are perceived as more likely to be studious, well behaved and cleverer — assumptions which are usually taken by educational researchers to enhance performance irrespective of whether they are accurate or not. It is possible that in some cases, however, lower expectations of ability may arise from low levels of English fluency and, of course, Asian girls may be subject to particular stereotypes of their own about their families' intentions for them (e.g. Wright, 1992). Eade et al. (1995) cite the encouragement by specific teachers as very significant in the success of some of their Bangladeshi respondents, while others mentioned low expectations and assumptions that an Asian girl's destiny was simply to be married off. Basit (1996) found the same assumptions seemed to be involved in work experience and careers advice. Research accounts of overtly negative responses to Asian pupils are rarer than for African-Caribbeans.

Racism from Pupils

> '. . . when we used to go to school we were always frightened of being attacked so most of our mind wasn't on education.' (Eade, 1995, p. 18)

The extent of racial bullying, name-calling and harassment cannot be discovered on a national scale since it is not easily accessible to large scale questionnaire type surveys, nevertheless the major studies of the past ten years consistently show a pattern of such harassment, more often suffered by Asian pupils (Akhtar, 1986; CRE, 1988; Troyna and Hatcher, 1992; Kelly and Cohn, 1988; Gaine, 1995). This is examined in more detail in Chapter 5, we would merely remark here that a climate of dislike is scarcely conducive to learning.

Counter School Sub-cultures

There is a great deal in the education literature about the formation of counter school cultures. This is explored in general terms and with reference to 'race' in Chapter 5 where several studies are reviewed which build upon earlier work about streaming/social class polarization and note the development of an additional racial dimension. These studies leave us in little doubt that the range of subcultures and peer groups available to pupils can have a marked effect upon their school achievement.

Wider Social Factors

Self-esteem

> ... black children can hardly avoid developing a deep sense of inferiority and worthlessness. . . . The black child raised on a mono-cultural diet in an English school experiences profound self-alienation. (Parekh, 1986, *cited* in Foster, 1990)

The notion expressed above was initially developed in the 1970s by Coard and more systematically by Milner (1975) though it extended to the whole of a child's life in Britain not just experience of schooling. This is a complex issue easily prone to over-simplification. It needs treating with some care since it risks pathologizing large numbers of children. The core of the argument is that in growing up in a society which devalues or even despises blackness, black and Asian children run a high risk of growing up with a degree of denial or dislike about a crucial part of themselves: their skin colour. Coard describes his own experience as a black teacher trying to get black children to colour in their self-portraits appropriately and the distress this evoked in them, even, in one case, to a boy disputing that Coard himself was black, so great was the mismatch between his concepts of black adults and teachers. Milner took this further in two studies (1975 and 1983) replicating work done in the USA in the 1940s (Clarke, 1947). His technique was to show various groups of 5–8 year-olds some dolls, white, African-Caribbean and Asian in appearance, and to ask the children 'Which doll is most like you?', 'Which dolls would you like to sit next to?' and so on. There was a striking pattern of denial and rejection of the black doll by black children, with 48 per cent identifying themselves as white and 72 per cent choosing mostly white 'friends', with no such mis-identification amongst white and interestingly, rather less by Asian children, though there was a similar pattern of rejecting their own group in some questions. Such marked results can be seen as indicating precisely what Parekh describes above, though it is questioned by Stone (1981) who argues that it takes too narrow a notion of self-esteem and cannot be seen as demonstrating a wide-spread wish to be white amongst black youngsters.

Whatever the strength of Stone's criticisms, one of the reasons this evidence from Milner needs to be treated with caution is that it is now comparatively old research. In the early 1970s being black was more overtly stigmatized than it is today, perhaps particularly in aesthetic terms. Black musicians and performers (especially women) tended to wear European-style straight-hair wigs because their own hair type was considered ugly. 'Skin-lightening' creams were widely available: they didn't work, but their mere presence was evidence of a market. An Enid Blyton book of the 1950s which had the three gollies, Willy, Woggy and Nigger rejoicing at the end 'because now they are washed clean and white' was not even considered controversial, but can hardly have made black children feel good about themselves.

This has changed, so if it was simplistic in the 1970s and 1980s to think of large proportions of black children wanting to be white, it is simply mistaken today. It is hard for white people in the 1990s to imagine the effect of the phrase 'black is beautiful' which crossed the Atlantic in the late 1960s. Indeed, it was much more than a phrase, encapsulating a movement, a whole aesthetic and cultural shift away from the idea of blackness as ugliness and signifying inferiority. This has been a key factor in the reduction of the incidence of low self-esteem reported by Milner himself in the second edition of his book in 1983. He also reports that by the early 1970s in the USA 'the misidentification phenomenon all but disappeared for good' (1997, p. 124).

Milner found that low self-esteem seemed to influence Asian children to a lesser extent. The usual explanations for this are that the difference and cohesiveness of their cultures, reinforced by language and religion, gave Asian children a relatively stronger sense of who they were in relation to the surrounding white society, a stronger bulwark against being devalued and demeaned.

Gender

In all British Asian sub-groups, gender has more overt salience than for most of the white population. This is most evident in religion: either different rooms or different parts of the same room being reserved for men and women whether the worship is Sikh, Hindu or Muslim. Socializing in homes often follows the same pattern (Jackson and Nesbitt, 1993; Shaw, 1988). Except for Gujeratis, mothers are less often in paid employment outside the home (Jackson and Nesbitt, 1993; Modood and Berthoud, 1997) In all groups there is likely to be more concern expressed for instance, about a daughter going away from home for higher education, but this will vary with sub-group, religious devoutness, social class, parents' gender, concern about reputation in the community, parental education and individual aspirations, rather than being either universal or on a simple traditional–modern continuum. It would be a gross oversimplification to assume that because a girl is Asian this will be the main determining factor in her educational aspirations and school success or of authoritarian parents dictating over- or under-ambitious careers for their daughters (Shaw, 1988; Brah, 1992; Eade, 1995; Basit, 1996).

In any case, while young Asian women may participate in past-16 education less than Asian young men, there is a *higher* rate of participation in post-compulsory education amongst Asian young women *of all backgrounds* and irrespective of social class than amongst whites (Drew, Gray and Sporton,

1994). There are women Bangladeshis, with working class and relatively un-educated parents who are not only academically successful but remain closely involved with their family, friends and community in Tower Hamlets (Eade, 1995). A small study by Basit (1996) of 24 working class Muslim girls from the three main roots in the Indian sub-continent found considerable aversion to manual work and aspirations to 'occupations which were unambiguously middle class' (p. 230). Because of the inadequacies of data gathering already referred to, there is patchy data about the achievement of 'Asian' girls, but what we do know suggests a complex mixture of very high aspirations (sup-ported by families) with a maintenance of expectations of adult lives in a joint family with a continuation of 'traditional' patterns of obligation and interac-tion with relatives. Arranged marriages and an expectation of motherhood are not necessarily antithetical to valuing a good education (see, for instance, Haw, 1995).

The recent pattern of girls' performance at GCSE overtaking and improv-ing faster than that of boys may or may not be true of Asian girls nationally — we simply do not know. The only national sample available is based upon data well over a decade old (Drew and Gray, 1990) and it showed Asian girls, whatever their social class, did not do as well as Asian boys (though even this national sample did not sub-divide 'Asian' and had a sample of professional Asians numbering only 17! (Gillborn and Gipps, 1996, p. 16). On the other hand, quite large numbers are involved in recent figures from Brent LEA, which show almost 50 per cent of 'Asian' (and white) girls gaining 5 or more high grade GCSEs compared with 30 per cent of Asian boys. (Fewer than 25 per cent of African-Caribbean girls achieved at this level, and about 16 per cent of African-Caribbean boys.)

In the case of African-Caribbeans, several studies, beginning with Driver (1979) have found a marked difference between the achievement of African-Caribbean boys and girls (see also Foster, 1990; Drew and Gray 1990). In Lambeth, with the country's largest proportions of African-Caribbean pupils, 1994 GCSE results show a marked gender effect. There is little difference between the performance of white and African-Caribbean girls, both of whom outperformed white boys, with African-Caribbean boys a higher grade pass behind them. As discussed in Chapter 5, it may be that African-Caribbean girls somehow manage a synthesis of rebellion and conformity in school which still enables them to do well, but that a combination of gender and racial stereo-types may make it more difficult for black young men to avoid being caught up in cycles of increasingly severe criticism and control (Gillborn and Gipps, 1996).

The Variation in Schools' Effectiveness

This current in educational research is explored a little more in the next sec-tion, though it is worth saying at this point that there is emerging evidence that, in terms of results, some schools are more effective with black and Asian students than others (Drew and Gray, 1991; Nuttall et al., 1989; Maughan and Dunn, 1988).

Part of this complex picture is to do with 'contextual effects', though an as yet unexplored contextual effect may be the ethnic composition of the school. White parents, it seems, often assume such an effect in their assumptions that their children will do worse in a largely Asian school (Naylor, 1989; Bagley, 1996) and perhaps there *are* schools in which some Asian groups do better, others which serve white girls best, and others where African Caribbeans are likely to get worse results. At the moment we simply do not know in very much detail, but it is highly likely that the web of factors in the diagram will combine in different ways in different schools.

Conclusions

As we have consistently argued in this section, generalizations are dangerous. For this reason we will not attempt an overall summary of current findings but concentrate on processes. Clearly one conclusion echoes this section's starting point: complexity. Single factor explanations are unlikely to be very informative, groups often lumped together need examining separately, and even treating the sub-groups identified as homogenous will be misleading and runs the risk of simply generating more sophisticated stereotypes. The flow diagram (Figure 6.1) summarizes patterns for which evidence can be found in the research literature, it does not suggest that they all bear down on every individual (indeed we know they affect some groups more than others) and it is important to remember the difference between *attainment* and *rate of progress.* Some factors in the Figure are probably no longer relevant, except in so far as they show up in old research which can still colour teachers' perceptions and assumptions. Some of the factors and influences discussed call for continuing social and political action. Others demand institutional awareness of how things can go wrong, together with individual awareness of the need to juggle knowledge of sociological patterns with individual needs and classroom processes. We also need to take note of the existing research and to be prepared to ask more sophisticated questions.

Note

1   For this reason we have not discussed the school achievement of other ethnic minorities. To illustrate the difficulties once more with the Chinese, though in total making up 5 per cent of Britain's minority population, they are so scattered that LEA evidence cannot really show patterns of attainment in comparison with other groups. Gillborn and Gipps illustrate this graphically with the case of Lambeth. It has the country's second largest Chinese population of school age, yet in real terms this means a sample population at GCSE age of 25 pupils. What evidence there is suggests that these and particularly the Vietnamese are doing exceptionally well.

Class and Achievement

The Extent of Change

Social class has long been a critical element in school achievement, although a century ago this was barely seen as a problem. At that time educational policy assumed certain ideas about 'breeding' and that classes had different abilities and destinies: just as there were 'naturally' different kinds of schools for boys and girls, so there were for the children of the poor and for those of the better off. The allied curriculum assumptions are touched upon in Chapter 4. Post-1944, however, the playing field was supposed to be levelled. Primary schools were supposed to aim at bringing out the best in *every* child, places in selective secondary schools were supposed to be allocated on merit, and higher education was meant to be open to all irrespective of parental income.

During the 1950s, however, evidence began to mount that despite the dismantling of the more obvious barriers of the past, children of working class parents were still doing dramatically less well in schooling than those of the middle class. Even the new and trusted tool of IQ testing confirmed this: despite its in-built cultural bias conferring an apparently greater IQ on the middle class it nevertheless revealed that working class children were performing less well than middle class ones with similar or indeed lower IQ scores (Benn and Simon, 1972).

At this point it is important to consider terms once again. During the 1950s and 1960s, when a good deal of key research into class and achievement was undertaken, the researchers' distinction between 'middle class' and 'working class' echoed a clearer distinction in society than can be made today when there is considerable blurring of class groups in the middle of the class scale (see Chapter 2) and differences in achievement within this central band are not very great — indeed they are barely detectable in some schools. To stress this we want to depart from the terminology used for decades in such discussions which uses 'working class' and 'middle class' as a shorthand, implicitly reinforcing the notion that everyone from a home where parents are manual workers are different and destined to different educational outcomes from others. This is plainly untrue. We do want, however, to maintain a contrast between what might be called the 'lower working class' (in practice, unskilled and many semi-skilled manual workers) and the 'upper middle class' (professionals and managers). 'Lower' in this context means lower income and job status and job security, hence lower probably in terms of housing class and access to other social and material goods. In the discussion which follows, therefore, we are contrasting, if not polar extremes, then certainly groups some way apart in terms of most of the attributes of class.

At first, it was hoped that the persisting class differences would be remedied by further reforms in the structure of schooling, most notably the introduction of comprehensive secondary schools, i.e. schools which contained the whole span of ability (though in practice it took until the mid-1970s until these catered for the majority). This reform was suggested by the wealth of evidence which demonstrated that the 1944 dream of schools for different kinds of children being held in equal esteem was simply not happening, and that success or failure at 11 plus produced matching expectations in both teachers and pupils.

Persisting Differences

Yet differential rates of success have continued in comprehensives, just as they have in primary schools containing a mix of social classes, even though *overall* results have risen (Mackinnon et al., 1995). Differences between schools are also evident, with schools with a large upper middle class intake typically producing higher examination passes than those in poorer districts, and these differences accumulating to produce marked differences between urban, poorer LEAs like Barnsley and ones with a higher average standard of living like West Sussex. These persistent and intransigent differentials were a preoccupation of educational sociology throughout the 1960s and a good deal of the 1970s, being added to by concerns about 'race' and gender. They have been a concern of policy-makers too, though as is explored later and in Chapter 7 their response to the problem changed markedly in the 1980s. One of the consequences of this change at the level of policy has been that funded research into class differences in attainment has diminished considerably, and the most detailed research is now some years old. Mackinnon et al. (1995) observe:

> One reason for this relative neglect may be that so many earlier surveys gave such clear and unequivocal results: at virtually every stage of education, by virtually every criterion of achievement, middle class children had higher levels of achievement than working class children. (p. 182)

Nevertheless, we know that GCSE passes at ordinary and advanced level are still highly correlated with parental occupation, and despite a huge increase in the proportion of 18 year olds going to higher education, the sons and daughters of professionals are over ten times more likely to get there than those of unskilled manual workers (Mackinnon et al., 1995).

While this is not an entirely deterministic picture, the pattern is clear from these figures. The puzzle, then, is why *on average* pupils of apparently similar intellectual ability achieve differently depending upon their social class. Traditionally, explanations have focused around either the home or the school, citing factors which pupils bring with them (or return to) which affect their school performance, or processes which operate within school.

Home Factors

Culture

We explored some potential home factors in Chapters 2 and 5, namely the suggested influence of culture and orientation towards work and the future, the argument being that a particular orientation in lower working class homes may disadvantage children in school. We should explicitly compare this with what is considered to be a more middle class orientation (not just *upper* middle class) of looking to the future expecting some improvement, living in the assumption of higher earnings, better housing, a series of steps upwards rather than a plateau of earnings. Parents whose own lives follow this pattern and who shape their decisions accordingly are likely to pass these on to their children. Values of deferring gratification, putting off satisfaction and reward to a future date, sustained application to a future goal, are all attributes and dispositions which fit in well with the demands of schooling.

If the research suggesting these 'ideal types' in the past is reliable, the question still remains whether they are still valid. The relatively stable (and relatively isolated) community centred around a particular kind of work is far less in evidence than it once was. Monotonous manual work still exists of course, so there is no reason to suppose that the kind of world view which makes such work manageable is not still passed on to children. The task for teachers is how to recognize if this may be the case, to see it as the rational response to some people's life experiences and chances that it is, and yet not consign the children to a kind of 'what can you expect from them' ghetto. In any case, this would be an example of the overlapping distributions discussed in Chapter 1, not discontinuous and separate groups. And, as ever, it should not be viewed deterministically, as if those brought up in such a cultural outlook are incapable of adopting a different one.

Parental Skills

We are separating this from culture because they are often carelessly blurred. The issue here is not whether or not parents inculcate values which promote school success, but whether they are in a position to help develop the necessary skills. If parents were not successful at school themselves, if they are not confident with the written word, if they do work in an environment where they need to read, write and negotiate with texts, then they are unlikely to be confident in this kind of activity. When their children have homework involving comprehension, research, or working in a foreign language they may feel a gap between wanting to help and knowing the best way to do so. This is not to say that computers, homework clubs, relatives and advice cannot get round these obstacles, but they are obstacles nevertheless, and ones not experienced by parents who are, say, accountants or managers. These obstacles are increased if the parents have low levels of literacy themselves.

Poverty

Culture and skills aside, there are persisting economic and material differences between different occupational groups, as discussed in Chapter 2. Without wishing to enter into arguments about the nature and extent of poverty, there are significant numbers of children growing up lacking what most would consider necessary for full participation in social life. The effects of lack of resources can be manifested in play and work space, facilities such as books and computers, educational visits and the like. Poor housing is clearly relevant: contrast, for instance, an ageing tower block or crumbling estate with newer detached housing, where every house has use of a car, children have their own rooms, there is some choice about whether to work with the TV on, and so on.

Language

In Chapter 3 the role of language in school success and failure was considered, and the effect both of a different pattern and code of language use (if it exists) as well as the *belief* that it exists. We treated this as in principle a separate issue from children and young people who are linguistically deprived in terms of poor stimulation and low levels of parental literacy. These latter factors are not ones which can be considered relevant to most of the school population, but for those for whom it *is* relevant, especially when combined with poverty, then it must clearly be a factor in school performance. (In Chapter 3, we referred to what could be called a crude 'Bernstein-ism' sometimes employed to characterize and stigmatize large numbers of parents, hence producing a set of stereotypes of communities and their children to 'explain' underachievement in terms of linguistic inadequacy. In our view, this is not a 'home' factor at all, but one which has more to do with the perceptions and assumptions of teachers.)

Special Needs?

Several of the preceding factors can be taken together to produce special educational needs, which in fact can be a coded term for 'poor' or 'lower working class'. This may seem an over-statement, but the commonest method in use by LEAs for allocating extra SEN funding to schools is the proportion of children on free school meals — on the face of it, a measure solely of parental poverty. The reason why such a measure works is that it serves as a proxy for many of the overlapping factors already mentioned. It is also closely entangled with gender, in that a higher proportion of boys are involved in the various stages of SEN support under the Code of Practice, both for language and behaviour-related problems. While making this connection between special needs and class runs the risk of reinforcing stereotypes, it certainly does not cause them. We have often had the experience of teaching groups of students who argue that class divisions have gone, that it is no longer relevant in today's world, that they never think in class terms themselves, only to find that when teaching practice placements are announced there is much talk of 'good schools', nice areas, rough schools, difficult children, council estates, social problems, and special needs.

School Factors

Curriculum

In Chapter 4 the formal or taught curriculum and its class assumptions was explored. Bourdieu developed the idea that the assumptions and values embedded within the curriculum contributed to the relative failure of lower working class children at school insofar as the curriculum valued and focused upon experiences and ideas which were alien to or far removed from their experiences. The argument goes that this produces two barriers, one in terms of motivation and interest but another more subtle one in terms of understanding. It is not necessarily that they lack the financial capital to access the benefits and rewards of schooling, they may lack the *cultural capital*. Here again, a simple distinction between home and school factors breaks down.

Hidden Curriculum

Chapter 5 explored the hidden curriculum and its effect upon achievement. In particular, we looked at the role of peer group cultures in constructing a dynamic within schools whereby disruptive activities and an anti-school orientation become an attractive option to young people. This changes the focus from locating the origins of lower working class school failure in the home to processes within the school. In this respect the perspectives and assumptions of teachers are crucial since they are intricately involved in the processes of labelling and spirals of interaction which can lead to the formation of counter-school cultures.

We are also conscious of the role of teacher expectation and the complex web of (potentially) mutual assumptions and preconceptions in which both teachers and lower working class pupils can become ensnared. We are aware that we may be contributing to this ourselves: the more one repeats that children from a certain group have historically performed less well in school the more one runs the risk that unthinking teachers will expect the same in the future. Low expectations are certainly pernicious and can become a part of teacher culture, the profession's folk wisdom. The challenge is to recognize the pattern and its causes in a critical and creative way so as to change it.

Neither regarding it as a foregone conclusion or denying that it happens at all is likely to produce a change for the better.

Effective and Less Effective Schools

We referred earlier to a decline in detailed research into lower working class underachievement. Whatever else was happening, this coincided with the arrival of the Conservative government in 1979 and their dominance of British politics in the 1980s and 1990s. The political emphasis shifted from assumptions about structured inequalities and a concern with injustice to an emphasis focusing on individual and collective effort. Attention shifted from identifying individual factors in relation to class towards identifying what it was which made effective, or ineffective schools.

The ILEA's Junior School project (Mortimore et al., 1988) demonstrated, with more detail and clarity than hitherto, that schools varied in respect of what is now commonly called 'value-added'. The Project compared a large number of factors in a large number of schools, finding (amongst many other things) that children with the same social class and ability profile did better in some schools than others. This work was added to by Smith and Tomlinson (1989) in *The School Effect*, sampling 18 schools from different areas of the country, 'some thought to be successful and others less so'. A larger study of 87 schools in seven LEAs was carried out for the Association of Metropolitan Authorities (AMA) in 1994. While most schools performed close to their expected level, it was also the case that with similar pupils, some were simply more effective at getting the best from them than others, and that this varied between departments within schools as much as it did between schools, and it may be that schools which seem to be effective for their most able pupils are less so for the less able.

These kinds of findings could be taken to mean that social class factors had more or less salience in different school environments, that different climates or regimes managed to diminish their importance and impact on children's performance. Perhaps this is not very surprising. The fact that some schools were able to offset the demotivating effect of ability labelling, or that some groups of teachers had fewer stereotypes about lower working class children or were able to motivate and interest them more, or did not have a simplistic and negative idea about inferior speech codes is perhaps only to be expected. We have said several times that the forces being described are not deterministic in terms of individual children, the same has to be true of schools and teachers.

In our view, however, some have taken the school effectiveness credo too literally and decontextualized the key factors with which a school has to engage. It is as if all the factors discussed in relation to class have no effect, all one has to do is have high expectations and good school management and all differentials in achievement will disappear (NCE, 1996). This has suited politicians of the Right rather well, who have tended to adopt the line that they know of very successful schools in disadvantaged areas and that teachers must stop using 'social background' as an excuse for low attainment. In consequence the patterned differences between schools and authorities can be attributed, if not to lazy and feckless parents then to poor teachers who do not expect enough of their pupils. In an elegant ideological move the Right then criticize the alleged stereotyping of poorer parents by left-liberals and claim to be liberating the working class by aiming at the provision of classless schooling. This 'move' tries to reclaim the educational high ground with the argument that there is no reason for extra attention or resources to be devoted to working class children, and that their true oppressors are those who persist with the idea that there are systematic inequalities and disadvantages to overcome. By this means any differences in overall LEA results between areas of higher average income and relatively poorer ones are attributed to poorly managed LEAs. It can even be pointed out that such LEAs typically receive more money per pupil in any case, thus giving weight to the argument that they waste it.

Nevertheless, we have no doubt that high (and low) expectations play a part in school success, and schools which display the characteristics of effective and well-led schools will serve *all* their pupils better. The same applies to LEAs: there are patterned differences between 'middle class' and 'working class' LEAs, but there are also differences in attainment between LEAs with very similar populations with no correlation between this and levels of funding (Audit Commission, 1998). There are also many schools which have entered a spiral of decline, low morale and low expectations. We doubt, however, that lower achievement levels in relation to class can be wished away by such measures. This chapter suggests areas of concern where such measures may have an effect but also some where they may not. An interesting aspect of the 'school effectiveness movement' is that it appears to regard the curriculum as irrelevant — it does not appear to matter whether it is archaic, riddled with class assumptions and biases, racist and sexist — as long as clear goals of success are set then all pupils can do well.

School Image and Reputation

This section prefaces some of the points made in Chapter 7, namely that a school's reputation and hence its popularity with parents is itself part of a feedback loop which affects overall results, and that this again is connected with class.

At one level it is to be expected that a school which is doing well in its published results may get better — morale may rise, targets may be set higher, spurs to further achievement are available. It can be correspondingly difficult for a school with worse results to improve. If the construction of public images of different schools are accompanied, however, by parental choices, then the gap may widen. It was argued in Chapter 7 that in fact the notion of 'choice' is heavily laden with class 'baggage', and that in reality active choice is skewed towards middle class parents. This aside, we would argue that class consciousness is still a relevant factor in parental choice of school, either where lower working class parents feel out of their depth and their children feel they don't belong, or where middle class parents dread their children going to a 'rough' school. In popular consciousness we would argue there is a loose connection between these categories, as noted above in relation to some students. People believe they know that there is a connection between certain areas or estates and higher rates of crime, unemployment, poorer housing, single parenthood and lower school results.

7 Policy: Separatism by Default, Design or Exclusion

In this chapter we want to explore a critical issue for British education at the end of the twentieth century, the pressures towards various kinds of separate provision which could variously be called diversity, increased choice, separatism, exclusion or stratification in schooling. We will consider these issues in relation to gender and 'race' first and use a consideration of class issues to problematize the notion of 'choice'.

Under each heading is also presented a series of parents' views, so that rather than rehearse the arguments in the conventional way the opposing views will speak for themselves in personalized accounts. While these are 'real' views, they are not quotations from specific people but syntheses of different real individuals compiled from research reports, the general literature, *TES* articles and personal experiences and conversations (the names are therefore fictitious). The danger of this approach is that while we are confident these constructions represent a real continuum of views, it is not possible to say the size of the constituencies, as it were, that they all represent.

Gender and Separate Schooling

The history of separate schooling for girls and boys has some contradictory strands. At one time single sex schooling was assumed as the norm for the upper classes and everyone else (where they had access to education) in the virtually universal belief that the sexes were fundamentally different, probably unequal, and therefore needed different kinds of education. The dominant assumption in all classes was that boys would become breadwinners and needed to learn the various skills and attributes to equip them for whatever section of the labour market was their destiny, and girls would need the knowledge to enable them to be good wives and mothers (Lavigeur, 1980).

There were some noteworthy challenges to this in the nineteenth century, with some private schools being established to rival the boys' public schools, but the degree to which they were out of step with contemporary thinking is shown by how few of their girls were even allowed into the universities afterwards, and even when they were (to study medicine in one celebrated case) they were not allowed to graduate. As women's place as workers was gradually recognized some grammar schools continued this tradition, aiming to prepare women for some (not all) of the professions and the pattern was continued into state education, with girls' secondary moderns in particular explicitly preparing them for 'women's work' (Board of Education, 1923). At this time, however, there were some proponents of co-educational schooling, but they tended to be 'the middle class progressives' who were more concerned with the social relationships between men and women than academic prowess. Their demand was for a form of liberal schooling which enabled self development and freedom of expression, which was linked with the democratic ideals of equality of opportunity. Other supporters of co-educational schooling saw this form of schooling in terms of the many advantages it held for boys:

- a reduction in homosexuality amongst the boys;
- boys' behaviour would be less rough because of the 'civilizing influence' of girls;
- the replication of family-like relationships and would contribute to bringing about healthier marriages.

In reality, the case for co-ed schooling during this time was a fragile one based on romanticism and individualism rather than one based on challenging social injustices. Co-educationalists lacked any real recognition of the deep rooted nature of the male dominance over women in society (Brehoney, 1984).

By the 1970s the assumption that single sex schooling was the most appropriate form of school organization was being challenged, and the pursuit of equality was thought by some to be best served by making schools co-educational, giving girls the benefits of the kind of education more often reserved for boys (as well as giving the boys the benefits of the girls' 'civilizing influence' and producing economies of scale). As a result, not one single sex state primary school survives, and the majority of secondary schools have become co-educational[1] from a position in 1968 when about 60 per cent of London secondary schools were still single sex (Benn and Simon, 1972, p. 414). Evidence from the Equal Opportunities Commission (1982) concluded that neither single sex schooling nor co-educational schooling as such favoured gender equality, and an inquiry undertaken by the Inner London Education Authority (1982) maintained that academic success had little to do with single sex schooling.

While there was a view at this time that gender inequalities would disappear, given time, many co-educational schools remained 'boys' schools with girls in them' (Sarah et al., 1988, p. 59). Co-education did not seem to be bringing appreciable benefits to girls and many feminists (e.g. Spender, 1982) felt that the social structure of mixed schools may drive children into *more* stereotyped behaviours and choices rather than less. Sharpe (1976) found that girls were inhibited by the presence of boys and their attitude to their success. In addition, the curriculum was seen to be directed towards boys, as was teacher attention which, although seen to be negative at times, also encouraged boys to question more. Girls achieved poorer results, barely experienced some areas of the curriculum at all, and had to tolerate sexual harassment into the bargain (see Chapter 5 and Spender and Sarah, 1988; Lees, 1986; Mahony, 1985; Measor and Sikes, 1992). At worst, some schools were preparing girls for all aspects of an unequal adult life.

At the same time a number of girls' grammar schools were providing a modern state version of the few academic girls' public schools of the nineteenth century. Fiercely academic and successful, these schools, arguably, had resisted the 'egalitarian' impulse to co-educate and were providing a space where girls could aspire to be doctors, mathematicians and politicians. Of course they were selective, so any extrapolation from their success is hazardous, but they probably provide the core of schools in which it became evident in the 1980s that girls in single sex schools might do better (Bone, 1983; Deem, 1984). By the mid to late 1980s, some co-educational schools had begun to experiment with segregated classes for boys and girls, and some were witnessing improvements in both performance and in attitude to subjects areas where previously there had been poor participation by girls.

The 1990s

Today, girls are outstripping boys in almost every subject at GCSE, and the advantages and disadvantages of single sex or co-educational schooling is the subject of scrutiny and debate. Conclusions from reports from 5,000 inspections carried out by the Equal Opportunity Commission and Ofsted (1996) put girls' schools firmly ahead of boys' schools in terms of achievement, judging girls' schools to be more successful than either boys' or mixed schools regardless of the social class of the intake. In the most under privileged group (between 40 per cent and 100 per cent of pupils eligible for free meals) 24 per cent of pupils in girls' schools obtained 5 or more GCSEs at grade A–C compared with 16 per cent in both boys' and mixed schools. Within the most privileged group, 91 per cent of pupils from girls' schools were achieving five A–C grades, compared with 85 per cent in boys' schools and only 60 per cent in mixed schools. In terms of ethos and the curriculum boys' schools were generally judged more favourably than mixed, though less favourably than girls' schools, and behaviour was much poorer in boys' schools. Attendance records were similar in the single sex schools and both better than mixed (TES, 20 October 1998).

A later study, carried out jointly by Ofsted and the EOC (1996/7), suggests that the comparison between mixed and single sex schooling is contentious and complex, with no straightforward answer as to whether one type of school is more successful than another because of the variables involved. This report maintains that girls' schools on the whole seem to do well because of the girls' attitude to work and their desire to achieve higher standards, finding that the schools were more likely to promote high aspirations, to develop a curriculum content which validates girls' experiences and dispositions, and to encourage girls to participate in lessons and to engage with the subject. They also found that the performance of schools had much to do with the economic and social context plus the ability profile of their intakes. Many of the high performing girls' schools are either selective or they have retained the kudos and catchment of having been a grammar school and the schools judged best were girls' schools in advantaged areas.

Questioning the widespread assumption that female educational performance is steadily improving everywhere, McCrum analysed final degree examination statistics over the last two decades and claims to have traced a link between girls' poorer performance in finals to the decline in girls' schools after the mid 1970s.

> Twenty years ago state educated girls were the strongest group, ahead of boys from the independent schools; now they are the weakest. This is true even in subjects seen as 'female-friendly'. Girls were getting 25 per cent more As and Bs in modern languages in 1965; in 1985 this had fallen to 0.87 per cent. (TES, 20 October 1998)

Studies of successful women suggest that many have common aspects to their upbringing and education, one of which may be attendance at girls only schools. Figes (1994) argues they are:

> ... more likely to make it to the top of their chosen field, will more readily assume they have the right to occupy the job they do, and will continue working in greater numbers after they have had children. In mixed schools the emphasis tends to be on exams, whereas girls' schools encourage women to think for themselves and do what they want to do. The majority of schools being co-educational are asking girls to sacrifice the one educational advantage they had, in the controversial hope that their presence will civilize the boys. (p. 213)

The case for single sex schooling is becoming more complex rather than going away. Whereas in 1990 there was some pressure to retain or even increase the number of girls' schools, not in the tradition of keeping girls in their place but in order to raise their achievement, this is (arguably) no longer needed since girls' average attainment at GCSE has overtaken that of boys (EOC/Ofsted, 1996). It may be that we will see a resurrection of the argument that co-education should be supported in the interests of the boys, they no longer just need civilizing, they need motivating and being around more studious role models. But the competing demands are not compatible: it is not possible to have single sex schools for girls and co-educational schools for boys as the following points of view demonstrate.

John Smith

I want my daughter to go to a single sex school because I keep up enough with the news to know that girls are doing better in school. On average they seem to have more positive attitudes and to have higher long-term motivation.

The climate in which a young person goes to school is important, peer groups matter a lot during adolescence, and it will make my job easier as a parent if she is in a climate where working and trying to get good results is considered fairly normal and not something to be mocked. The worst scenario would be if she was in a school where most of her class messed about, didn't do their homework and gave her a hard time if she didn't join in with them. Obviously not all boys mess about and don't care about their school work and not all girls are really studious, but she will only have one chance so I will play safe in choosing her school.

I know in the past one of the reasons girls' schools seemed to have better results was because many were grammar schools, so their results skewed the average and made it higher, but I don't think this is the case any more. Whatever the reason, on average girls display more motivation, so that's the kind of atmosphere I want her to go to school in.

Some people say that girls in single sex schools lose out by not being with the opposite sex, that they don't learn to socialize and they get distracted by the absence of boys. Personally I think they get far more distracted when boys **are** *around, and there's plenty of opportunity in this day and age for girls and boys to mix socially. A single sex school is not a convent, after all.*

Jane Griffiths

Some of the most confident, successful women I know went to single sex girls schools, so I believe in them for my daughter. I know some of those schools were girls' grammar schools, but I believe their success was due to more than the fact that they just selected clever girls who passed the 11+. It is as if those years away from the presence of boys, from being in their shadow, from measuring their performance against them, almost having to define themselves in relation to boys, has given them the self-confidence to be themselves as women. I know it sounds a bit nebulous and vague, but growing up as a girl in a climate of male dominance is difficult. There has always been the unspoken (or even spoken) assumption that a girl's real place is subservient to boys and men. Girls need to get away from that during their formative years and develop the strength to be themselves — they will need it. If single sex schools could do that in the past, when sexism was more blatant and obvious, if they could provide a kind of solid basic identity as a female which enabled girls to successfully take on a male world, then they must still be a good idea today.

It's all very well saying that things have changed and that everyone now has equal opportunities, but for my daughter's sake I think I'll reserve judgment for a while yet.

Of course, some people might argue that girls' schools give girls an unfair advantage and that the motivated pupils (girls and boys) should be evenly spread throughout all schools to raise everyone's standards. People might moan that boys are left behind and that this isn't fair. My answer to that is that males have had the advantage for a long time (otherwise why did we have to have an Equal Pay Act and an Equal Opportunities Act?) so I think it is a bit soon for anyone to start complaining the minute it looks as though girls are getting an advantage for once.

There's a lot of nonsense talked about pupils in single sex schools not learning to mix with the opposite sex. People say they aren't prepared for adult life, but I think that's just the point: in mixed schools in the past girls and boys have been prepared for an adult life in which males are dominant. I think the way to prepare girls to be themselves and to assert their rights is to keep them out of a male dominated environment until they're sixteen or so. As for saying single sex schools are not like adult working life, well I don't know where those who say these things have been working for the past twenty years. In my experience workplaces are still very segregated. Some jobs are very largely done by one sex or the other and others are segregated vertically, i.e. the bosses are mostly men and the clerical and administrative staff are mostly women. In lots of manual work too, women do certain jobs and men do others.

You might say 'what about the boys?' but that's not my problem since I don't have any. As a parent it's my right to press for the best deal I can get for my own children, not everyone else's.

Mary Green

I believe in a single sex school for my daughter for religious and cultural reasons. It's not that I think boys are evil or anything but they are less responsible than girls and every culture in the world has always protected its girls more than its boys. When it boils down to it, it is girls who get

135

pregnant and have a reputation to lose, and it is women who tend to have the main responsibility for looking after children and maintaining the family's values. I'm not traditional enough to think that girls and boys should have a different curriculum or anything, but I think it's better that they don't get distracted into early pairing up and so on by being with each other all day every day.

This is how it's been for centuries, it's only recently that people have been letting the sexes mix freely at all ages, and look at the results — lots more young pregnancies and young people being pressured into having sex before they're old enough to know what it's all about, or to take the responsibility.

People might say that boys and girls mixing equally like this is normal in this country and that I ought to accept the normal way of doing things, since I'm only an immigrant. But although I was born somewhere else, I am a British citizen, I have worked and paid taxes here for thirty years and I think I have the right to have my wishes respected for my own children. No-one said to me when I was first welcomed here to work in the health service that part of the deal was to give up everything that was important to me, to bring up my children the way 'the majority' told me I had to. Anyway, I notice that many of the upper classes still send their sons and daughters to single sex schools, at least up to the age of sixteen. If it's good enough for them if they pay for it, I can't see why I can't have the same rights in state schooling, just because I'm an Irish Catholic.

Terry Johnson

I can see lots of arguments for girls' schools, both on the grounds of girls' social/personal development and their academic success, but I have a wider concern, and it's not just because I have two sons. We need to think beyond the wishes of individual parents if we are to build a decent society where people respect each other and can get along.

The plain fact is that many boys' schools are awful (not all of them, obviously). Some of the worst aspects of testosterone-based macho behaviour goes on unchecked by any civilizing female influence, and long term that does nobody any good, girls and women included. I know some people would argue that it's unfair to expect girls to act as civilizing influences on boys, that it treats them as less important, but I think this is the same kind of argument as the argument for the 11+ and selective schools. If you pick pupils who on average are more motivated, more studious, more focused on doing well and getting good exam results, then keeping them separate may work for them, but what about the others? One of the original aims for comprehensive schools was to produce 'grammar schools for all'. The idea was that you raise everyone's achievement by putting all children together in the same school. Well, I think it's the same thing with co-educational schools.

It is no good the parents of girls simply thinking of what may be best for their daughters, we have to think of wider social needs, and lots of schools with the worst elements of boys' schools and 'laddish' culture will not bring about a society where men and women respect each other more.

'Race' and Separate Schooling

The presence of significant numbers of black or Asian pupils, often in fairly localized areas of towns and cities has led to three distinct pressures or tendencies:

- the inevitable concentration in some schools simply because they are the local schools to black and Asian children's homes;
- the exacerbation of this by 'white flight', white parents seeking other schools for their children (Bagley, 1996);
- the interest among some ethnic minorities in favouring schools serving their particular interests and concerns, informally by choosing schools which try to counter racism, and sometimes formally promoting religiously based schools.

There was once an official policy decision responding to at least the first two of these, a Department of Education and Science (DES) circular in 1965 which advised LEAs to disperse black and Asian pupils into neighbouring schools when their numbers exceeded 30 per cent of the school roll (DES, 1965a). Once public, this was quickly rescinded because of its assumption of the inherent undesirability of concentrations of black and Asian pupils and its tacit deference to white sensibilities — it was officially justified on language grounds, but in fact no language tests were carried out to select children for bussing (Troyna, 1982). It may that some LEAs have continued a 'thinning out' policy by their construction of catchment area boundaries, but as in many other respects they now have less power to do this. The current makeup of schools is still determined primarily by geography (and hence housing class) and then by 'market forces', both minority and majority parents making 'choices' to the extent that they are able. These various forces currently result in about 500 schools where the majority of pupils are black or Asian and a smaller number where the white pupils are a small minority. There are perhaps a hundred state schools with virtually no white pupils. Demographic trends (i.e. the higher birth-rate of the black and Asian population because it is younger than the white population) are likely to make this number increase, but it may also be subject to black and Asian families becoming gradually more dispersed (Skellington and Morris, 1992).

The law provides some constraints:

- It is unlawful under the Race Relations Act to restrict entry to a state or private school to members of a specific ethnic group (e.g. Indians, Bangladeshis, Chinese, Europeans);
- Giving priority to members of a particular faith or sub-sections of it *is* legal (e.g. Roman Catholics, Anglicans, Jews, Muslims). Any such school can legally turn away members of other faiths *if it is full*;
- There are many private schools of this sort in Britain, mostly representing different branches of Christianity (from Quakers to Seventh Day Adventists) but also some Muslim schools, several Jewish schools, a Sikh school and one Buddhist school. The Seventh Day Adventist school is in practice an African-Caribbean school;
- State schools can have religious affiliations too, most often they are Anglican or Roman Catholic (they are technically called either voluntary aided or voluntary controlled);
- There are about 16 Jewish voluntary aided/voluntary controlled schools: some primary, some secondary;
- Several Muslim private schools and one Sikh private school have tried to enter the state system and become voluntary aided or voluntary controlled. The main motive is funding: if they were successful they would be able to provide the kind of schooling they want without the parents having to pay fees;
- So far, only two of these attempts have been successful (both in 1998), and there is considerable resentment (especially in the Muslim schools) at what they see as unfair treatment compared with Christians;
- The Swann Report (DES, 1985) came out against any separate schooling, but this was the subject of the only formal dissent in the Report: all but one of the black and Asian members insisted on a footnote saying they disagreed but were outvoted (p. 515);
- There have been some celebrated cases of white parents explicitly objecting to their children's schools on the basis of the proportion of Asian or black pupils. The law allowing parental choice has been ruled to take precedence over the Race Relations Act, though in practice few parents have made public a racially based choice (Naylor, 1989; Hughes, 1988; Vincent, 1992; Morris, 1995);
- This issue does not fall neatly into conventional political groupings. Some Labour LEAs have opposed separate schools on the grounds of wanting young people to mix on equal terms. Some right-wing

members of Conservative think-tanks support separate schools because of their belief in market choice and the preference for a faith being taught explicitly (usually Christianity) rather than a multifaith approach (Walford, 1994; 1996).

As the following points of view demonstrate, the reasons people want separate schools are deeply felt and mutually incompatible, so it is not an easy policy issue to resolve.

Gilbert Whyte

The evidence is that our black children get poorer school results than other children. Why is this? In my community we think there are five main reasons:

- *racism from other pupils;*
- *racism from the staff directly in higher suspensions and indirectly in lower expectations;*
- *non-recognition of the language issue with some of our kids;*
- *too few black role models in schools;*
- *a curriculum which is Eurocentric, that glorifies whiteness and makes black people look inferior or on the sidelines.*

Our children do not do worse because their parents don't care. There are dozens of black supplementary schools all over the country, paid for by parents and communities and staffed by volunteers who give hours of their own time. These schools tend to offer two main things:

- *additional work and support on the basics, the 3 Rs;*
- *an emphasis on black history and culture.*

Children go to them from primary age right up to GCSE. The supplementary schools make up two shortfalls in the children's mainstream schooling, the low expectations of their teachers so they fall behind in the basics, and the lack of any information which allows them to be proud of themselves and their history, and to know about their parents' roots in the Caribbean and before that in Africa. We put huge effort into this and it works. We believe that children who come to supplementary school do significantly better, so what does that say about the mainstream?

Ideally, we would like not to have to do this. Ideally we would like mainstream schooling to meet all our kids' needs in the way it meets the needs of most white children. But in the meantime we will keep the supplementary schools going and press LEAs to help us — at least by giving us free use of premises at weekends. They should help until they can prove they are doing a good job for our children.

We don't want separatism, we want an equal chance to succeed. We know there can't be a school for black children as such, but we do know the John Loughborough Seventh Day Adventist School in north London attracts black parents from a huge area. There they have traditional teaching and good black role models and the results are really good. . . .

Ruth Solomon

I went to a Jewish voluntary aided school and I'm endlessly grateful that I had the chance, though it's not easy to explain why.

Jewish schools are in most respects the same as any other state schools. These days they have to follow the National Curriculum, though the curriculum is covered with more of a Jewish emphasis, with maybe more reference to Jewish history and literature. Religion is obviously different, the schools have Jewish prayers, recognize Jewish festivals and historic days, serve Kosher food. Hebrew is also taught, both as a link to the Jewish past but also as a link to modern Israel.

Many would claim that the 'atmosphere' of Jewish schools is different, more academic, and that this is due to the value placed in Jewish culture on learning and scholarship. This may be true, but people also often say that Church of England schools are 'better'. I think at least part of the more positive attitude towards school is that most of the children (or at least their parents) have made an active and conscious choice to be there, and wherever you get that degree of involvement and interest you probably get a more positive atmosphere.

The reasons I am so glad I went to a Jewish school are not academic ones. It was my primary school (after that I went to an ordinary comprehensive), so it was only six years, but I can honestly say that it has effected my sense of myself ever since (and I'm now in my 40s). Somehow it gave me a strong sense of identity as a Jew, it made me sure of who I was and confident about it. When people talk about 'integration' and ask whether it wouldn't be better for everyone to learn to get along in the same school, my answer is that my time at a Jewish school has helped me to integrate better. I feel I can meet non-Jews as an equal and on my own terms, rather than as someone who has always been part of a marginalized minority.

I say 'marginalized' but at times we are stigmatized too, and I was aware of that even at five or six. One of the other great things about my school was that it gave a safe haven from anti-Semitism, at least once I got there, because I might say that this establishment of my identity was not without some costs. I had to walk past two other primary schools in north London to get to my school, and our uniform was quite distinctive. I often had to run the gauntlet of other children calling us names and even threatening us, so I know that being visibly different carries some risks. But I am different, and I'm proud enough of my heritage not to want to hide it. The answer to other people's prejudices is not to accommodate yourself in every possible way so you don't inflame them. We will not make anti-Semitism go away by Jews keeping a low profile.

Ahmed Rafique

As a British Muslim I think I have the right to choose a state education in a Muslim context, just like Roman Catholics, Anglicans and Jews do. Ideally there should be some voluntary-aided Muslim schools, so Muslim parents have a real choice. I suspect that we have been denied this until recently because of a deep-seated idea that to be Muslim is somehow not really British, or the belief that Muslim schools would be more repressive than others — indeed the Swann report hinted at this in its section on separate schooling.

Muslim voluntary aided schools would obviously be state schools, they would have to teach the National Curriculum, they would be in many ways like other schools (and indeed there may well be non-Muslim children in them). The work in the school would obviously be in English, but:

- *there would be an Islamic ethos;*
- *RE would be mainly Islamic — it would have the purpose of educating children in the Muslim faith of their families;*
- *pupils would learn Arabic and the Qu'ran;*
- *the uniform would fit in with Muslim values;*
- *sex education would fit in with Muslim values;*
- *art and dance would be taught in such a way as to not go against Muslim beliefs.*

Other values important to Muslims would be promoted:

- *not charging too much interest;*
- *giving alms to the poor;*
- *fasting during the holy month of Ramadan;*

- *not drinking or smoking or taking drugs;*
- *valuing scholarship and learning;*
- *older girls and boys would not mix freely;*
- *strong family life;*
- *Halal food.*

I should stress that Muslims are not an ethnic group or a 'race'. Most Pakistanis, Bangladeshis, Arabs, Malaysians and many Africans in this country are Muslims. We do not all speak the same language, dress in the same way or cook the same kinds of food (just as in Catholic schools there are children with Italian, Polish and Irish backgrounds, as well as an English background).

Many of us fear that our children could do better in school than they are doing at the moment, and academic results aside, we fear for our children's morality and sense of values, just like many Christian parents do.

I do not think all Muslim children should go to Muslim schools, and it would make no difference if I did because lots of Muslim parents disagree with me. I do not think there should be such a strict segregation, but parents should have the choice, where numbers allow. We aren't talking here about a situation where no Muslim and non-Muslim children go to school together. And you can't tell us about making segregation worse, or racism worse — we don't need advice on that score from people who don't have to experience it. We know there are risks, but my way of dealing with them is to face them as a Muslim.

Another thing which needs pointing out is that there already are, in effect, Muslim schools, not by our choice but as the result of the choices made by others. People take their children out of schools or don't send them there in the first place 'because there are too many Asians', and in some places the school has become entirely Asian. When these children are Pakistani and Bangladeshi we already have a Muslim school.

Lastly, who gets to decide? Do we, as Muslims, get to decide for ourselves, even if you think we are wrong, or do we always have to accept the ruling of the white majority who think they know what's best for us? I don't know any Greek, but I thought 'democracy' meant protecting the rights of minorities as well as going along with the wishes of the majority. . . .

Jasprit Singh

I would regard myself as a very religious man. I want my children to grow up as practising Sikhs. I want them to:

> *be well informed about Panjabi culture;*
> *speak and read Panjabi;*
> *have a strong sense of family and community loyalty;*
> *contribute to the life of the Gurudwara.*

But these are private matters, they are for families to take care of and look after, not the state or the education system. I think all schools should be secular, non-religious. I don't think anyone's religion should be preached in school, or valued more than anyone else's. I don't expect my son and daughter to learn much about Sikhism in school. Perhaps a little, and a little about Islam, Christianity and all the others, but I don't think a school can teach someone to be a Christian, a Jew, or Sikh and it shouldn't try.

Many people are surprised to learn that in India, where religion is a big part of most people's everyday life, most of the schools are secular. It's mostly a Hindu country, but it's not an official Hindu state because there are huge minorities, especially Muslims and Sikhs, so the state took the decision at Independence that with so many religious divisions Indians would stand a far better chance of getting on with each other if children learned to mix, easily and naturally.

I think the same is true here with religion and with colour too. I've encountered racism, so have my children, it's an evil fact of life, but I think a better future will come from us working it out together, not separately.

I ought to say that just because I oppose separate religious schools, I don't think that everything about the present system is good. I don't think it is right that there are Church of England schools where Sikh children are treated as odd, or an embarrassment. And I don't think all schools do enough to promote good contact between groups or to work against racism actively, but I don't think having separate schools will help this — it may make it worse.

I ought also to add that this is not a 'Sikh' view. I know many Sikhs who want voluntary aided Sikh schools, and some who send their children to a private Sikh school. I know another who deliberately moved his son to a different local school where, as it happened, most of the pupils were Sikhs — so he was educated in more of a Sikh atmosphere.

Susan Harrison

I am proud of being white and British and I don't like the way Britain has changed. It seems to me that if immigrants choose to come into this

*country they shouldn't seek to change it, and that includes schooling. I
don't necessarily expect them to become Christians and I don't have a
problem with them going out of Christian assemblies, but I don't see why
we should adapt our schools to suit their ways (and it's not just religion,
they have writing on the wall in their languages and they read children's
stories about India). In British schools the main culture ought to be British.*

*As just a parent there isn't much I can do about what schools teach, but
I can have my way about which school my daughter goes to. Two local
schools have got large numbers of Asians and there's no way she's going
to a very mixed school so I've put her down for the other one. I think we
should integrate, neither one should dominate the others in school, numbers wise. There is supposed to be parental choice, so I am making mine.
I'm not strongly Christian but the one I'm choosing is the Church of
England school. After all, they want their separate Muslim schools, so
what's the matter with separate Christian schools? There's got to be a
language problem as well. I know some people say Asians do better in
school, but that doesn't apply to all of them, and I know for a fact that
some of the kiddies in the local schools are well behind English kids in
their English.*

Class and Separate Schooling

Having separate schools for different social classes goes back to the origins of
British education. It was widely believed that not only were there a limited
number of occupations requiring education and literacy there were also a
limited number of people capable of filling them, and these were almost
invariably the sons of those who had them already. Though a greater need for
literacy was recognized by the mid-nineteenth century it was still only limited
literacy and for specific purposes, one of which was not social mobility.

By the middle of this century there was some recognition that talent was
being wasted and that more could benefit from an education beyond the
elementary stage than had received it hitherto. The 1944 Education Act enshrined this belief in law and hoped to further it by the use of the then trusted
intelligence tests: by setting all children a test at 11 it was believed that potential could be recognized and children allocated accordingly to the schools to
which they were best suited: grammar, technical or 'modern', irrespective of
parental ability to pay.

It did not take long to realize that the selection taking place was in fact
heavily influenced by social class and that the secondary schools (particularly

he grammar and 'modern' schools, since few technical schools were built) were replicating the class divides of the adult world. The objection, let us be clear, was not that there were different schools preparing children for different adult work roles (though some did regret the consequent social segregation) but that the basis for school allocation (the 11+) was unfair. The intention of he reform to comprehensive education was primarily to enhance opportunity and mobility to all who were capable of it: it was a meritocratic ideal (Benn and Simon, 1972) and by no means as radical or as coherent as its detractors maintained (Ball, 1984). There remained, of course, the private sector, which has consistently taken about 6 per cent of children.

Though in the 1990s it is often believed otherwise, the comprehensive reform was potentially a very successful one. In Scotland, where the private sector is smaller and comprehensivization universal (there is a handful of English LEAs who always resisted it) results have markedly improved for all social classes, laying to rest the claim that standards inevitably suffered especially, as is often alleged, for the brightest. Why then has there been persistent criticism of the reform from the time when it really took hold? (This could be dated at around 1976, which was the first year that comprehensive schools began to take more than 50 per cent of the age range — the numbers went from only 10 per cent in 1970 to 84 per cent in 1979.)

Both Ball and Hunter (in Ball, 1984) argue that a crucial factor was a stalled national economy and a decline in pupil numbers which enabled large cuts to be made in education budgets. The consequences were serious because they were very uneven and decimated the start-up funding and morale necessary for the amalgamations and working through of many disparate and competing 'comprehensive' philosophies.

We would suggest that the 'moral panic' about comprehensives in the late 1970s and early 1980s was also fuelled by the fact that grammar schools were closing apace, and in London, the home of many politicians, journalists and commentators, the last few had not long been reorganized (in 1972 perhaps 12 per cent of 11 year olds in inner London had attended selective schools). The middle class no longer had their separate schools into which their children gained entry 'on merit' and many of the schools they were now going to were experimenting with new curricula and a limited amount of mixed ability teaching (though many were not and remained very traditional, in effect retaining a selective system under one roof). It was no coincidence that this was the period of Callaghan's 'Great Debate'. There was no new crisis in the mid- to late-1970s, the class and untechnological bias of British elite education (which were partly in Callaghan's sights) were already well known. What was new was that for the first time large numbers of middle class parents did not have available for their children a particular kind of prestigious secondary school, where in practice they mixed with few lower working class (and black) children. Inner London in particular, because numbers allowed it, had a complex system administered by the LEA to try to ensure a balanced ability intake at every school, but extensive efforts were also made by other LEAs to achieve this.

As the 1980s began, the new Conservative administration grew in confid
ence and became more influenced by sections of its right wing. Traditional
ists and free marketeers found a way of combining their concerns in the notion
of parental choice. Self-evidently, to them, all right thinking people would
choose schools which looked most like the prestigious schools they them
selves had experienced or aspired to: grammar schools modelled upon public
schools. If such parents therefore had the choice such schools would have
strong support, hence achieving elitism under the guise of populism. This
became Conservative policy and then the law. Schools had to let children in if
their parents so chose until they were full, parents were to be informed of the
best schools to choose by the publication of exam and test results, popular
schools were to be allowed to grow or to introduce selection (the latter step
being initially hotly denied by Baker, the Secretary of State who brought in
the 1988 Act), and the allegedly bureaucratic, over-egalitarian LEAs were to
have their powers reduced. This opened the door to a coded system of class
segregated education (Ball et al., 1995; 1996; Gewirtz et al., 1995).

It is notoriously difficult to find policy consensus on this issue. Clearly
parents will want the best schools for their children, whatever they conceive
that to be, and they will want some say in the decision. Clearly also, if a
hierarchy of schools becomes explicit and public then some will be seen as
worse and less desirable, yet many children will still have to go to them,
presumably against their parents' choice.

At this point we have to examine the concept of 'choice' critically and
recognize how problematic it is. The parental views presented in the two
preceding sections are just that, points of view, presented decontextualized
from the situations in which people have to make their choices. Even the
simplest shopping choices are constrained by geography and transport, let
alone spending power and information, yet much of the rhetoric in favour of
school choice barely mentions their importance (perhaps because while few
people suggest private schooling is a real choice for many of the population
since state schooling is free it is easy to represent the choice as unrestricted).

There is considerable recent evidence that the 'choice' is problematic for
many parents, that in practice it is a section of parents who might loosely be
called 'middle class' who are the most 'active choosers' (David et al., 1994) and
shoppers in the education market. It is not difficult to see why. In Hillingdon
for example, the former system of catchment areas and overall co-ordination
of secondary school places by the LEA has been replaced by LEA responsibility
for only four schools and the obligation for parents to apply separately to nine
grant maintained schools and two church schools. In the most popular school
the ratio of applications to places is approaching 10:1. The single most import
ant criterion applied is the proximity of the home to the school, but this stands
as a proxy for class since it is in the most expensive part of the borough. In
practice, most children end up going to the school nearest their home, but not
until after a long and largely illusory process of exercising their 'choice'. This
should not surprise anyone. It is instructive to read an account such as Ben

and Simon's, written in 1970, which clearly understands the social causes and consequences of a skewed social class intake into particular schools (p. 454) and a ten year old study in Scotland (where 'choice' was introduced first) which showed that 'strong relationships between social class and movements between schools . . . had a considerable effect on the social composition of some schools' (reported in Adler, 1997, p. 299).

Reay (1996) comments:

> . . . for working class mothers it is the constraints rather than the opportunities that overshadow their relationships with their children's schooling. (p. 582)

and

> The 'pick and mix' selection of contemporary education policies comes with a price tag beyond the purchasing power of most working class parents and their children. (p. 594)

The constraints the mothers refer to are straightforward ones of worrying whether they will have any money at the end of the week.

This is not solely an issue which affects secondary schools. Reay's work can be seen as demonstrating that the reinforcement through the education market of traditional images and notions of what constitutes a good school (discipline, clear subject boundaries, uniform, exam results) affects primary schools in that they can become incubators for the 'right' schools (she reports that in one school 50 per cent of year six took selective exams while not a single child did in another). We are not arguing against these traditional images *per se*, but that the emphasis upon them in the 'choice' process and the attendant efforts of the schools to secure the 'best' children can produce a distortion of schools' central values, a prioritizing of potential high achievers, a narrowing of the curriculum and an over-emphasis on symbols and appearances (Deem et al., 1994). Adler's (1997) older study predicted this: 'There was strong evidence of 'band-wagon' effects, i.e. of parents opting for particular schools because they perceive other parents to be doing so . . .' (p. 299). Again, Reay provides several examples of these pressures affecting teachers' decisions (p. 584).

The process also produces clear winners and losers — not surprisingly, since in any market some consumers are more advantaged, adept and lucky than others (this is masked in political rhetoric with phrases about all parents 'naturally' being concerned parents). When the pressure is on schools to improve their raw results in relation to neighbouring schools then the pressure is on them in turn to look carefully at the parents/children who choose them. Schools in a strong 'market position' can partly reverse the power relations in choosing by setting entrance exams for all or part of its intake, requiring parental interviews, and giving clear signals about the kinds of pupils they want. Schools seeking to improve their market position have no market interest in children with special needs or those whose test results may be depressed by working in their second language. The 'quasi market' in schools (Le Grand and

Bartlett, 1993) has been presented as schools competing to raise standards, but in practice it is also parents who must compete for the scarce resource of schools who can be increasingly choosy about who they let in.

Another problematic element of the notion of 'choice' is that it ignores cultural capital as well as financial advantage. This was explored in the section about class and attainment in relation to parents' understanding of and engagement with their children's education in day to day terms, but it has clear relevance to how parents negotiate overall school choice. Confidence and knowledge of the system are correlated with social class, the 'practical mastery of the social structure as a whole' (Bourdieu, 1985, p. 728) is a key variable in successfully steering one's way through the system and decoding the complex messages, producing, Ball et al. suggest, 'skilled', 'semi-skilled' and 'disconnected' choosers (1996, p. 92). We should beware, however, of assuming that there is a single overarching set of criteria to which everyone subscribes. Boys potentially going to a 'good' school may be facing a very different experience in ostensibly the same school as girls; black children and their parents may choose an academically weaker school with more black children and a strong equal opportunities culture in preference to another; children from one social class may dread being in a small minority, whatever a school's apparent advantages. Thus 'what constitutes a rational choice about secondary schooling differs according to social class' (Reay, 1996, p. 592) and this fact should not be obscured by depoliticized terms like 'diversity' and claims that selection and 'specialization' are simply to break up the 'uniformity' of comprehensives.

Our final point reiterates one raised in the sections on gender and 'race': one person's choice limits other people's. If a significant number of parents choose single sex schools they deny the choice of co-education to others; if sufficient numbers of Muslim parents prefer secular schools for their children they will deny the option of a religious school to other Muslims; parents who influence a school to remain or to become selective affect the kind of schooling available to others' children. This problem is not solved by market theory because the theory applied to schools harnesses parental self interest rather than a more general commitment towards wider social goals ('the tyranny of small decisions' Adler (1997) refers to in his overview of arguments about choice. See also Walford, 1996). We would argue that the coded class advantage in the policy of 'choice' is a central problem which will become increasingly explicit as its effects permeate the education system and schools become stratified in all but name. In our judgment it will increasingly become *the* critical issue in education policy.

Linda Bell

I feel completely bewildered by the choices I am supposed to be making. There are six schools to choose from and they all produce glossy brochures.

They all have open evenings too. I've been to three, but it's hard to know if you've picked up the things that really matter from a quick tour of the buildings with some pupils and a talk from the Head — though I liked the atmosphere of one much more than the others. I mean, I spent much longer looking at and thinking about the little house we live in than I could about the school, yet schools are much more complicated things and I know less about them. What you end up doing is playing safe: what do you recognize, what sorts of things seem familiar? You can under-stand traditional looking desks and classrooms, don't you, so you feel safer with a school that has them.

I know that last year's results can't tell me what my son would have got, let alone what he'll get at a particular school in five years' time. I know that a school which seems to have worse results may have done a really good job with children who weren't so bright, but it's hard to actually choose somewhere which isn't as high in the league tables.

I've also heard that lots of children don't get their choice anyway, so sometimes I feel like just going for the nearest. If he's likely to end up there whatever I do, what's the point?

James Harrison

I have every intention of using my choice to get my daughter into the best school. Liberal do-gooders can say what they like, but I want her mixing with loutish kids and potential delinquents as little as possible. Lots of people I know will not come out and say it, but basically they know as well as I do that there are more rough and difficult kids in the council estates and they want to avoid them. Basically we all know there are some kids who don't want to work and there are others who aren't very bright and it stands to reason that if they are the majority in a school they will set the tone. My daughter is not brilliant, but I think she is above average. I think she will do better surrounded by others of the same or higher ability so I want her to go to a school where that's possible.

I also want a school where other things are valued, like politeness and good manners and speaking well. We value these things but they aren't valued by all parents, why should our work as parents be undermined by denying us a choice in the kind of children our daughter should mix with?

The school we think is best also has lots of extra-curricula activities like a debating society, drama, music clubs and sports teams. She will make friends with similar interests in activities like this and these activities will also teach her to use her time wisely.

I can't afford to go private and I don't think I should even have to consider it — the state education service ought to provide the kind of school which will bring the best out of my daughter and I should have the right to choose it.

Lynne Stevenson

I don't know what to say about choosing schools for our son because, to be honest, I feel out of my depth with all the parents evenings and the different heads going on about what their school has to offer.

We went through it a bit with his elder sister but this time we're just going to opt for the nearest — which is where she got sent anyway. We can't really afford five years of bus fares to the other side of town and anyway he wants to go to the local one because that's where most of his friends are going. From what I read in the papers and from listening to other parents I don't think we've done so badly.

I don't know if he's bright or not — his teachers say he is, but no-one in our family has ever done really well at school and they've all managed to get jobs. I reckon it's important to be happy at school and if you've got the brains you'll do all right. It's not as if the local school is really rough or anything — though I know some people say it is. I sometimes wish we all just sent our kids to the nearest school, I'm sure that's what we used to do . . .

Dilip Chauhan

I completely support the ideas of parental choice and selection by ability, that's to say my choice is for selection.

This is not necessarily because I think my children will prove to be very bright and get into the selective school. It's very obvious to anyone who has been out in the world of work that people need to have very different skills and also that people have very different abilities. Some people love working with numbers and making sure everything balances, some people are good with people, others are good with their hands. It doesn't seem possible to me that they should all have the same kind of schooling, or that they are all capable of benefiting from it. I mean, why make someone do Latin when they're not even very good at English and are barely even going to use that in their jobs? And why teach someone lots of practical skills when they are just not interested or any good at them?

Different schools should set out to develop what children are best at. They are not all good at everything and some aren't good at much at all. It doesn't seem fair to me to pretend this isn't true — young people need realistic goals, not an idealistic dream that everyone is the same.

I'm not pretending that all different abilities are valued equally: people have always valued doctors more highly than people who mend the roads, paid them more and given them higher social status, but that's inevitable. I'm sure that as a result selective schools have more status that the others, but what can you do? It doesn't mean that other kids have to feel like failures — and after all, those 'other kids' might be mine — I'm sure it's possible to give a realistic judgment of a pupil's ability without destroying their self-esteem. After all, they have to face up to their limits sooner or later.

I know people say that in the past there was a lot of wastage of talent because the 11 plus wasn't very accurate so quite a lot of children were sent to the wrong school. Perhaps eleven is a little young? Perhaps all children could be at the same kinds of schools until 13 or so and then go to separate ones depending on how they've got on in the previous two years?

Jennifer Browne

What worries me about so-called 'parental choice' is that although all the schools around here are comprehensives there's a kind of unspoken conspiracy about which school is 'best' and why. People talk about it as being 'good' and the children as being 'nice' and the head as believing in 'standards', but it seems to me they're just saying it's pretty middle class. It's the school that many of the brighter children seem to get to, so of course its results are higher, and they are becoming a bit of an academic hothouse, having articles in the paper about how many pupils went to Oxford or Cambridge last year, that kind of thing. They've also gone back to being much more strict about uniform: five or six years ago they had a school sweatshirt and it was okay to wear that. Now they have a blazer with a badge on it, and everyone has to wear a tie.

I live near enough the school to stand a good chance of getting my son in, but he's dyslexic. I have been to a meeting at the school and really got the impression that they're not interested in someone with special needs like his, however bright he is. I can't help thinking it's because their main concern is with good exam scores, so they put less effort into a child who needs more time and care. You can't blame them in a way, I suppose. If they can fill up the school with kids who are almost certain to do well, why take anyone who is more risky? The trouble is the effect that has on all the other schools. They have more of the difficult cases. The teachers may be just as good and work just as hard, and actually they may get more out a son like mine than the 'good' school, but they end up with the image of being second class.

*This has been hanging over us since the beginning of my son's last year in primary school, and my overall feeling is that I don't really have the 'choice' I'm supposed to have. I feel like **we're** being chosen — or not. It doesn't seem to me like a comprehensive system where all schools have a bit of a mix. I think that would be ideal, to spread out the bright kids, and the ones who want to work but have got some difficulties, and the villains, if you concentrate any of them in one school you get problems.*

Note

1   There are now about 234 state girls' schools (including grammar and grant main-tained schools) compared to 2,000 thirty years ago, and the number in the private sector is also diminishing as the fashion for co-educational schools combine with economic pressure in the private sector. Some schools became co-educational by amalgamating, with bizarre results in some cases, though perhaps not as bizarre as the situation which preceded it. A secondary school one of us knows was built as two single-sex secondary moderns on the same site, indeed sharing a party wall, either side of which were buildings an exact mirror image of each other (though the uses to which the labs and practical subjects' rooms were put were different). The party wall divided two halls, two gyms and two parallel corridors. There was one communicating door, allegedly never opened.

Bibliography

ALTARF (1984) *Challenging Racism*, London: All London Teachers Alliance against Racism and Fascism.

ACKER, S. (ed.) (1989) *Teachers, Gender and Careers*, Lewes: Falmer Press.

ACKER, S. (1994) *Gendered Education*, Buckingham: Open University Press.

ADLER, M. (1997) 'Looking backwards to the future: Parental choice and education policy', *British Educational Research Journal*, **23**, 3, pp. 297–314.

AKHTAR, S. (1986) 'They call me Blacky', *TES*, 19.9.86.

ALBANY VIDEO (1987) *Being White*, London: Albany Video.

ALHIBAI, Y. (1987) 'The child racists', *New Society*, 4/12/87.

ALLCOTT, T. (1992) 'Antiracism in education: The search for policy in practice', in GILL, D., MAYOR, B. and BLAIR, M. *Racism and Education: Structures and Strategies*, London: Sage.

ALTHUSSER, L. (1971) 'Ideology and ideological state apparatus: Notes towards an investigation', in COSIN, B.R. (ed.) *Education: Structure and Society*, Harmondsworth: Penguin Books.

ARNOT, M. and WEINER, G. (eds) (1987) *Gender and the Politics of Schooling*, London: Hutchinson.

ARNOT, M., DAVID, M. and WEINER, G. (1995) *Educational Reforms and Gender Equality in Schools*, Manchester: Equal Opportunities Commission.

AUDIT COMMISSION (1988) *The Performance of Education Authorities*, reported in the Guardian, 12/3/98: p. 1.

BAGLEY, C. (1996) 'Black and white unite or flight? The racialised dimension of schooling and parental choice', *British Educational Research Journal*, **22**, 5, pp. 569–80.

BALL, S.J. (1981) *Beachside Comprehensive*, Cambridge: Cambridge University Press.

BALL, S.J. (ed.) (1984) *Comprehensive Schooling: A Reader*, Lewes: Falmer Press.

BALL, S.J. (1990a) *Politics and Policy Making in Education*, London: Routledge.

BALL, S.J. (1990b) *Markets, Morality and Equality in Education*, Brighton: Hillcole Group.

BALL, S.J. (1994) *Education Reform*, Buckingham: Open University Press.

BALL, S.J., BOWE, R. and GEWIRZT, S. (1995) 'Circuits of schooling: A sociological exploration of parental choice in social class contexts', *Sociological Review*, **43**, pp. 52–78.

BALL, S., BOWE, R. and GEWIRZT, S. (1996) 'School choice, social class and distinction: The realization of social advantage in education', *Journal of Education Policy*, **11**, 1, pp. 89–112.

BASIT, T.N. (1996) '"I'd hate to be just a housewife": Career aspirations of British Muslim girls', *British Journal of Guidance and Counselling*, **24**, 2, June, pp. 227–42.

BBC (1995) *Men aren't working*, TV, Panorama (October), London: British Broadcasting Corporation.

BBC (1996) *East: Relative Values*, TV (April), London: British Broadcasting Corporation.

BELL, C. and ROBERTS, H. (eds) (1984) *Social Researching: Politics, Problems, Practice*, London: Routledge & Kegan Paul.

BENJAMIN, H. (1971) 'The sabre-toothed curriculum', in HOOPER, R. (ed.) *The Curriculum: Context, Design and Development*, Edinburgh: Oliver and Boyd.

BENN, C. and SIMON, B. (1972) *Half Way There*, Harmondsworth: Penguin.

BERKSHIRE LEA (1989) *Education is the Key*, Reading: Berkshire Education Dept. Resources Unit.

BERNARD, M. and MEADE, K. (eds) (1995) *Women Come of Age*, London: Edward Arnold.

BERNSTEIN, B. (1958) 'Some sociological determinants of perception. An enquiry into sub-cultural differences', *British Journal of Sociology*, **9**.

BERNSTEIN, B. (1959) 'A public language: Some sociological determinants of linguistic form', *British Journal of Sociology*, **10**.

BERNSTEIN, B. (1960) 'Language and social class', *British Journal of Sociology*, **11**.

BERNSTEIN, B. (1961a) 'Social structure, language and learning', *Educational Research*, **3**.

BERNSTEIN, B. (1961b) 'Social class and linguistic development: A theory of social learning', in HALSEY, A. et al., *Education, Economy & Society*, New York: Free Press.

BERNSTEIN, B. (1970) 'Social class, language and socialisation', in GIGLIOLI, P. (ed.) *Language and Social Context*, Harmondsworth: Penguin.

BHACHU, P. (1985) *Parental Educational Strategies: The Case of Punjabi Sikhs in Britain*, University of Warwick: Centre for Research in Ethnic Relations.

BOALER, J. (1997) 'Reclaiming School Mathematics: The girls fight back' in *Gender and Education*, **9**, 3, pp. 285–305.

BOARD OF EDUCATION (1923) *Report of the Consultative Committee on Differentiation of the Curriculum for Boys and Girls Respectively in Secondary Schools*, London: HMSO.

BOARD OF EDUCATION (1923) *Report of the Consultative Committee on Secondary Education, with special reference to grammar and technical high schools* (The Spens Report), London: HMSO.

BOARD OF EDUCATION (1926) *The Education of the Adolescent* (The Hadow Report), London: HMSO.

BODINE, A. (1975) 'Androcentrism in prescriptive grammar', *Language in Society*, **4**, 2, pp. 129–56 (reprinted in CAMERON, D. (ed.) (1990) *The Feminist Critique of Language*, London: Routledge.

BONE, A. (1983) *Girls and Girls-Only Schools: A Review of the Evidence*, London: Equal Opportunities Commission.

BONES, JAH (1986) 'Language and Rastafari', in SUTCLIFFE, D. and WONG, A. *The Language of the Black Experience*, Oxford: Blackwell.

BORNSTEIN, D. (1978) 'As meek as a maid: A historical perspective on language for women in courtesy books from the Middle Ages to Seventeen magazine', in BUTTURFF, D. and EPSTEIN, E. (eds) *Women's Language and Style*, Department of English, University of Akron (cited in Swann, 1992).

BOURDIEU, P. (1973) 'Cultural reproduction and social reproduction', in KARABEL, J. and HALSEY, A.H. (eds) (1977) *Power and Ideology in Education*, New York: Oxford University Press.

BOURDIEU, P. (1985) 'Social space and the genesis of groups', *Theory and Society*, 14, pp. 723–44.

BOURDIEU, P. and PASSERON, J-C (1977) *Reproduction in Education, Society and Culture*, London: Sage.

BOWLES, S. and GINTIS, H. (1976) *Schooling in Capitalist America*, London: Routledge & Kegan Paul.

BOWLES, S. and GINTIS, H. (1981) 'Contradiction and reproduction in educational theory', in DALE, R. et al. (eds) *Education and the State*, vol. 1, Lewes: Falmer Press.

BRAH, A. (1992) 'Difference, diversity and differentiation', in DONALD, J. and RATTANSI, A. *'Race', Culture and Difference*, London: Sage.

BRAHAM, P., RATTANSI, A. and SKELLINGTON, R. (1992) *Racism and Antiracism*, London: Sage.

BRANDT, G. (1986) *The Realization of Anti-Racist Teaching*, Lewes: Falmer Press.

BREHONY, K. (1984) 'Co-education: Perspectives and debates in the early twentieth century', in DEEM, R. (ed.) *Co-education reconsidered*, Milton Keynes: Open University Press.

BRIGHT, M. (1998) 'Boys Performing Badly', *The Observer*, 4 January.

BROPHY, J. and GOOD, T. (1970) 'Teachers' communication of differential expectations', *Journal of Educational Psychology*, 61, pp. 365–74.

BROWN, C. (1984) *Black and White Britain*, Aldershot: Gower/Policy Studies Institute.

BROWN, CLAIRE et al. (1990) *A Spanner in the Works*, Stoke on Trent: Trentham Books.

BROWN, COLIN (1992) 'Same difference: The persistence of racial disadvantage in the British employment market', in BRAHAM, P., RATTANSI, A. and SKELLINGTON, R. (eds) *Racism and Antiracism*, London: Sage.

BROWN, P. and LEVINSON, S. (1987) *Politeness*, Cambridge: Cambridge University Press.

BROWNE, N. and FRANCE, P. (eds) *Untying the Apron Strings: Anti-sexist Provision for the Under Fives*, Milton Keynes: Open University Press.

CAMERON, D. (1990) *The Feminist Critique of Language*, London: Routledge.

CARICOM (1995) *Towards Equity in Development: A Report on the Status of Women in Sixteen Commonwealth Caribbean Countries*, Caribbean Community Secretariat.

CARRINGTON, B. and SHORT, G. (1989) *'Race' and the Primary School*, Slough: NFER/Nelson.

CARRINGTON, B. and SHORT, G. (1995) 'What makes a person British? Children's conceptions of their national culture and identity', in *Educational Studies*, **XXI**, 2, pp. 217–38.

CENTRAL STATISTICAL OFFICE (1995) *Social Focus: Women*, London: HMSO.

CENTRE FOR CONTEMPORARY CULTURAL STUDIES (eds) (1978) *Women Take Issue*, London: Hutchinson.

CHAUHAN, C. (1988) 'Anti-racist teaching in white areas, a black perspective', *Multicultural Teaching*, **VI**, 2, pp. 35–7.

CHEVANNES, M. and REEVES, F. (1987) 'The black voluntary school movement', in TROYNA, B. *Racial Inequality and Education*, London: Routledge.

CHITTY, C. (1989) *Towards a New Education System: The Victory of the New Right?*, London: Falmer Press.

CLARRICOATES, K. (1978) 'Dinosaurs in the classroom — A re-examination of some aspects of the "hidden curriculum" in primary schools', *Women's Studies International Quarterly*, **1**, pp. 353–64, Routledge & Kegan Paul.

CLARK, K. and CLARK, M. (1947) 'Racial identification and preference in negro children', in NEWCOMB, T.M. and HARTLEY, E.L. (eds) *Readings in Social Psychology*, New York: Holt.

CLARKE, E. (1966) *My Mother Who Fathered Me*, London: Allen & Unwin.

COARD, B. (1971) *How the West Indian Child is Made Educationally Sub-normal in the British School System*, London: New Beacon Books.

COATES, J. (1993) *Women, Men and Language*, London: Longman.

COATES, K. and SILBURN, P. (1970) *Poverty, the Forgotten Englishmen*, Harmondsworth: Penguin.

COHEN, G. et al. (eds) (1986) *The New Right, Image and Reality*, London: Runnymede Trust.

COHEN, P. (1989) *Tackling Common Sense Racism*, University of London Institute of Education, Centre for Multicultural Education.

COHEN, P. (1992) 'It's racism what's dunnit', in DONALD, J. and RATTANSI, A. *Racism and Antiracism*, London: Sage.

COHEN, P. and HADDOCK, L. (1991) *Anansi Meets Spiderwoman*, University of London Institute of Education, Cultural Studies Project.

COMMISSION FOR RACIAL EQUALITY (1985) *Birmingham LEA and Schools: Referral and Suspension of Pupils*, London: CRE.

COMMISSION FOR RACIAL EQUALITY (1988a) *Medical School Admissions*, London: CRE.

COMMISSION FOR RACIAL EQUALITY (1988b) *Learning in Terror*, London: CRE.

COMMISSION FOR RACIAL EQUALITY (1992a) *Keep Them in Birmingham*, London: CRE.

COMMISSION FOR RACIAL EQUALITY (1992b) *Secondary School Admissions: Report of a Formal Investigation into Hertfordshire County Council*, London: CRE.

CONNELL, R.W. (1987) *Gender and Power*, London: Polity Press.

CONNELL, R.W. (1989) 'Cool guys, swots and wimps; the interplay of masculinity and education', *Oxford Review of Education*, **15**, 3, pp. 291–303.

CONNELL, R.W. (1995) *Masculinities*, Sydney: Allen and Unwin.

CONNOLLY, P. (1995) 'Reconsidering multicultural/antiracist strategies in education: Articulations of "race" and gender in a primary school', in GRIFFITHS, M. and TROYNA, B. *Antiracism, Culture and Social Justice in Education*, Stoke on Trent: Trentham.

CORRIGAN, P. (1979) *Schooling the Bash Street Kids*, London: Macmillan.

CORSON, D. (1993) *Language, Minority Education and Power*, Clevedon: Multilingual Matters.

COX, B. (1991) *Cox on Cox: An English Curriculum for the 1990s*, London: Hodder & Stoughton.

COX, B. and DYSON, A. (1971) *The Black Papers on Education*, London: Davis Poynter.

CROWTHER COMMITTEE (1959) *15 to 18: A report of the Central Advisory Council for Education (England)*, London: Ministry of Education.

CRYSTAL, D. (1987) *Cambridge Encyclopaedia of Languages*, Cambridge: Cambridge University Press.

DALPHINIS, M. (1985) *Caribbean and African Languages*, London: Karia Press.

DARLING, J. and GLENDINNING, A. (1996) *Gender Matters in Schools; Pupils and Teachers*, London: Cassell.

DAVID, M., WEST, A. and RIBBENS, J. (1994) *Mother's Intuition? Choosing Secondary Schools*, London: Falmer Press.

DEEM, R. (1981) 'State policy and ideology in the education of women', *British Journal of Sociology of Education*, **2**, 2, pp. 131–43.

DEEM, R. (ed.) (1984) *Co-education Reconsidered*, Milton Keynes: Open University Press.

DEEM, R., BREHONY, K. and HEATH, S. (1994) 'Governors, schools and the miasma of the market', *British Education Research Journal*, **20**, 5, pp. 535–48.

DELAMONT, S. (1976) *Interaction in the Classroom*, London: Methuen.

DELAMONT, S. (1984) *Sex Roles and the School*, London: Methuen.

DEPARTMENT OF EDUCATION AND SCIENCE (1965a) *The Education of Immigrants* (Circular 7/65), London: HMSO.

DEPARTMENT OF EDUCATION AND SCIENCE (1965b) *The Organisation of Secondary Education* (Circular 10/65), London: HMSO.

DEPARTMENT OF EDUCATION AND SCIENCE (1981) *West Indian Children in Our Schools* (The Rampton Report), London: HMSO Cmnd 8273.

DEPARTMENT OF EDUCATION AND SCIENCE (1985) *Education for All* (The Swann Report), London: HMSO Cmnd 9453.

DEPARTMENT FOR EDUCATION AND EMPLOYMENT (1997) *Statistics of Education; Teachers in England & Wales*, 1996 Edition, London: HMSO.

DHONDY, F. (1974) 'The Black explosion in schools', *Race Today*, February, pp. 44–7.

DIXON, B. (1977) *Catching Them Young: Sex, Race and Class in Children's Fiction*, Vol. 1, London: Pluto.

DONALD, J. and RATTANSI, A. (1992) *'Race', Culture and Difference*, London: Sage.

DONALD, P. et al. (1995) 'No problem here: Action research against racism in a mainly white area', *British Educational Research Journal*, **21**, 3.

DORLING, D. (1997) reported by David Brindle in *Guardian*, 11 August, p. 3.

DOUGLAS, J.W.B. (1964) *The Home and the School*, London: MacGibbon & Kee.

DREW, D. and GRAY, J. (1990) 'The fifth year examination achievements of Black young people in England and Wales', *Educational Research*, **32**, 3, pp. 107–17.

DREW, D. and GRAY, J. (1991) 'The Black-White gap in examination results: A statistical critique of a decade's research', *New Community*, **17**, 2, pp. 159–72.

DREW, D., GRAY, J. and SPORTON, D. (1994) unpublished paper cited in GILLBORN, D. and GIPPS, G. (1996) *Recent Research on the Achievements of Ethnic Minority Pupils*, London: Ofsted/Institute of Education.

EADE, J. (1995) *Routes and Beyond: Voices from Educationally Successful Bangladeshis*, London: Centre for Bangladeshi Studies.

EDELSKY, C. (1976) 'The acquisition of communicative competence: Recognition of linguistic correlates of sex-roles', *Merrill-Palmer Quarterly*, **22**, 1, pp. 47–59.

EDWARDS, T., GEWIRTZ, S. and WHITTY, G. (1992) 'Whose choice of schools? Making sense of city technology colleges', in ARNOT, M. and BARTON, L. (eds) *Voicing Concerns*, Wallingford: Triangle.

EDWARDS, V. (1979) *The West Indian Language Issue in British Schools*, London: Routledge & Kegan Paul.

EDWARDS, V. (1986) *Language in a Black Community*, Clevedon: Multilingual Matters.

EGGLESTON, S.J., DUNN, D. and ANGALI, M. (1986) *Education for Some: The Educational and Vocational Experiences of 15–18 year old Members of Minority Ethnic Groups*, Stoke on Trent; Trentham.

ENCA (1992) SHORROCKS, D., DANIELS, S., FROBISHER, L., NELSON, N., WATERSON, A. and BELL, J. *The Evaluation of National Curriculum Assessment at Key Stage I, Final Report*, Leeds: University of Leeds School of Education.

EPSTEIN, D. (1993) *Changing Classroom Cultures*, Stoke on Trent: Trentham.

EPSTEIN, D. (1993) 'Too small to notice? Constructions of childhood and discourses of "race" in prodominantly white contexts', *Curriculum Studies*, **1**, 3, pp. 317–34.

EPSTEIN, D. (ed.) (1994) *Challenging Lesbian and Gay Inequalities in Education*, Buckinghamshire: Open University Press.

EPSTEIN, D. and SEALEY, A. (1990) *Where it Really Matters*, Birmingham: Birmingham DEC.

EQUAL OPPORTUNITIES COMMISSION AND OFFICE FOR STANDARDS IN EDUCATION (1996) *The Gender Divide: Performance Differences Between Boys and Girls at School*, London: HMSO.

EVANS, T. (1988) *A Gender Agenda*, Australia: Allen & Unwin.

EYTARN (1994) *Focus on Equality*, London: Early Years Anti-Racist Training Network.

FARRELL, P. (1990) *Multicultural Education*, Leamington Spa: Scholastic Publications.

FIGUEROA, P. (1984) 'Race relations and cultural differences: Some ideas on a racial frame of reference', in VERMA, G. and BAGLEY, C. (eds) *Race Relations and Cultural Differences*, London: Croom Helm.

FIGES, K. (1994) *Because of Her Sex. The Myth of Equality for Women in Britain*, London: Macmillan.

FISHER, J. (1991) 'Unequal voices: Gender and assessment', in Open University P535 *Talk and Learning 5–16*, Milton Keynes: Open University.

FISHMAN, P. (1978) 'Interaction: The work women do', *Social Problems*, **25**, pp. 397–406.

FOSTER, P. (1990) *Policy and Practice in Multicultural and Antiracist Education*, London: Routledge.

FOUCAULT, M. (1979) *Discipline and Punish*, Harmondsworth: Penguin.

FRASER, F. (1995) *The Bell Curve Wars*, New York: Basic Books.

FRENCH, J. and FRENCH, P. (1984) 'Gender imbalance in the primary classroom: An interactional account', *Educational Research*, **26**, 2, pp. 127–36.

FRYER, P. (1984) *Staying Power*, London: Pluto Press.

FULLER, M. (1980) 'Black girls in a London comprehensive school', in DEEM, R. (ed.) *Schooling for Women's Work*, London: Routledge & Kegan Paul.

GAINE, C. (1987) *No Problem Here*, London: Hutchinson.

GAINE, C. (1995) *Still No Problem Here*, Stoke on Trent: Trentham.

GAINE, C. and PEARCE, L. (eds) (1988) *Anti-Racist Education in White Areas*, 1987 NAME Conference Report, Chichester: NAME.

GEORGE, R. (1993) *Equal Opportunities in Schools: Principles, Policy and Practice*, Harlow: Longman.

GEORGE, R. and MAGUIRE, M. (1997) ' "What if they ask me how old I am?" Older women training to teach.' Paper presented at the *10th International Women's Studies Conference*, London: Institute of Education, University of London.

GEWIRTZ, S., BALL, S. and BOWE, R. (1994) 'Parents, privilege and the education market place', *Research Papers in Education*, **IX**, 1, pp. 3–30.

GEWIRTZ, S., BALL, S. and BOWE, R. (1995) *Markets, Choice and Equity*, Buckingham: Open University Press.

GIGLIOLI, P. (ed.) (1972) *Language and Social Context*, Harmondsworth: Penguin.

GILL, D., MAYOR, B. and BLAIR, M. (1992) *Racism and Education: Structures and Strategies*, London: Sage.

GILLBORN, D. (1990) *'Race', Ethnicity and Education*, London: Unwin Hyman.

GILLBORN, D. (1995) *Racism and Antiracism in Real Schools*, Buckingham: Open University Press.

GILLBORN, D. and GIPPS, C. (1996) *Recent Research on the Achievements of Ethnic Minority Pupils*, London: Office for Standards in Education/Institute of Education.

GIROUX, H. and MCLAREN, P. (eds) (1989) *Critical Pedagogy, the State and Cultural Struggle*, New York: State University of New York Press.

GLASS, D. (1954) *Social Mobility in Britain*, London: Routledge & Kegan Paul.

GOODMAN, M. (1964) *Race Awareness in Young Children*, New York: Collier Books.

GRADDOL, D. and SWANN, J. (1989) *Gender Voices*, Oxford: Blackwell.

GREEN, P. (1985) 'Multi-ethnic teaching and the pupils' self-concepts', in DES *Education for All (The Swann Report)*, London: HMSO.

GRIFFITHS, M. and TROYNA, B. (1995) *Antiracism, Culture and Social Justice in Education*, Stoke on Trent: Trentham.

HALSEY, A.H. (1972) *Education Priority: Report of a Research. Vol. 1 EPA Problems and Priorities*, London: HMSO.

HALSEY, A.H., HEATH, A.F. and RIDGE, J.M. (1980) *Origins and Destinations*, Oxford: Clarendon.

HARGREAVES, A. (1989) 'Changes, choices and challenges in secondary education', in CLOUGH, E. and NIXON, J. (eds) *The New Learning*, Basingstoke: Macmillan Education.

HARGREAVES, D. (1967) *Social Relations in a Secondary School*, London: Routledge & Kegan Paul.

HARGREAVES, D. (1982) *The Challenge for the Comprehensive School*, London: Routledge & Kegan Paul.

HARGREAVES, D., HESTOR, S. and MELLOR, F. (1975) *Deviance in Classrooms*, London: Routledge & Kegan Paul.

HARNETT, A. and NAISH, M. (1986) *Education and Society Today*, London: Falmer Press.

HAW, K. (1995) 'Why Muslim girls are more feminist in Muslim schools', in GRIFFITHS, M. and TROYNA, B. (eds) *Antiracism, Culture and Social Justice in Education*, Stoke on Trent: Trentham.

HEATH, S.B. (1983) *Ways With Words*, Cambridge: Cambridge University Press.

HILL, D. (1989) *The Charge of the Right Brigade*, Brighton: Hillcole Group.

HILLGATE GROUP (1986) *Whose Schools? A Radical Manifesto*, London: Hillgate Group.

HILLGATE GROUP (1987) *The Reform of British Education*, London: The Claridge Press.

HIRO, D. (1973) *Black British, White British*, Harmondsworth: Penguin.

HOLMES, J. (1992) *An Introduction to Sociolinguistics*, London: Longman.

HOME OFFICE (1975) *Sex Discrimination Act*, London: HMSO.

HUGHES, R. (1988) *A Report by the Chief Executive on the Dewsbury Schools Affair 1987–8*, Huddersfield: Kirkees Metropolitan District Council.

HUNTER, C. (1984) 'The political devaluation of comprehensives', in BALL, S. (ed.) *Comprehensive Schooling: A Reader*, Lewes: Falmer Press.

INNER LONDON EDUCATION AUTHORITY (1982) 'Sex difference and achievement', *Research and Statistical Report RS823/83*, London: Inner London Education Authority.

INSTITUTE OF PUBLIC POLICY RESEARCH (1997) *Report on a Survey on Prejudice*, London: IPPR/NOP.

ITZIN, C.L. (1990) Age and sexual divisions: A study of opportunity and identity in women, University of Kent (PhD thesis).

JACKSON, B. and MARSDEN, D. (1966) *Education and the Working Class*, Harmondsworth: Penguin.

JACKSON, R. and NESBITT, E. (1993) *Hindu Children in Britain*, Stoke on Trent: Trentham.

JAMES, A. and JEFFCOATE, R. (eds) (1981) *The School in the Multicultural Society*, London: Harper and Row.

JONES, T. (1993) *Britain's Ethnic Minorities*, London: Policy Studies Institute.

KANT, L. (1985) 'A question of judgement', in WHYTE, J. et al. (eds) *Girl Friendly Schooling*, London: Routledge & Kegan Paul.

KEDDIE, N. (ed.) (1973) *Tinker, Tailor . . . The Myth of Cultural Deprivation*, Harmondsworth: Penguin.

KELLY, A. (1986) 'Gender differences in teacher–pupil interactions: A meta-analytic review', *Research in Education*, **39**, pp. 1–23.

KELLY, E. and COHN, T. (1989) *Racism in Schools — New Research Evidence*, Stoke on Trent: Trentham.

KENWAY, J. (1995) 'Masculinities in schools: Under siege, on the defensive and under reconstruction?', *Discourse*, **16**, 1, pp. 59–80.

KING, A. and REISS, M. (1993) *The Multicultural Dimension of the National Curriculum*, London: Falmer Press.

KIRKBY, J. (1746) *A New English Grammar*, Menston: Scolar Press, 1971.

KLEIN, G. (1993) *Education Towards Race Equality*, London: Cassell.

LABOV, W. (1972a) 'The logic of non-standard English', in GIGLIOLI, P. *Language and Social Context*.

LABOV, W. (1972b) *Sociolinguistic Patterns*, Philadelphia: University of Pennsylvania Press.

LACEY, C. (1970) *Hightown Grammar: The School as a Social System*, Manchester: Manchester University Press.

LAVIGEUR, J. (1980) 'Coeducation and the tradition of separate needs', in SPENDER, D. and SARAH, E. *Learning to Lose* (2nd edition 1988), London: Women's Press.

LAWTON, D. (1968) *Social Class, Language and Education*, London: Routledge & Kegan Paul.

LE GRAND, J. and BARTLETT, W. (1993) *Quasi Markets and Public Policy*, London: Macmillan.

LEE, J. (1989) 'Social class and schooling', in COLE, M. (ed.) *The Social Contexts of Schooling*, London: Falmer Press.

LEES, S. (1986) *Losing Out: Sexuality and Adolescent Girls*, London: Hutchinson.

LEES, S. (1987) 'The structure of sexual relations in school', in ARNOT, M. and WEINER, G. (eds) *Gender and the Politics of Schooling*, Milton Keynes: Open University.

LEVITAS, R. (ed.) (1986) *The Ideology of the New Right*, Cambridge: Polity Press.

LEWIS, J. (1984) *Women in England 1870–1950*, Hemel Hempstead: Harvester Wheatsheaf.

LINGUISTIC MINORITIES PROJECT (1985) *The Other Languages of England*, London: Routledge & Kegan Paul.

LOBBAN, G. (1974) 'Sex roles in reading schemes', in WEINER, G. and ARNOT, M. (eds) (1987) *Gender Under Scrutiny*, London: Hutchinson.

LOUIS, K. and MILES, M. (1990) *Improving the Urban High school: What Works and Why*, New York: Teachers' College Press.

MAC AN GHAILL, M. (1988) *Young, Gifted and Black*, Milton Keynes: Open University Press.

MACDONALD, I. et al. (1990) *Murder in the Playground*, London: Longsight Press.

MACINTOSH, M. (1990) ' "Caught between the two": Gender and race in a Scottish school', in PATERSON, F. and FEWELL, J. (eds) *Girls in their Prime: Scottish Education Revisited*, Edinburgh: Scottish Academic Press.

MACKAY, D. and FULKERSON, D. (1979) 'On the comprehension and production of pronouns', *Journal of Verbal Learning and Verbal Behaviour*, **18**, pp. 661–73.

MACKINNON, D., STATHAM, J. and HALES, M. (1995) *Education in the UK: Facts and Figures*, London: Hodder & Stoughton.

MAGUIRE, M. and WEINER, G. (1994) 'The place of women in teacher education: Discourse of power', *Education Review*, **46**, 2, 194, pp. 121–41.

MAHONY, P. (1985) *Schooling for the Boys*, London: Hutchinson.

MARTYNA, W. (1980) 'The psychology of generic masculine', in MCCONNELL-GINET, S. et al. (eds) *Women and Language in Literature and Society*, New York: Praeger.

MASSEY, I. (1987) 'Hampshire happening: Working towards change', *Multicultural Teaching*, **V**, 2, pp. 6–8.

MASSEY, I. (1991) *More Than Skin Deep, Developing Multicultural Anti-racist Education in All-White Schools*, Sevenoaks: Hodder & Stoughton.

MAUGHAN, B. and DUNN, G. (1988) 'Black pupils' progress in secondary school', in VERMA, G. and PUMFREY, P. (eds) *Educational Attainments: Issues and Outcomes in Multicultural Education*, London: Falmer Press.

Measor, L. and Woods, P. (1984) *Changing Schools*, Milton Keynes: Open University Press.

Measor, L. and Sikes, P. (1992) *Gender and Schools*, London: Cassell.

Menter, I. (1989) ' "They're too young to notice": Young children and racism', in Barrett, G. (ed.) *Dissaffection from School? The Early Years*, Lewes: Falmer Press.

Merrett, F. and Wheldall, K. (1992) 'Teachers' use of praise and reprimands to boys and girls', *Educational Review*, **44**, pp. 73–9.

Metcalfe, H. and Thompson, M. (1989) *Older workers, Employers' Attitudes and Practices.* Brighton: Institute of Manpower Studies.

Midwinter, E. (1972) *Social Environment and the Urban School*, London: Ward Lock Educational.

Millard, E. (1997) *Differently Literate. Boys, Girls and the Schooling of Literacy*, London: Falmer Press.

Milner, D. (1975) *Children and Race*, Harmondsworth: Penguin.

Milner, D. (1983) *Children and Race — 10 Years On*, London: Ward Lock.

Milner, D. (1997) 'Racism and childhood identity', *The Psychologist*, **10**, 3 March, pp. 123–5.

Minns, H. (1991) *Language, Literacy and Gender*, Sevenoaks: Hodder and Stoughton.

Mirza, H. (1992) *Young Female and Black*, London: Routledge.

Modood, T. (1992) *Not Easy Being British*, London: Runnymede Trust/Trentham.

Modood, T. and Berthoud, R. (1997) *Ethnic Minorities in Britain*, London: Policy Studies Institute.

Modood, T. and Shiner, M. (1994) *Ethnic Minorities and Higher Education*, London: Policy Studies Institute.

Morris, R. (1995) *School Choice in England & Wales: An Exploration of the Legal and Administrative Background*, Slough: NFER.

Mortimore, J. and Blackstone, T. (1982) *Disadvantage in Education*, London: Heinemann Educational.

Mortimore, P., Sammons, P., Stoll, L., Lewis, D. and Ecob, R. (1988) *School Matters: The Junior Years*, Wells: Open Books.

Moynihan, D. (ed.) (1968) *On Understanding Poverty*, New York: Basic Books.

Myers, K. (1987) *Genderwatch; Self Assessment Schedules for Use in Schools*, London: SCDC & EOC.

Naidoo, B. (1992) *Through Whose Eyes?*, Stoke on Trent: Trentham.

National Commission on Education (NCE) (1996) *Success Against the Odds: Effective Schools in Disadvantaged Areas*, London: Routledge.

National Union of Teachers (1992) *Anti-Racist Curriculum Guidelines*, London: NUT.

Naylor, F. (1989) *Dewsbury, The School Above the Pub*, London: Claridge Press.

Newson Committee (1963) *Half Our Future*, A report of the Central Advisory Council for Education (England), London: Ministry of Education.

Nilsen, A. et al. (1977) *Sexism and Language*, Urbana, Illinois: National Council of Teachers of English.

Nixon, J. (1984) *A Teacher's Guide to Multicultural Education*, Oxford: Blackwell.

Norwich and Norfolk Racial Equality Council (1994) *Not in Norfolk: Tackling the Invisibility of Racism*, Norwich: NNREC.

Nuttall, D., Goldstein, H., Prosser, H. and Rasbash, B. (1989) 'Differential school effectiveness', *International Journal of Educational Research*, **13**, 769–76.

Office for National Statistics (1996; 1997; 1998) *Social Trends*, London: HMSO.

Office for National Statistics (1997) *Health Inequalities*, London: HMSO.

OFFICE FOR STANDARDS IN EDUCATION (1996) *The Gender Divide*, London: HMSO.

OPEN UNIVERSITY (1983) *The Changing Experience of Women: Educating Girls*. U221, Unit 10–11, Milton Keynes: Open University Press.

OPEN UNIVERSITY (1989a) *Exploring Educational Issues: Class and Educational Inequality*, E208, Unit 23, Milton Keynes, Open University Press.

OPEN UNIVERSITY (1989b) *Exploring Educational Issues: The Changing Experience of Education*, E208, Unit 1, Milton Keynes, Open University Press.

OXFORD DEC (1987) *Books to Break Barriers, A Review of Multicultural Fiction 4–18*, Oxford: Development Education Centre.

PETERS, W. (1987) *A Class Divided*, New Haven: Yale University Press.

PENELOPE, J. (1990) *Speaking Freely*, Oxford: Blackwell.

PILCHER, J. and WAGG, S. (1996) *Thatcher's Children? Politics, Childhood and Society in the 1980s and the 1990s*, London: Falmer Press.

PRING, R. and WALFORD, G. (eds) (1997) *Affirming the Comprehensive Ideal*, London: Falmer Press.

PURVIS, J. (1991) *A History of Women's Education in England*, Milton Keynes: Open University Press.

RAMPTON, B. (1995) *Crossing: Language and Ethnicity Among Adolescents*, London: Longman.

REAY, D. (1991) 'Working with boys', *Gender and Education*, **III**, 3, pp. 269–82.

REAY, D. (1996) 'Contexualising choice: Social power and parental involvement', *British Educational Research Journal*, **22**, 5, pp. 581–96.

REDBRIDGE COMMUNITY RELATIONS COUNCIL (1978) *Cause for Concern — West Indian Pupils in Redbridge*, London: Redbridge CRC.

RICHARDSON, R. (1992) 'Race policies and programmes under attack: Two case studies for the 1990s', in GILL, D., MAYOR, B. and BLAIR, M. *Racism and Education: Structures and Strategies*, London: Sage.

RIDDELL, S. (1992) *Gender and the Politics of the Curriculum*, London: Routledge.

ROBERTS, A. (1988) *Gaining Commitment: Developing Anti-racist Multicultural Development in Bohont School*, Winchester: Hampshire Education Authority.

RODHEAVER, D. (1990) 'Labor market progeria: On the life expectancy of presentability among working women', in GLASSE, L. and HENDRICKS, J. (eds) *Gender and Ageing*, New York: Baywood.

ROGERS, M. (1994) 'Growing up lesbian: The role of the school', in EPSTEIN, D. (ed.) *Challenging Lesbian and Gay Inequalities in Education*, Buckingham: Open University Press.

ROGERS, R. (ed.) (1986) *Education and Social Class*, Lewes: Falmer Press.

ROSE, E. et al. (1969) *Colour and Citizenship; A Report on British Race Relations*, London: Oxford University Press.

ROSEN, H. (1972) *Language and Class, a Critical Look at the Theories of Basil Bernstein*, Bristol: Falling Wall Press.

ROSENTHAL, R. and JACONSON, L. (1968) *Pygmalion in the Classroom*, New York: Holt, Reinhart & Winston.

ROSS, K. (1992) *Television in Black and White*, University of Warwick: Centre for Research in Ethnic Relations (Research Paper 19).

RUBERY, J. (1993) 'The gender pay gap: Some European comparisions.' Paper for conference on women, minimum pay and the wage councils.

RUDDUCK, J. (1994) *Developing a Gender Policy in Secondary Schools*, Milton Keynes: Open University Press.

RUNNYMEDE TRUST (1983) *Different Worlds*, London: Runnymede Trust/Borough of Lewisham.

RUNNYMEDE TRUST (1993) *Equality Assurance*, Stoke on Trent: Trentham Books.

RUNNYMEDE TRUST (1994a) *Multi-ethnic Britain: Facts and Trends*, London: Runnymede Trust.

RUNNYMEDE TRUST (1994b) *Multi-ethnic London: A Place to Live and Work*, London: Runnymede Trust.

RUNNYMEDE TRUST (1994c) *Submission to the Home Affairs Committee: Racially Motivated Attacks and Harassment*, London: Runnymede Trust.

SADKER, M. and SADKER, D. (1985) 'Sexism in the schoolroom of the '80s', *Psychology Today*, March, pp. 54–7.

SARAH, E., SCOTT, M. and SPENDER, D. (1988) 'The education of feminists: The case for single sex schools', in SPENDER, D. and SARAH, E. (eds) *Learning to Lose*, London: The Women's Press.

SARUP, M. (1986) *The Politics of Multiracial Education*, London: Routledge & Kegan Paul.

SARUP, M. (1991) *Education and the Ideologies of Racism*, Stoke on Trent: Trentham.

SCOTT, S. (1984) 'The personable and the powerful: Gender and status in sociological research', in BELL, C. and ROBERTS, H. (eds) *Social Researching: Politics, Problems, Practice*, London: Routledge & Kegan Paul.

SEARLE, C. (1989) *Your Daily Dose — Racism and the Sun*, London: CPBF.

SEBBA, M. (1983) Language change among Afro-Caribbeans in London, *Papers from the York Creole Conference*, University of York.

SEWELL, T. (1995) 'A phallic response to schooling: Black masculinity and race in an inner city comprehensive', in GRIFFITHS, M. and TROYNA, B. *Antiracism, Culture and Social Justice in Education*, Stoke on Trent: Trentham.

SEWELL, T. (1997) *Black Masculinities and Schooling*, Stoke on Trent: Trentham.

SEXTON, P. (1969) *The Feminized Male: Classrooms, White Collars and the Decline of Manliness*, New York: Vintage.

SHARPE, S. (1976) *Just Like a Girl*, Harmondsworth: Penguin.

SHAW, A. (1988) *A Pakistani Community in Britain,* Oxford: Blackwell.

SIANN, G. and KHALID, R. (1984) 'Muslim traditions and attitudes to female education', *Journal of Adolescence*, **7**, 191–200.

SIRAJ-BLATCHFORD, I. (1994) *The Early Years: Laying the Foundations for Racial Equality*, Stoke on Trent: Trentham.

SILVEIRA, J. (1980) 'Generic masculine words and thinking', *Women's Studies International Quarterly*, **3**, pp. 165–78.

SINGH GHUMAN, P. (1994) *Coping With Two Cultures*, Clevedon: Multilingual Matters.

SINGH RAUD, H. (1997) British Asian girls: Education, employment and aspirations. Paper presented at European Conference on Educational Research, Frankfurt.

SKELLINGTON, R. and MORRIS, C. (1992) *'Race' in Britain Today*, London: Sage.

SKELTON, C. (1980) *Whatever Happens to Little Women? Gender and the Primary School*, Buckinghamshire: Open University Press.

SMITH, D. and TOMLINSON, S. (1989) *The School Effect — A Study of Multi-racial Comprehensives*, London: PSI.

SMITH, P. (1985) *Language, the Sexes and Society*, Oxford: Basil Blackwell.

SMITHERS, A. and ZIENTEK, P. (1991) *Gender, Primary Schools and the National Curriculum*, London: NASUWT and the Engineering Council.

SPENDER, D. (1978) 'Don't talk, listen!', *Times Educational Supplement*, 3 November, p. 19.

SPENDER, D. (1980) *Man Made Language*, London: Routledge & Kegan Paul.

SPENDER, D. (1982) *Invisible Women: The Schooling Scandal*, London: Writers and Readers Co-operative.

SPENDER, D. and SARAH, E. (1988) *Learning to Lose*, London: The Women's Press.

STANWORTH, M. (1981) *Gender and Schooling*, London: Hutchinson.

STONE, M. (1981) *The Education of the Black Child*, London: Fontana.

STONES, R. (1983) *'Pour Out the Cocoa, Janet': Sexism in Children's Books*, York: Longman.

STUART, S. (1996) 'Female-headed families: A comparative perspective of the Caribbean and the developed world', *Gender and Development*, **4**, 2, pp. 28–34.

SUGERMAN, B. (1970) 'Social class, values and behaviour in schools', in CRAFT, M. (ed.) *Family, Class and Education*, London: Longman.

SUTCLIFFE, D. (1982) *British Black English*, Oxford: Blackwell.

SUTCLIFFE, D. (1992) *System in Black Language*, Clevedon: Multilingual Matters.

SUTCLIFFE, D. and WONG, A. (1986) *The Language of the Black Experience*, London: Blackwell.

SWANN, J. (1992) *Girls, Boys and Language*, Oxford: Blackwell.

TAKING LIBERTIES COLLECTIVE (1989) *Learning the Hard Way. Women's Oppression in Men's Education*, Basingstoke: Macmillan.

TAYLOR, J. (1976) *The Halfway Generation: A Study of Asian Youths in Newcastle*, Slough: NFER.

TAYLOR, M. (1979) *Caught Between?* Slough: NFER/Nelson.

TAYLOR, M. (1987) *Chinese Pupils in Britain*, Slough: NFER/Nelson.

TAYLOR, M. with HEGARTY, S. (1985) *The Best of Both Worlds?* Slough: NFER/Nelson.

TES (1996) 'The lads may not be all right', *Times Educational Supplement*, 28 June.

TES (1998) 'Females do better on reflection', *Times Educational Supplement*, 20 October.

TES (1998) 'Forget gender, class is still the real divide', *Times Educational Supplement*, 23 January.

TES (1998) 'Able boys succumb to complex pressures', *Times Educational Supplement*, 23 January.

TES (1998) 'Boys should sit next to girls', *Times Educational Supplement*, 9 January.

TES (1998) 'Poverty gap beats gender divide', *Times Educational Supplement*, 16 January.

THORNE, B. (1993) *Gender Play. Girls and Boys in School*, Buckingham: Open University Press.

THORP, S. (1991) *Race, Equality and Science Teaching*, London: Association for Science Education.

TOMLINSON, S. (1990) *Multicultural Education in White Schools*, London: Batsford.

TOWER HAMLETS (1994) *Analysis of 1994 GCSE Results*, London: Tower Hamlets.

TROYNA, B. (1982) 'The ideological and policy response to black people in British schools', in HARTNETT, A. (ed.) *The Social Sciences in Educational Studies*, London: Heinemann.

TROYNA, B. (ed.) (1987) *Racial Inequality and Education*, London: Tavistock.

TROYNA, B. and HATCHER, R. (1992) *Racism in Children's Lives*, London: Routledge.

TROYNA, B. and WILLIAMS, J. (1986) *Racism, Education and the State*, London: Croom Helm.

TRUDGILL, P. (1995) *Sociolinguistics*, Harmondsworth: Penguin.

TWITCHIN, J. and DEMUTH, C. (1981 and 1985) *Multicultural Education*, London: BBC.

TWITCHIN, J. (1988) *The Black and White Media Book*, Stoke on Trent: Trentham.

VAN DIJK, T.A. (1993) *Elite Discourse and Racism*, Newbury Park: Sage.

Vernon, P.E. (1957) *Secondary School Selection: A British Psychological Enquiry*, London: Methuen.

Vincent, C. (1992) 'Tolerating intolerance? Parental choice and race relations — the Cleveland case', *Journal of Education Policy*, **7**, 429–43.

Walford, G. (1994) 'The new religious grant-maintained schools', *Educational Management and Administration*, **22**, 2, pp. 123–30.

Walford, G. (1996) 'Diversity and choice in education: An alternative view', *Oxford Review of Education*, **22**, pp. 143–57.

Walkerdine, V. (1981) 'Sex, power and pedagogy', *Screen Education*, **38**, pp. 14–25.

Weiner, G. (1976) Girls' Education, the Curriculum and the Sex Discrimination Act, unpublished MA dissertation, London University, Institute of Education.

Weiner, G. (1985a) 'Equal opportunities, feminism and girls' education', introduction in Weiner, G. (ed.) *Just a Bunch of Girls*, Milton Keynes: Open University Press.

Weiner, G. (ed.) (1985) *Just a Bunch of Girls*, Milton Keynes: Open University Press.

Weiner, G. (ed.) (1990) *The Primary School and Equal Opportunities*, London: Cassell.

Weiner, G. (1992) 'Enterprise culture, Victorian values or equality: Ideology in the National Curriculum', *Internationale Schullbuch Forschung / International Textbook Research*, **14**, pp. 59–70.

Weiner, G. (1994) *Feminism in Education*, Buckingham: Open University Press.

Whyte, J., Deem, R., Kant, L. and Cruickshank, M. (1985) *Girl Friendly Schooling*, London: Methuen.

White, B., Cox, C. and Cooper, C. (1992) *Women's Career Development: A Study of High Flyers*, Oxford: Blackwell.

Wickham, A. (1986) *Women and Training*, Milton Keynes: Open University Press.

Willis, P. (1977) *Learning to Labour*, Farnborough: Saxon House.

Wilson, T. (1724) *The Many Advantages of a Good Language to Any Nation*, Menston: Scolar Press 1969.

Wolfson, N. and Manes, J. (1980) 'Don't "dear" me!', in McConnell-Ginet, S. et al. (eds) *Women and Language in Literature and Society*, New York: Praeger.

Wollstonecraft, M. (1792) (1975) *A Vindication of the Rights of Women*, Harmondsworth: Penguin.

Wong, A. (1986) 'Creole as a language of power and solidarity', in Sutcliffe, D. and Wong, A. *The Language of the Black Experience*, London: Blackwell.

Woolfe, N. (1990) *The Beauty Myth*, London: Vintage.

Wright, C. (1986) 'School processes: An ethnographical study', in Eggleston, J., Dunn, J. and Anjuli, M. *Education for Some*, London: Trentham Books.

Wright, C. (1992) *Race Relations in the Primary School*, London: David Fulton.

Yates, L. (1997) 'Gender equity and the boys debate: What sort of challenge is it?, *British Journal of Sociology of Education*, **18**, 3, pp. 337–47.

Young, M.F.D. (1971) *Knowledge and Control*, London: Collier-Macmillan.

Index

academic selection 6
accent 34, 51, 54
Acker, S. 83, 84
Adler, M. 147, 148
ageism 15
Akhtar, S. 117
A-level 85
Althusser, L. 78
anti-racist 73, 74, 79, 116
anti-sexist 64
Aphra B. 62
Arnot, M. and Weiner, G. 65
Asian Culture and Gender 25
Asian family patterns 23, 113
assimilation 69, 72
Association of Metropolitan Authorities 127
attendance records 132
Audit Commission 128

Bagley, C. 121, 137
Baker 80, 146
Balfour Act 76
Ball, S.J. 3, 73, 74, 80, 97, 145, 146, 148
Basit, T.N. 119
behaviour 39, 44, 45, 82, 83, 89, 91, 93, 95, 103, 116, 117, 125, 131
Benjamin, H. 75
Benn, C. 146
Benn, C. and Simon, B. 122, 131, 145
Bernard, M. and Meade, K. 15
Bernstein, B. 56, 57, 58, 125
bilingualism 47, 48, 49
Birmingham LEA 116
black British 53
Black Papers 78, 79
black parents 114
Boaler, J. 103
Board of Education 131
Bodine, A. 41
Bornstein, D. 45

Bourdieu, P. 78, 98, 99, 126, 148
Bowlby 13
Bowles, S. and Gintis, H. 78, 98
boys' schools 131, 132, 137
Brah, A. 119
Brandt, G. 73
Brehoney, K. 131
Brent 18, 109, 112, 120
British Asian groups 17, 49, 111
British culture 11, 70, 72
Britishness 19, 23, 68
Brophy, J. and Good, T. 83
Brown, C. 18, 73

Callaghan, J. 66, 145
careers 15, 16, 34, 63, 64, 93, 103
career opportunities 15, 16
Caribbean families 26
Caribbean language and schooling 50
CARICOM 27
Carrington, B. and Short, G. 23
Chauhan, C. 71
Chevannes, M. and Reeves, F. 114
child care 11, 24, 27
Clarke, E. 27
Clarricoates, K. 82
Class and Code 56
Class and Language 54
Classroom Interaction and Gender 39, 44, 47, 82
Classroom Interaction and 'Race' 88, 89, 90, 93, 94, 120
Classroom Interaction and Class 96, 97, 126
class-segregated education 146
Coard, B. 106, 115, 118
Coates, J. 45
Coates, K. and Silburn, P. 30
co-educational 62, 131, 132, 133, 137, 152
Cohen, G. 9
Cohen, P. 73

166

colonial 60, 72, 74
Commission for Racial Equality 10, 23, 90, 94, 116, 117
Commission for Social Justice 105
Commonwealth 18
communities 20, 24, 26, 30, 54, 58, 100, 114, 125, 139
comprehensive schools 1, 2, 5, 77, 99, 103, 123, 137, 140, 145, 152
Connell, R.W. 83, 84, 104
Connolly, P. 90, 116
Conservative 1, 2, 3, 5, 9, 33, 34, 74, 80, 127, 139, 146
correspondence theory 78, 98
Corrigan, P. 97
Cox, B. 74
Creole 51, 52, 53
Crowther Committee 62
Crystal, D. 50, 60
cultural capital 98, 111, 126, 148
cultural deprivation 97, 100
cultural resistance 52
cultural restorationists 80
culture and gender 84, 106
culture and 'race' 5, 19, 23, 24, 25, 26, 27, 28, 29, 51, 60, 70, 71, 72, 113, 143, 144
culture and class 34, 60, 75, 78, 98, 99, 100, 124, 148

Dalphinis, M. 51
Darling, J. and Glendinning, A. 61, 63, 83, 84, 87
David, M. 146
Delamont, S. 82
Demography 17
DES 108
DfEE 14
Dhondy, F. 116
dialect 49, 52, 53, 54, 55, 56, 57, 59, 60
discrimination 1, 4, 16, 63
diversity 25, 71, 72, 73, 130, 148
division of labour 11, 61
Dixon, B. 115
Dixon, C. 103
domestic labourers 11
Dorling, D. 33
Douglas, J. 83
Drew, D. and Gray, J. 119, 120, 121

Eade, J. 19, 26, 109, 113, 117, 119, 120
economy 31, 61, 75, 78, 85, 105, 145
Edelsky, C. 45
Education Acts 77, 144
Educational Action Zones 100
Educational Priority Areas 100
Edwards, V. 51, 53
EEC 63
effective schools 127
elaborated code 56, 57, 58
eleven plus 103, 123, 134, 136, 145, 151
elite 30, 76, 79, 80, 145
employers 15
employment and gender 15, 63, 87, 102, 103, 105
employment and 'race' 5, 10, 20, 21, 49, 52, 94, 111, 119
employment and class 32, 34, 57, 99
English Heritage 78
Enid Blyton 70, 119
EOC 14, 103, 106, 132, 133
Epstein, D. 93
Epstein, D. and Sealey, A. 73
equal access 63, 86
Equal Opportunities 64, 65, 87, 131, 135
Equal Opportunities Act 135
Equal Opportunities Commission 64, 131, 132
Equal Opportunities Consortium 66
equal pay 14
Equal Pay Act 13, 135
Equality of Opportunity 4
ethnicity 5, 9, 19, 21, 37, 68, 74, 92, 108, 113, 116
exclusion 3, 69, 90, 94, 130

family 11, 15, 16, 17, 21, 23, 24, 25, 26, 27, 31, 36, 48, 57, 70, 89, 94, 100, 111, 113, 114, 115, 120, 143
Farrell, P. 73
femininity 42, 86
Figes, K. 14, 15, 16, 64, 133
Figueroa, P. 22
First World War 12, 13
Fisher, J. 46
Fishman, P. 45
Foster, P. 89, 107, 116, 118, 120
Foucault, M. 79
free school meals 112, 125

French, J. and French, P. 46
Fryer, P. 27
Fuller, M. 91

Gaine, C. 5, 19, 23, 69, 71, 73, 74, 95, 117
gay 6, 19, 25, 79, 86
GCSE 2, 9, 81, 87, 102, 103, 104, 113, 120, 121, 123, 132, 133, 139
Genderwatch 64
George, R. and Maguire, M. 14, 16
Gillborn, D. 90, 91, 116
Gillborn, D. and Gipps, C. 90, 109, 111, 117, 120, 121
girl-friendly curriculum 102
Girls and Mathematics 64
Girls into Science and Technology 64
girls' schools 132, 133
glass ceiling 15, 16
Glass, D. 30
Goodman, M. 93
Graddol, D. and Swann, J. 45, 46
grammar schools 1, 5, 76, 77, 99, 103, 131, 132, 133, 134, 137, 145, 146
Green, P. 90

Hadow Report 76
Halsey, A.H. 100
harassment 20, 86, 117, 132
Hargreaves, D. 96, 97
Haw, K. 25, 120
Head Start 100
Heath, S.B. 57
heterosexual 87
hidden curriculum 73, 82, 96, 98, 126
higher education 1, 5, 99
Hill, D. 73
Hiro, D. 27, 111
Holmes, J. 60
home and school 102, 111, 124
homophobic 86, 87
housing 4, 5, 20, 26, 29, 30, 31, 33, 34, 72, 94, 100, 111, 122, 124, 125, 129, 137

identity 15, 19, 20, 38, 49, 52, 53, 78, 82, 91, 114, 135, 140, 141
ideology 11, 13, 61, 62, 63
ILEA 112, 127

immigration 1, 18, 50, 69, 70, 71, 92, 95, 108, 114, 136
inclusion 39, 41, 63, 70, 73
income 5, 11, 15, 16, 29, 30, 31, 32, 34, 35, 111, 122, 128
independent schools 104
Indian sub-continent 18, 38, 69, 107, 120
industry 12, 30, 66, 105
Institute of Education 66
IQ testing 122
Itzin, C.L. 15

Jackson, B. and Marsden, D. 99
Jackson, R. and Nesbitt, E. 19, 24, 29, 111, 119
James, A. and Jeffcoate, R. 72
Jones, T. 29
Joseph, K. 74, 80, 81
Junior School Project 112, 127

Kant, L. 63
Keddie, N. 99, 100
Kelly, A. 83, 94
Kelly, E. and Cohn, T. 117
King, A. and Reiss, M. 74
Klein, G. 69

Labour 5, 34, 138
Labov, W. 58
Lacey, C. 97
Language and inequality 36
Lavigeur, J. 130
Lawton, D. 56, 57, 58
LEAs 1, 2, 5, 66, 67, 74, 102, 109, 123, 125, 127, 128, 137, 138, 140, 145, 146
Lees, S. 43, 86, 132
Levitas, R. 9
Lewis, J. 12
liberalism 6
life chances 21, 31, 33
linguistic 19, 20, 45, 47, 50, 52, 53, 54, 57, 60, 125
linguistic codes 56
Linguistic Minorities Project 48
living standards 30, 31, 32
Lobban, G. 85

Mac an Ghaill, M. 88, 89, 90, 91, 92, 93, 116

Macdonald, I. 74, 88
MacIntosh, I. 83
MacKay, D. and Fulkerson, D. 40
Mackinnon, D. 123
Maguire, M. and Weiner, G. 14
Mahony, P. 132
manual work 13, 14, 30, 31, 32, 33, 34, 58, 76, 101, 106, 111, 120, 122, 123, 124, 135
market 1, 6, 11, 12, 15, 16, 32, 80, 85, 92, 105, 119, 130, 137, 139, 146, 147, 148
marriage 4, 12, 13, 14, 25, 27, 29, 62, 63
Martineau, H. 62
Martyna, W. 39
Mary Seacole 74
masculinity 40, 42, 44, 84, 86, 91, 98, 105
Massey, I. 95
Maughan, B. and Dunn, G. 111, 112, 121
McCrum, G. 133
Measor, L. and Sikes, P. 65, 67, 85, 132
Measor, L. and Woods, P. 82
Menter, I. 93
meritocratic 30, 145
Merrett, F. and Wheldall, K. 83
Metcalfe, H. and Thompson, M. 16
middle class women 11
Midwinter, E. 100
migration 17, 19, 50, 108, 114
Milner, D. 93, 118, 119
minorities 37
Mirza, H. 88, 89, 92, 113, 116
Modood, T. 19, 23, 28, 29, 35, 108, 111, 119
Modood, T. and Berthoud, R. 19, 20, 21, 22, 24, 31
Modood, T. and Shiner, M. 109
Moynihan, D. 27
multicultural 71, 72, 73, 116
multiculturalism 65, 71, 72, 73
myths 18, 26, 31, 95, 107

Naidoo, B. 73
name-calling 5, 94, 117
National Curriculum 61, 67, 74, 80, 85, 103, 140, 141
New Right 6, 80
Newsom Report 63
Nilsen, A. 44
Nixon, J. 72

non-manual 13, 30, 32, 34
Norwood Report 62, 67, 76
nuclear family 24, 70
nursery 84, 86, 90

occupation 31, 32, 74, 85, 104, 108, 112, 123
Office for National Statistics 33
Ofsted 109, 132, 133
old age 15

Parekh 113
parental choice 2, 129, 138, 144, 146, 150, 151
part-time workers 14
peer groups 87, 90, 96, 97, 118, 134
Penelope, J. 39, 44
Plummer, J. 103
policy makers 12, 61, 62, 63, 68, 102
positive action 4
Positive discrimination 4
poverty 16, 100, 111, 125
primary school 2, 14, 77, 83, 84, 85, 90, 92, 95, 97, 131, 140, 152
public schools 30, 75, 76, 130, 146
public sphere 11
Purvis, J. 11, 12

'race' 1, 4, 5, 9, 19, 29, 37, 47, 68, 69, 71, 72, 74, 87, 106, 137, 138
Race Relations Act 4, 9, 59, 138
racial abuse 94
racial bullying 117
racism 5, 21, 22, 88, 93, 117
racism and disadvantage 21
Rampton, B. 53
Rastafarianism 27, 28, 52, 53
Reay, D. 147, 148
Registrar General 32
religion 5, 19, 20, 21, 23, 28, 29, 49, 68, 69, 70, 72, 75, 107, 119, 140, 143, 144
restricted code 56, 57, 58
Riddell, S. 84
right wing 6
Roberts, A. 95
Rodhever, D. 15
Rogers, M. 86
Rose, E. 111

Rosenthal, R. and Jacobson, L. 96
Rousseau 61
Runnymede Trust 22, 29, 74, 108, 111
Ruskin, J. 12

Sadker, M. and Sadker, D. 46
Sarup, M. 69
Saturday schools 114
school assemblies 2
school performance 2, 52, 111, 113, 114, 123, 125
school population 69, 71, 125
school suspension 116
Searle, C. 23
Sebba, M. 53
Second World War 13, 18
secondary schools 8, 14, 53, 86, 90, 95, 97, 99, 107, 122, 123, 131, 144, 147
Secretary of State for Education 74, 81, 106, 146
selection 2, 21, 61, 65, 73, 76, 77, 117, 136, 144, 146, 147, 148, 150
self-fulfilling prophesy 107
separate schooling 130, 138, 141
separatism 130, 140
Service occupations 14
settlement 18, 20, 108
sex and gender 4
Sex Discrimination Act 1, 16, 63
sexism 5
sex-stereotyped 85
Sexton, P. 83
sexual relations 11, 86
sexuality 43, 82
Sharpe, S. 131
Shaw, A. 24, 29, 111, 119
Siann, G. and Khalid, R. 25
Silveira, J. 40
Singh Ghuman, P. 24, 29
Singh-Raud, H. 25, 28
single parent 31
single sex schools 67, 132, 133, 135
Siraj-Blatchford, I. 93
Skellington, R. and Morris, C. 18, 22, 29, 138
slavery 26, 27, 50, 51, 74
Smith, D. and Tomlinson, S. 90, 127
Smith, P. 41, 44
Smithers, A. 84

Social Class 29
social engineering 2
Somerville, M. 62
special educational needs 125
Spender, D. 40, 41, 46, 61, 62, 83, 131
Spender, D. and Sarah, E. 132
Spens Report 76
Standard English 52, 54, 56, 59
Stanworth, M. 82
state 1, 2, 11, 13, 31, 49, 63, 68, 72, 73, 74, 76, 78, 80, 102, 131, 132, 133, 136, 138, 140, 141, 143, 146, 150, 152
state schools 68, 131, 138
stereotyping 24, 63, 67, 85, 100, 114, 128
Stone, M. 114, 118
Stones, R. 85
streaming 73, 97, 118
Stuart, S. 27
sub-cultures 83, 90, 91, 97, 117
Sugarman, B. 34
supplementary schools 139
Sutcliffe, D. and Wong, A. 53
Swann Report 73, 94, 95, 106, 107, 113, 116, 138, 141
Swann, J. 40, 45, 46, 52, 74

Taylor, M. and Hegarty, S. 21
teacher expectation 89, 96
Thatcher, M. 1, 2, 79, 80
The 1991 Census 29
The General Household Survey 35
Thorp, S. 73
Through the Glass Ceiling Network 16
Tomlinson, S. 73
Tower Hamlets 18, 109, 113, 120
tradition 2, 6, 80, 131, 133
Troyna, B. and Hatcher, R. 94, 95, 117
Trudgill, P. 56, 60
TUC 34
TVEI 66, 67
Twitchin, J. 115
Twitchin, J. and Demuth, C. 73

underachievement 2, 68, 73, 83, 87, 104, 105, 109, 116, 125, 127
underclass 32
unemployment 14, 21, 22, 26, 66, 72, 104, 111, 129
unequal outcomes 3

United Nations 63
university 66
un-waged employment 11

van Dijk, T.A. 115
Victorian 11, 12, 29, 30, 34, 75, 76
vocational 62, 63, 66, 67, 77

Walford, G. 139, 148
Walkerdine, V. 86
Wandsworth 112, 113
Weiner, G. 63, 64, 67, 102
white British 23, 49, 108

Wickham, A. 13, 15
Willis, P. 97, 98, 105
Wolfson, N. and Manes, J. 45
Wollstonecraft, M. 62
Women and the Economy 11
Wong, A. 20, 53
Woolfe, N. 14
Woolfe, V. 62
working class women 11, 12, 105
Wright, C. 88, 90, 92, 94, 116, 117

Yates, L. 106
Young, M. 78

4818